They Eat Horses, Don't They?

They Eat Horses, Don't They?

The Truth About the French

PIU MARIE EATWELL

Thomas Dunne Books
St. Martin's Press
New York

To Alek, Oscar and Noah,
my Franco-British sons,
who cheer for France and England
(depending on who's winning)

THOMAS DUNNE BOOKS.
An imprint of St. Martin's Press.

www.thomasdunnebooks.com
www.stmartins.com

The Library of Congress Cataloging-in-Publication Data
is available upon request.

ISBN 978-1-250-05305-3 (hardcover)
ISBN 978-1-4668-5493-2 (e-book)

St. Martin's Press books may be purchased for educational, business, or promotional use. For information on bulk purchases, please contact the Macmillan Corporate and Premium Sales Department at 1-800-221-7945, extension 5442, or write to specialmarkets@macmillan.com.

First published in Great Britain by Head of Zeus Ltd

First U.S. Edition: December 2014

10 9 8 7 6 5 4 3 2 1

Contents

Introduction

At the point where the River Seine snakes like a gleaming ribbon between the genteel 15th and 16th *arrondissements*—the ancient sectors in which the city of Paris is divided—there is a long, narrow strip of an island called the Île aux Cygnes (Island of the Swans). Here, a tree-lined avenue leads to a view of Paris that is all the more astonishing for being so little known: the Statue of Liberty, torch aloft, with the Eiffel Tower soaring behind her. Of course, this is not the original Liberty; she is in fact a one-fourth scale replica, facing in the direction of her larger and more celebrated sibling. Liberty's younger, Parisian sister was built in 1889, three years after the New York statue. She was a gift to the city from the American community in Paris, in commemoration of the centenary of the French Revolution. In truth, she represented the exchange of gifts: for the original Liberty was, of course, a gift to the United States from the people of France, in commemoration of the American Declaration of Independence. The Liberty of the Île aux Cygnes carries a joint inscription commemorating both American Independence Day and Bastille Day, the defining moment of the French Revolution:

IV Juillet 1776 = XIV Juillet 1789

In fact, France boasts more replicas of the Statue of Liberty than any other country. Paris alone is home to four. In addition to the statue on Île aux Cygnes, the bronze model used by the sculptor, Frédéric Auguste Bartholdi, as a study for the New York statue stands in the graceful, tree-lined avenues of the Luxembourg Gardens; a plaster version is displayed in the Arts and Crafts Museum; and a life-size copy of Liberty's torch can be seen at the entrance to the Pont d'Alma tunnel. Copies of Liberty gaze down on French citizens in regional cities as far flung as Bordeaux, Barentin, Colmar, Saint-Cyr-sur-Mer, Poitiers,

Châteauneuf-la-Forêt, and Lunel. They remain as powerful symbols of the strong and emotive tie between two nations united in a struggle against oppression, wedded to the ideal of freedom.

As far as the United States was concerned, France lost its original status as a powerful ally against British colonial oppression centuries ago. However, over the years Paris has remained, in American eyes, the cultural and historical capital of Europe. Never has this been more strongly articulated than during the period between the two World Wars, when America's literary and artistic elite gathered in Paris like moths to a candle flame. Gertrude Stein, Ernest Hemingway, and F. Scott Fitzgerald all found the cafés of the Left Bank sources of endless inspiration. 'If you are lucky enough to have lived in Paris as a young man,' Hemingway remarked, 'then wherever you go for the rest of your life, it stays with you, for Paris is a moveable feast.' Similarly, F. Scott Fitzgerald was of the view that: 'the best of America drifts to Paris. The American in Paris is the best American. It is more fun for an intelligent person to live in an intelligent country. France has the only two things toward which we drift as we grow older—intelligence and good manners.'

In the decades after the swinging '20s, however, Franco-American relations became more fraught. Many of the negative stereotypes that Americans hold about the French people even today—that they don't wash, for example—date from the immediate aftermath of the Second World War, when American GIs started coming home with tales of appalling French plumbing and a stinky Parisian metro. This was the heyday of the Looney Tunes character Pepé Le Pew, the skunk (coincidentally with a French accent) who put off the members of the female sex that he passed his time endlessly chasing, due to his pungent odour. The French, for their part, were appalled at the drunkenness and rowdiness of many of the American soldiers. Nor, after the war, were they suitably obsequious or grateful (at least, in American eyes) for the deluge of U.S. dollars poured into their coffers by the Marshall Plan. The poet Sylvia Plath, visiting Paris in the 1950s, noticed the sullenness and rudeness of the native population towards visiting Americans. A certain frostiness and mistrust set in between the two peoples, hitting an all-time low in the dark years of the Gulf War in the early 2000s.

These days, however, the French seem to be back in favour with the American people. A 2013 Gallup poll found that 73 percent of Americans have a positive view of France. Yet still, many of the old stereotypes remain; nor are these necessarily all negative. In fact, many of them are exactly the opposite, reflecting a paradoxical countertendency of Americans to hero-worship the French—especially in matters relating to style, cuisine, and culture—running at least as strong as the tendency to condemn them.

It is this cacophony of conflicting national stereotypes that this book seeks to investigate, picking a bright line through the muddle of competing myths, exposing the truth about what contemporary France is really like. In so doing, whilst I recognize the existence of a shared Anglo-American 'mythology' about the Gallic race, I have also tried to show where British and American attitudes diverge, as a result of each country's own, unique relationship with this very special—and complicated—ally. Do French women get fat? Do French children throw food? Do French women shave? Do the French wash? The answers, often, are not what we might expect. Truth, after all, is frequently stranger than fiction. . . .

Prologue

It was on a sunny August bank holiday that I checked into a hotel in the Latin Quarter of Paris for a weekend break. Almost ten years later, I am still in France. The story is the usual one for many expats in France: meet, fall in love, marry. I never did get to stay in the hotel in the Latin Quarter (spending that whole first weekend with my future husband). But I did get to live in several dodgy apartments in the seedier *arrondissements* of Paris. Over the years, I have spent sweltering summers queuing in traffic jams on the motorways leading to the French coast, and many a winter in the deepest Gallic countryside. Now ensconced in a quiet French village, that first Paris bank holiday seems a world away. Another life.

During my first few years in France, I was excited and enticed by everything around me that seemed quintessentially French. A freshly baked croissant – how French! The rudeness of the waiter at the bistro – how French! The thin and glamorous women who tottered down the Parisian boulevards – how French! A glass of wine at lunchtime – how French! Shopping in the local market – how French!

Gradually, however, I began to notice cracks in this 'French' experience. Not all, or even most, of the women I saw were particularly beautiful or glamorous. Every so often, there was a polite waiter. The croissant in the café was tired and crusty. There were McDonald's and fast-food joints jostling for space beside the cute bistros, with their checked red tablecloths. The supermarkets were stuffed with rows of canned goods. Somehow, however, I ignored these things. They weren't really 'French'. The beautiful and glamorous women, the freshly baked croissant, the local market, on the other hand – all these things *were* 'French'. It was as though I yearned after, needed this romantic, glamorous, 'French' world to which to aspire, closing my eyes to the reality which was, often, very different.

But the fast-food joints, ordinary-looking women, and supermarkets with rubbishy food were there, all the same. They were, unmistakably, 'French'. What they were not part of was what I considered the 'French experience'.

The more I considered this 'French experience', the more it seemed to me to consist of certain specific ideas. For example, it most definitely included rude waiters, bistros, glamorous women, smoking and dangerous liaisons. It most definitely did not include fast food, fat women and sandwich lunches. Yet these were things I encountered every day.

And so gradually, I began to see around me more and more the *exceptions* to the so-called 'French experience'. I began to see how my ideas about France and the French, although some of them were true, were also often a construction of my imagination. I asked around my English-speaking friends back home, and found that they shared a lot of these same preconceptions. And not only that, but there was a whole sub-genre of writing, a mini-industry of 'Froglit' – mainly consisting of books written by foreigners who had spent a couple of years in Paris – busy propagating, promulgating, and disseminating the myth of the 'French experience'. So I listed these common ideas about the French in my notebook and set out to investigate them, poring over tomes in the local libraries and talking to everybody – English or French – that I could persuade to give me some minutes of their time. Were these myths about the French true or false? The results, as you will see, were often quite unexpected.

Apéritif

The archetypal Frenchman wears a beret and striped shirt and rides a bicycle festooned with onions

'You aren't one of those French onion sellers, are you?' the woman asked Hercule Poirot.

AGATHA CHRISTIE, ENGLISH CRIME WRITER (1890–1976), *THE VEILED LADY*, 1923

This is a myth that everybody knows, few believe, and even fewer will admit to having witnessed. This is not surprising, since if you do recall having seen a Frenchman wearing a beret and striped shirt on a bike festooned with onions, you are very likely either to frequent naff fancy-dress parties or to be very advanced in years. In my ten years of living in France, I have never seen any Frenchman on a bike festooned with onions, and only occasionally the odd ageing artist by the *Sacré Coeur* in a striped shirt and beret (and those clearly donned for the benefit of the tourists). And yet the image is ingrained in the Anglo American imagination as that of the stereotypical Frenchman. Where, exactly, does it come from?

The answer is that the image is a British invention. It does, however, ultimately derive from a Frenchman: one Henri Ollivier. In 1828, Monsieur Ollivier, a Breton peasant farmer, made the hazardous trip to the shores of Albion from his home – the fishing village of Roscoff – to travel around door to door, selling his strings of onions to British housewives. He made such a packet that many of his fellow Roscoff peasant labourers quickly followed suit. Soon, hundreds of them were crossing the Channel every year with their harvest of onions, which they would store in rented barns while they travelled from village to village, peddling their wares on rickety old bicycles. The English called them 'Onion Johnnies', since most of them seemed to be called 'Jean', and some of them were as young as teenagers. They would arrive in July and depart the following December or January, sleeping in barns on top of their piles of onions. This 'unofficial' Anglo-French trade boomed until the outbreak of the Second World War. It peaked in the late 1920s – when 9,000 tons of onions were sold in England by 1,400 Johnnies – before gradually petering out in the postwar period. For many English people, the Onion Johnny was as close to France or the French as they ever got. Soon, he became in British minds the image of the stereotypical Frenchman, immortalized on everything from packets of cheese to the TV series *'Allo 'Allo!* This was ironic because, hailing as they did from Brittany, most of the original Onion Johnnies did not actually speak French. Breton being a Celtic language related to Welsh, the itinerant costermongers naturally bonded with the Welsh as a united fringe against the Anglo-French enemy. Even to this day, some former Onion Johnnies continue to meet up with their old Celtic pals at that forum for self-assertion against colonial oppression, the Welsh Eisteddfod.

Onion Johnnies wore the *béret*, the traditional 'cloth cap' of the French peasantry. This originated in the Southwest of France, the Basque beret being worn by shepherds in the Pyrenees from the seventeenth century onwards. In the twentieth century the beret came to be associated with left-wing intellectuals and radical artists, including, most famously, Pablo Picasso and Salvador Dalí. It also became, in the 1960s, a powerful symbol of rebellion and radical chic: Che Guevara was rarely seen without one (the image of his trademark black version with a red star found a post-revolutionary afterlife on millions of posters and T-shirts the world over), and the beret became the accessory *de choix* of radical and paramilitary groupings as diverse as the Black Panthers in the USA, the Provisional IRA in Northern Ireland, and the Basque separatist group ETA in Spain. Until the 1970s the beret, along with the cloth cap, was one of the types of headgear traditionally worn by film directors, until it was ousted by the now-ubiquitous American baseball cap.

In France nowadays, though, berets are seldom to be seen – except on the occasional octogenarian playing *pétanque* in a dusty village of the Southwest. Certainly not in Paris, where

it would just be… well, *pas comme il faut*.* The average French workman these days is just as likely to be wearing a *casquette*, or baseball cap, turned jauntily backwards in the manner of his favourite rap star, as the traditional headgear of the French peasantry. In July 2012, the last traditional French beret manufacturer in the Southwest was bought out in the nick of time, saving the jobs of the twenty-odd remaining artisan beret-

* Even so, there are exceptional circumstances where the beret is still *de rigueur*: for example, berets are sometimes worn by French rugby fans (particularly at away games in Britain), presumably to advertise their national allegiance.

makers.[1] The beret is nowadays mainly used as an item of army uniform, and as such is still going strong around the world. In fact, it is a crowning irony that today's principal market for the ultimate sartorial symbol of the nation of 'cheese-eating surrender monkeys' (see page 41) is… the US Army.*[2] At the Opening Ceremony of the 2012 Olympic Games in London, it was the American athletes who sported the beret. The French team – somewhat unsportingly – did not make an appearance on bikes with berets, striped shirts and onions, but rather in outfits created by that ambassador of French chic, the German sportswear brand Adidas.

Onion Johnnies also frequently wore striped black or blue and white boat-necked shirts: the traditional garb of Breton fishermen. The Breton shirt was created as an official garment of the French Navy in 1858, according to tradition because the stripes made it easier to spot a man overboard. They were not considered remotely stylish at the time (striped garments were also worn by lepers and convicts). In a display of tricolour-tinted nostalgia, the original Navy shirt featured 21 stripes, one for each of Napoleon's victories. The striped shirt was spotted on Breton fishermen by Coco Chanel on a weekend break to Deauville and inspired a nautical collection by her in 1917, subsequently becoming one of the most famous fashion icons in the world. Once an item of peasant garb – a sign of the outcast and dispossessed – the striped shirt now became the ultimate in modern chic, sported by the likes of Brigitte Bardot, Jean Seberg and Jeanne Moreau. It has subsequently been rehashed and reinterpreted hundreds of times by fashion houses from Gucci to Givenchy, incarnating everything from the hunky sailor as gay icon in Jean-Paul Gaultier's 1993 campaign for the perfume *Le Male*, to the retro innocence of a traditional childhood in the classic child's yellow and striped fisherman's coat by *Petit Bateau*.

---

* Though even the US Army is beginning to phase out the beret in favour of the cheaper and more practical baseball cap. In June 2011, the Pentagon announced that the US land army was to renounce the beret in favour of the cap for ordinary workwear, keeping the beret only for ceremonial use. The move was welcomed by the troops. 'I can't stand a wet sock on my head,' was the comment of one officer to the *Army Times*.

Today, however, Onion Johnnies have all but disappeared from the British landscape. After the Second World War, increased competition from rival producers and English protectionism, together with the fact that wandering Johnnies did not qualify for the new French postwar state welfare benefits, meant that most hung up their berets. Now there are only a handful left who regularly make the trip to sell onions door to door in English streets. Today's Onion Johnnies, however, are as likely to send a round-robin by e-mail to alert customers to their arrival, and make their rounds in a van (although they might keep a bike in the back for special appearances). The Onion Johnnies have been immortalized with their own museum in Roscoff (*La Maison des Johnnies et de l'oignon*): here one can see fading photographs of this curious, all-but-forgotten second French invasion of England, have a master class in onion-plaiting by a real Onion Johnny, and listen to nostalgic folk songs and poems (all with a strong onion theme to bring tears to the eyes). There is even an annual Roscoff Onion Festival, where local delicacies such as onion tart and onion crêpes can be sampled. Most powerful of all, the image of Onion Johnny lives on in the minds of millions of Japanese, American and British tourists, as the quintessential mythical Frenchman.

The French for their part are entirely nonplussed by the foreign stereotype of the Onion Johnny. Given that the original Johnnies were nationalistic Bretons who considered the French an alien race, this is hardly surprising. It is as though the national stereotype of an Englishman were a Welshman selling leeks with a daffodil tucked behind his ear. An absurd thought. But then, the French invented the philosophical concept of 'the Absurd' and the novelist Albert Camus, its most famous proponent, could hardly have come up with a more meaninglessly random national stereotype. In its absurdity if nothing else, the image of the Onion Johnny is archetypically French.

Myth Evaluation: *False*

1

The King of Cuisines and the Cuisine of Kings

Myths about French Food and Drink

French cuisine is the best in the world

Lunch kills half of Paris, supper the other half.
CHARLES-LOUIS DE SECONDAT,
BARON DE MONTESQUIEU (1689–1755)

It has been taken as gospel for many years that French cuisine is the best in the world. Whether it is regional, bourgeois or *haute cuisine* (and in truth, these all feed off each other), French cuisine is the *crème de la crème* of the world's gastronomic heritage, unbeatable for its distinguished history, refinement and *savoir-faire*. The priority accorded by the French to what they ingest over everything else, including the achievements of science, cannot be doubted: 'The discovery of a new dish,' the eighteenth-century French wit and gastronomic critic Jean-Anthelme Brillat-Savarin observed, 'creates greater happiness for the human race than the discovery of a new star.' The great French playwright Jean Anouilh (1910–87) summed up the ultimate goal of French social interactions thus: 'Everything ends this way in France – everything. Weddings, christenings, duels, burials, swindlings, diplomatic affairs – everything is a pretext for a good dinner.' Just as eating has traditionally dominated French life, so French cuisine has traditionally dominated the world's restaurants. No other single cuisine has exerted such an influence on the world's palate. Until now, perhaps.

Enchant, stay beautiful and graceful, but do this, eat well. Bring the same consideration to the preparation of your food as you devote to your appearance. Let your dinner be a poem, like your dress.
CHARLES PIERRE MONSELET, FRENCH JOURNALIST (1825–88)

That French gastronomy has historically dominated European cuisine is certainly true, at least since the reign of the illustrious King Louis XIV (1643–1715). The *Roi Soleil* ('Sun King') was himself a legendary gourmand, capable of putting away gigantic quantities of food at a sitting. His repasts were gargantuan. Lunch – known as *le petit couvert* ('the little table'), although there was nothing little about it – would typically consist of four different bowls of soup, a whole stuffed pheasant, a partridge, chicken, duck, mutton with garlic gravy, two pieces of ham, hard-boiled eggs, three enormous salads and a plateful of pastries, fruit and jam (and on top of all this the king would go on to demolish a further forty dishes at dinner). On Louis' death, his stomach and intestines were found to be twice the size of an ordinary man's.

Under such belt-busting leadership, it is not surprising that French cuisine burgeoned during Louis' reign. It was during this period that the famous chef François Pierre La Varenne published the first major cookbook, *Le Cuisinier français*, Dom Pérignon invented champagne, the ritual of the dinner service became established, and a distinct new method of French cookery evolved. This new culinary style broke with the medieval tradition of the heavy use of spices, adding herbs instead to bring out the natural flavour of the food. Then, as always, the chef's calling was a matter of the highest honour. Take, for example, the noble case of François Vatel, chef to the Prince of Condé (Vatel was portrayed on screen in a 2000 feature film of the same name by – who else? – Gérard Depardieu). According to the Marquise de Sévigné, to whom we owe an account of the events, in 1671 Vatel was given charge of preparations for an enormous feast to receive Louis XIV at the Château de Chantilly. Having barely slept for twelve nights during the frantic preparations, Vatel was beside himself when only two of the fish deliveries for the dinner turned up. Not realizing that the rest were on their way, he exclaimed: 'I cannot outlive this disgrace!', retired to his room, set the hilt of his sword against the door, and after two ineffectual attempts succeeded in the third, forcing the sword through his heart. At that very moment, the missing fish arrived. Dinner went ahead as planned.*[1]

The French Revolution put many of the French master chefs out of a job, with the result that they either went to cook for foreign monarchs (thus exporting French cuisine around the world), or opened one of the new breed of eating establishments that were taking root around Paris: restaurants. The word 'restaurant' originally referred to a type of soup called a *bouillon restaurant* ('restorative *bouillon*'), served in the world's first such hostelry, founded by a Monsieur Boulanger in Paris in 1765. Previously, guests at inns would partake of a meal together at the innkeeper's table, but Boulanger introduced the innovation of guests dining at separate, small marble tables. This idea caught on, and soon restaurants were mushrooming all over the capital. It was at this point that the lawyer and journalist Alexandre Balthazar Laurent Grimod de la Reynière – the father of modern food journalism – published his restaurant guide, *L'Almanach des gourmands* (1803–12). An early ancestor of Michelin and Zagat, the *Almanach* was a periodical in which Grimod evaluated cafés and restaurants in Paris: he established 'tasting panels' of distinguished testers to whom restaurateurs, pâtissiers and charcutiers would send their dishes for evaluation and subsequent listing, with a rating, in the *Almanach*.† At the same time, food philosophers like Brillat-Savarin (see page 67) wrote compendiums of meditations about the pleasures of gourmandism, containing such aphorisms as: *Dis-moi ce que tu manges et je te dirai ce que tu es* ('Tell me what you eat and I shall tell you what you are').

There are five divisions of the fine arts: painting, poetry, music, sculpture, and architecture, of which final category the principal branch is pâtisserie.
ANTONIN CARÊME (1784–1833)

* Noble gesture or case of overkill, Vatel's act seems to have started something of a tradition of honour among French chefs. Centuries later, in February 2003, the celebrated chef Bernard Loiseau committed suicide by shooting himself in the mouth with a shotgun over the prospect of losing a Michelin star.

† To obtain a rating it was sufficient to send the dish to M. Grimod at his address at the rue des Champs-Elysées, but it was made clear that all dishes for which transport costs were not discharged would be refused.

Over this period of growth in public dining, the principles and practices of French *haute cuisine* were being codified by one of the greatest of all French chefs: Antonin Carême, often dubbed the father of French cooking. Born the son of a destitute drunkard in 1784, Carême established himself as one of the foremost confectioners of his time, studying books on Greek and Roman architecture in the national library to give his sugary palaces, temples, follies and ruins stunning authenticity. A stint serving the English Prince Regent and future King George IV was a disaster (he couldn't cope with the London fog), and so for some years Carême worked for the Russian tsar Alexander I, who later remarked that 'he taught us how to eat'. Towards the end of his life, Carême focused on the *magnum opus* that was to become the Bible of French *haute cuisine*: *L'Art de la cuisine française*.* This weighty tome codified the principles and philosophies of French culinary art, including establishing the four 'mother sauces' that constitute its cornerstones. Burgundian by origin, Carême's work (like that of so many great French chefs) built upon the cuisine of his roots, elevating such earthy peasant fare as snails to the heady delights of the classic *escargots de Bourgogne*.

If Carême was the founding father of French *haute cuisine*, his successor Georges Auguste Escoffier was the first celebrity chef. Coming from a dirt-poor background (as was beginning to be a requirement for French chefs), Escoffier showed remarkable culinary genius from an early age. In 1884 he met the budding young hotelier César Ritz at the Hôtel National in Lucerne, Switzerland; the rest, as they say, is luxury. Escoffier and Ritz together took over the Savoy Hotel in London in 1890, then the Ritz in Paris, and subsequently the Carlton. Understanding opulence as only the sons of poor men can (Ritz also came from humble origins, having been a hotel groom), the pair redefined fine living for the élite. Escoffier's motto was 'keep it simple' (he never did), but he did streamline the overelaborate cuisine of Carême for a modern age, introducing revolutionary

* At least, until Escoffier's *Le Guide culinaire*, whereupon Carême became the Old Testament and Escoffier the New.

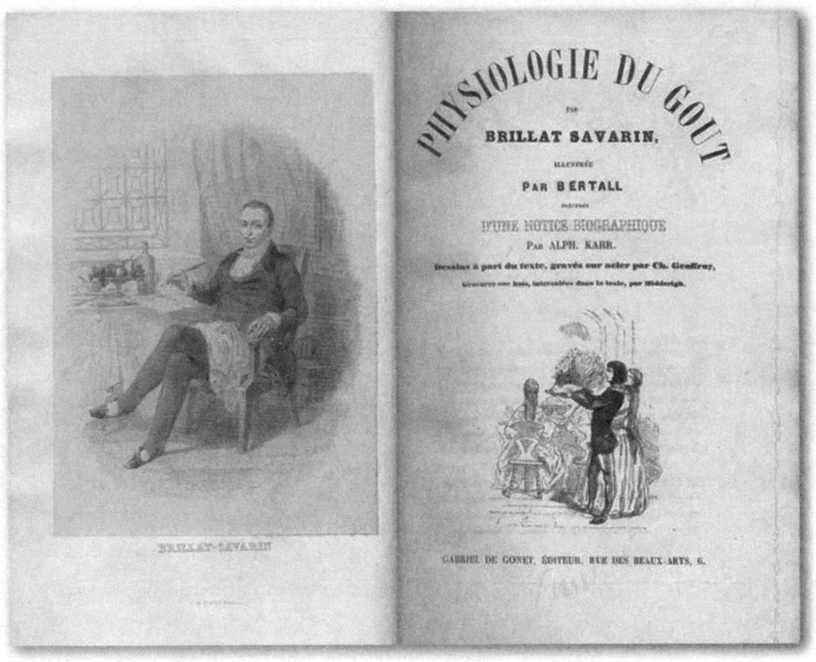

innovations still in use today. It is to Escoffier that modern restaurant kitchens owe the 'kitchen brigade' system of dividing tasks between separate sous-chefs working under the direction of a *chef de cuisine*, while he was also responsible for introducing the *à la carte* menu. Escoffier also worked on the new luxury liners, where it is said that once, having been served a superb dish of salmon steamed in champagne, Kaiser Wilhelm II asked him, 'How can I repay you?' His alleged reply was, 'By returning Alsace-Lorraine to France.'

In the later twentieth century French *haute cuisine* was 'simplified' yet again (although somehow, these progressive simplifications never really made it simple), this time by the *nouvelle cuisine* of the 1960s: smaller portions, lighter ingredients, fewer buttery sauces (or, as Elizabeth David cuttingly put it, 'lighter food, less of it, costing more'[2]).

French gastronomy undoubtedly has an illustrious history, but is it still the king of cuisines and the cuisine of kings? Many think not. French gastronomy has had to take a lot of heat in recent years. The artery-clogging richness of the food, the pernickety presentation, the grandiose self-importance of the French restaurant, the traditional *froideur* of the waiting staff – all have been subject to a grilling. The French just got too complacent, it is said, and their top chefs became too glitzy. Food fashion has supposedly moved elsewhere – to the simplicity and freshness of Italian cooking, the gutsy innovation of Spanish, or the modernist minimalism of Japanese. The buzzwords are no longer *French* (= stuffy and boring), but new and trendy concepts like *Fusion Food, Molecular Gastronomy* or – even better, combining two for the price of one (sorry, price of three) – *Science Fusion*. Who, after all, wants a plain old *escalope de saumon à l'oseille*, when you can have exploding milkshakes, foaming mushrooms or bacon and egg ice-cream?*

Even the 'Red Bible', France's own Michelin Guide, has recently given the cuisine of its homeland the cold shoulder. The 2012 Guide declared Tokyo the culinary capital of the world, awarding it a total of sixteen stars over Paris' fourteen.† Michelin itself has felt the heat recently for its alleged stuffiness, with a clutch of decorated chefs handing back their stars to great media acclaim (cynics might point out that giving back stars actually attracts more column inches than getting them). But it is not only Michelin that is sounding the death knell for French cooking. Every other food journalist has been proclaiming the demise of French cuisine, which judging by the stream of journalistic commentary in recent years, must have died more often than Darla in *Buffy the Vampire Slayer*. The fact that French food was

---

* 'Molecular Gastronomy' is a relatively recent fad in cooking, which aims to use scientific techniques and chemicals to create unusual or spectacular food. Leading proponents are the Spanish chef Ferran Adrià and the British chef Heston Blumenthal.

† The Michelin Guide, France's famous annual restaurant ratings book, was first published by car tyre tycoons the Michelin brothers in 1900 and given away as a free handout to motorists. Over the years it has garnered enormous prestige and become a French national treasure, but a fact often forgotten is that it is still essentially a marketing tool for selling car tyres. Underscoring the *bon viveur*-ishness of it all, the company's trademark, the rotund, rubbery figure whom we call the 'Michelin man' is known in French as *Bibendum*.

recently added to UNESCO's list of 'intangible cultural heritage' (along with Peking opera and Corsican polyphonic chant) seems only to have had the effect of laying a funeral wreath on a moribund institution that is now officially a museum piece.

But is French cuisine really dead? The French themselves don't seem to think so. Over the last few years, the nation's favourite dish has been consistently French, although the dish traditionally occupying the top spot, the hallowed *blanquette de veau* (veal in white sauce), has now been usurped by the upstart, smoky duck dish *magret de canard*, a child of 1960s *nouvelle cuisine*.* Nor do ordinary British people (as opposed to their journalists) seem to think French food is dead: French cuisine was ranked number two in a 2010 survey of British tastes in food, after Italian.[3] For the untrendy amongst us who are not rushing to pay a fortune for a prandial pyrotechnic display out of a test tube, regional French cuisine retains its timeless appeal: the crispness of a real *salade niçoise* in summer, with crunchy crudités and ripe Saint Pierre tomatoes; a hearty *bouillabaisse* with croutons and a fiery cayenne *rouille* sauce on a winter's day; Breton crêpes doused in burnt sugar and Calvados for a romantic *dîner à deux*.†

Bouillabaisse is only good because cooked by the French, who, if they cared to try, could produce an excellent and nutritious substitute out of cigar stumps and empty matchboxes.
NORMAN DOUGLAS, BRITISH NOVELIST (1868–1952)

The *caillette* olives in an authentic *salade niçoise* are found nowhere else on the planet except the area around Nice, and every French region boasts similar fruits of the earth, sea and sky unique to it (and as many government protection orders). French cuisine is really a thousand regional cuisines, of which

* Study by TNS Sofres for *Vie pratique gourmand*, 2011. With 21 per cent of votes, *magret de canard* was just ahead of the Belgian dish *moules-frites* (20 per cent) and the North African *couscous* (19 per cent).

† The ingredients of a real *salade niçoise* are the subject of hot debate, but the people of Nice – who can be presumed to know something about the subject – are adamant that only raw vegetables cut the mustard, and that cooked potatoes are therefore a Parisian bistro abomination.

haute cuisine is a rarefied distillation. Whether contemporary French cuisine retains the global top spot remains an argument between food critics, but France's contribution to the history and development of cuisine remains unmatched. And having given the world its first restaurant, menu, restaurant ratings service, food critic, philosophy of cuisine and back office system, not to mention the delights of *tournedos Rossini*, *caille en sarcophage* and a myriad other exquisite dishes, does French cuisine really have anything for which to apologize?

Myth Evaluation: *Arguably true. French cuisine is certainly one of the greatest in the world, although competition is increasingly stiff, notably from the Orient, and its primacy is contested by a new brand of edgy cuisine which banishes garlic butter and the mother sauces in favour of liquid nitrogen and molecular mixology.*

They eat horses, don't they?

I'm so hungry, I could eat a horse.
ENGLISH SAYING

Everybody knows the French are into hippophagy. What is hippophagy, you ask? Well, it's got nothing to do with devouring the large, foul-tempered pachyderm that inhabits the waterways of Africa (a step too far even for the omnivorous French). Rather, quite simply, it is the consumption of horses. The English seem to be convinced that the French regularly serve man's second-best friend at the dinner table with the insouciance that would accompany an ordinary *steak au poivre*. It goes with the general perception of the French as a people who are prepared to shoot (and eat) more or less anything that moves, and who consider all creatures great and small as being potentially part of the *mundus edibilis*. But is this perception correct?

It's a strange fact that horse consumption in France was socially engineered and a relatively recent phenomenon.[4] Hippophagy in ancient cultures has a long and distinguished history: it is said, for example, that the horse-eating Tartars or Mongols of Central Asia would put a piece of raw horsemeat under their saddles in the morning, to be pounded to a fine mince by the end of the day – allegedly the origin of the celebrated *steak tartare*. Sadly, this romantic myth is probably untrue, as it is thought that the dish owes its name to the more prosaic fact that it was originally accompanied by Tartar sauce. In the Christian world, however, hippophagy was traditionally strictly taboo, and until the mid-nineteenth century, the French were as squeamish about eating horses as anybody else in Europe. Hippophagy had been forbidden by Pope Gregory III in the eighth century as an 'abomination' – although the pope, needless to say, was at the time at least as interested in quashing the pagans of the North, who sacrificed and ate horses, as he was in animal welfare. Horsemeat was a food to be resorted to only by those in the direst straits – such as the French peasantry during the food shortages of the Revolution, or the armies of Napoleon on campaign in the depths of the Russian winter.

In fact, it wasn't until the 1860s or even later that the French really got into horsemeat, largely due to the efforts of a zoologist named Étienne Geoffroy Saint-Hilaire, and a fanatical military veterinarian, Émile Decroix. Decroix was obsessed with proving (to a sceptical public) that horsemeat was edible, and to this end he chomped his way through several hundred dead horses suffering from every conceivable disease, and even a mad dog by way of comparison – the purpose of the rabid canine *amuse-bouche* being presumably to prove that, if you could survive eating a mad dog, you could survive eating a horse. Taking a rational and unsentimental approach, Decroix and his fellow scientists argued that it was better for the poor of Paris to kill their horses than to starve. There may also, however, have been a less lofty motive to his campaign, in that offloading cheap horsemeat on the poor would have reduced the demand for beef and pork, thus making these classier meats less expensive for the rich.

The French public proved unreceptive to this idea, and so a number of 'horsemeat banquets' were thrown, to which the press were invited – including a particularly famous one in 1865 at the *Grand Hôtel* in Paris. At this fabulous (or freakish) repast, according to the respected authority the *Larousse Gastronomique*, the menu was as follows:[5]

Horse-Broth Vermicelli
Horse Sausage and Charcuterie
Boiled Horse
Horse à la Mode
Horse Stew
Fillet of Horse with Mushrooms
Potatoes Sautéed in Horse Fat
Salad Dressed in Horse Oil
Rum Gâteau with Horse Bone Marrow
*Wine: Château Cheval-Blanc**

* Those who imagine that they could stomach only the wine on this menu – *Château Cheval-Blanc*, one of the most sublime of the Bordeaux *Grands*

The horsemeat banquets in Paris inspired similar feasts in Britain, in Ramsgate in the 1860s, where the choice dishes were euphemistically described using the French term, as '*chevaline* delicacies'. Funnily enough, horsemeat in England did not catch on.[6]

On the other side of the Channel, despite all the press and campaigning – and the legalization of horsemeat for human consumption in 1866 – the poor of Paris remained unreasonably reluctant to consume their ageing nags. Until, that is, an event of seminal significance in French hippophagic history: the Siege of Paris during the Franco-Prussian War of 1870–71. Surrounded by the invading Prussian army, Parisians found themselves cut off from their customary food supplies. As a consequence, hunger and desperation led to some hitherto unconsidered creatures becoming part of the Parisian diet. Horses were the first to be served up on dinner tables, quickly followed by cats, dogs and rats. Finally – as Christmas approached with the bleak prospect of roasted rat as the star dish – it was the turn of the exotic animals in the Paris zoo. Camels, kangaroos and even the zoo's famous elephants Castor and Pollux – all were auctioned off to Paris butchers, who made a mint selling slices of zebra and chunks of elephant trunk (culinarily speaking the most prized part of an elephant's anatomy) to wealthy Parisians. (On 6 January 1871 the British writer, politician and diplomat Henry Labouchère noted in his diary: 'Yesterday, I had a slice of Pollux for dinner… It was tough, coarse and oily, and I do not recommend English families to eat elephant as long as they can get beef or mutton.')[7] The Christmas Day 1870 menu of the chic Parisian Café Voisin, in the rue Saint-Honoré, featured such intriguing delicacies as *éléphant consommé* and *jugged kangaroo* (see page 29). Cookery books appeared with recipes and instructions on how to cook everything from giraffe to wolf.

Now that the ancient taboo had finally been broken, hippophagy in France in the late nineteenth and early twentieth centuries went from strength to strength, with the consump-

Crus, totally horse-free its name notwithstanding – should remember that the only alternative for many Parisians at this time was to starve.

MENU OF THE CAFÉ VOISIN: 25 DECEMBER 1870, 99TH DAY OF THE SIEGE

Hors-D'Oeuvre:

Butter, Radish, Stuffed Donkey's Head, Sardines

Soups:

Red Bean Soup with Croûtons

Elephant Consommé

Entrées:

Roasted Camel à l'Anglaise with Fried Goujons

Jugged Kangaroo

Roasted Side of Bear with Pepper Sauce

Main Courses:

Roasted Leg of Wolf with Venison Sauce

Cat surrounded by Rats

Watercress Salad

Antelope Terrine with Truffles

Bordeaux Mushrooms

Buttered Peas

Dessert:

Rice Pudding with Jam

Cheese:

Gruyère

tion of horsemeat increasing by 77 per cent between 1895 and 1904.[8] In 1876 butchers in Paris marketed the flesh of over 9,000 horses, mules and donkeys, a total weight of more than 3.7 million pounds.[9] Prized for its high iron and nitrate content but relatively low in fat, horsemeat was regularly prescribed by doctors for all sorts of ailments from anaemia to tuberculosis. Owners of cavalry and shire horses were only too delighted to offload their old nags at the knackers' yards.

The first half of the twentieth century saw the apogee of horsemeat consumption: by 1913, native French horsemeat dealers were unable to keep up with demand and horsemeat had to be imported from abroad. Horsemeat butchers, or *boucheries chevalines* – with their distinctive horse's head above their doorways – burgeoned, particularly in working-class areas, such as the nineteenth *arrondissement* of Paris or the Nord-Pas-de-Calais region. Cheaper than other meat and shunned by hippophile aristocrats, horsemeat was always working-class fare: even at the peak of its consumption, it was associated with low status and poverty.[10]

From the 1950s onwards, though, the role of the horse changed. No longer a beast of burden or war (those roles having been taken over by the tractor and the tank respectively), the horse came to be regarded as a pet by the increasingly pony-mad French. Nevertheless, the average French consumer did not seem too fazed at the prospect of eating his new friend, as the horsemeat industry in France continued to thrive around the middle of the century (110,290 *tonnes équivalent-carcasse* or TEC, the industrial unit of measurement of horsemeat, were consumed in 1964).[11] But in the 1980s, something disastrous happened to the horseflesh trade: the Devil recreated the former 1960s sex symbol and fashion model Brigitte Bardot as a vegetarian animal rights activist. She vociferously denounced the act of eating an animal that had become man's loyal companion, and condemned the – admittedly ghastly – conditions in which horses were transported to slaughter. It is probably at least partly down to Bardot's influence that consumption of horsemeat in France fell dramatically in the 1990s.

Contrary to popular belief, then, the French are becoming increasingly *hippophile* and less and less *hippophage*. In 2004, for example, France consumed 25,380 tonnes of horsemeat (mainly imported from abroad) – less than half the amount consumed in Italy (65,950 tonnes). The Italian market remains the main export market for French horsemeat, valued at 90 million euros per year.[12] According to figures from the French livestock rearers' association OFIVAL (*L'Office national interprofessionnel des viandes, de l'élevage et de l'aviculture*), hippophagy dropped by 60 per cent between 1980 and 2001. And relative to other types of meat, the French don't consume much horsemeat at all – just 0.4 kg per French person per year in 2005, compared to 22.5 kg of beef.[13] The French, in fact – today as in the past – tend to eat horsemeat most when pushed by fear of something worse: Bovine Spongiform Encephalopathy, for example. (Rates of horsemeat consumption shot up during the mad cow disease crisis of the mid 1990s, which led to a ten-year ban on export of British beef to the rest of the European Union.) Even now, the average Frenchman would prefer to eat a horse than British beef. Many French people actually think that BSE stands for 'British Spongiform Encephalopathy'. Nothing, in fact, terrifies the nation of the Laughing Cow more than the spectre of *la vache folle*.

Meanwhile, the battle in France between *hippophiles* and *hippophages* continues unabated. An attempt in 2010 to ban the consumption of horsemeat by law failed, although the animal protection leagues did manage to get it taken off the shelves of many French supermarkets by organized campaigns of letter-writing. And the *boucherie chevaline* – previously a common sight on the French high street – appears to have had its day, with only a few dozen of them now remaining in the whole of Paris. There are horse retirement homes where old Dobbin can put his hooves up in luxury after a hard life of service, and there is even a legal provision for horse owners to stipulate on a sale that their horse is not to be sent to the knacker's yard (two-thirds of French light horses and ponies are now protected in this way).[14]

AN EXCEEDINGLY NOVEL USE FOR AN OLD NAG

'At Paris, where all eccentricities are found and even encouraged, one of the latest gastronomic innovations is the use of horse-flesh.

This social phenomenon of making the horse contribute to the nourishment of the human race is not altogether new. The ancient Germans and Scandinavians had a marked liking for horse-flesh. The nomad tribes of Northern Asia make horse-flesh their favourite food.

With the high ruling prices of butcher's meat, what think you, gentlemen and housekeepers, of horse-flesh as a substitute for beef and mutton?

Banquets of horse-flesh are at present the rage in Paris, Toulouse and Berlin. The veterinary schools there pronounce horse-bone soup preferable beyond measure to the old-fashioned beef-bone liquid, and much more economical.'
From *The Curiosities of Food; or the Dainties and Delicacies of Different Nations obtained from the Animal Kingdom*
Peter Lund Simmonds (London, 1859)

The French Horse Butchers' Association, of course, has taken up arms in opposition, marshalling arguments in support of the continued consumption of horsemeat. The most convincing of these is: 'mind your own business'. The least convincing is that the nine breeds of horse reared in France for meat would die out if people stopping eating them.* Hippophagy is supported by the French racing profession and stud farms, and even the renowned horse trainer and impresario Clément Marty, known to his adoring fans as 'Bartabas', is on record as urging, '*Si vous aimez les chevaux, mangez-en!*' ('If you love horses, eat them!'). An acrimonious debate on the horsemeat question is currently raging in France between tweedy traditionalists on one side, and urban reformers on the other. In some ways, this clash has parallels with the foxhunting debate of the early 2000s in Brit-

* One cannot, somehow, be convinced of an argument that says that the continued survival of a species depends upon its being eaten.

ain – the main difference being that, apart from a few diehard activists, the French public is nothing like as exercised by the rights and wrongs of eating horses as the British public was by the morality of hunting foxes with hounds.

The relatively *laissez-faire* attitude of most of the French public on the horsemeat issue was illustrated by the French reaction to the 'Horsegate' scandal of 2013. The crisis blew up when '100 per cent beef' products – including burgers, lasagnes and chilli con carne produced by Findus, Picard and other frozen-food manufacturers – were found to consist of anything up to '100 per cent horse'. Investigations across the European Union revealed a tangled network of abattoirs, subcontractors, traders, meat processors and frozen-food distributors. In France, a Languedoc-based meat-processing company was accused by the French government of selling horsemeat labelled as beef. The French government and consumers were enraged, like everybody else, over the issue of traceability: a government inquiry was immediately set up and calls made to the EU for the labelling of presumptive 'beef' by country of origin.

The French response to British expressions of outrage at the idea of consuming horsemeat, however, was a giant Gallic shrug of the shoulders at the incomprehensible sentimentality of the British towards animals. As the food critic of the newspaper *Le Monde*, Jean-Claude Ribaut, observed: 'It's an English ethnocentric attitude that applies also to rabbit, andouillette, frogs and calves' heads.' He added that, unlike the French, who legally define a horse as a farm animal, 'the English consider the horse a domestic animal. That's their right,' noting for good measure that horsemeat is low in fat and ideal for *steak tartare*.[15] *Le Monde* even dug up an expert on the history and culture of food to explain to its readers the weird British antipathy to eating horseflesh: according to the distinguished academic, this aversion is due to Britain's inception of the Industrial Revolution, which meant that horses lost their status as working animals and became pets at an earlier date than in other parts of Continental Europe.[16]

The reaction of French consumers interviewed in supermarkets by the national television news was not so much disgust and outrage at eating horse, as disgust and outrage at not knowing what they were eating. Perhaps the French have a point. After all, if one can tuck into octopus and pufferfish sashimi without batting an eyelid (these are now standard fare in the average hip London restaurant), should sliced raw horsemeat with grated garlic, miso paste and soy sauce really pose much of a problem? (In fact, the 'Horsegate' scandal revealed that a number of Asian restaurants in Britain had been discreetly but openly serving horsemeat successfully for years.) As a number of commentators on both sides of the Channel have pointed out, the true issue of 'Horsegate' is not so much the rights and wrongs of eating horses, as the fast-disappearing traceability of what we eat in a vast multinational production line.

Never may the French be accused of failing to turn a situation to their advantage, however. The solution to the crisis, according to their national media, is simple: *vive le boeuf français!*

Myth Evaluation: *Partly true. The French are divided between hippophiles and hippophages, but in any event they eat a lot less horse than the Italians.*

... AND FROGS' LEGS... AND SNAILS

If it's your job to eat a frog, it's best to do it first thing in the morning. And if it's your job to eat two frogs, it's best to eat the biggest one first.
MARK TWAIN, AMERICAN WRITER (1835–1910)

There is no doubt that frogs and snails are indelibly associated in the English folk imagination with the French, mainly because they are said to eat them. The names we give to our Gallic neighbours reflect this long-held metaphorical association: *Frogs, Froggies, Johnny Crapaud...* But whether the Froggies do indeed consume the vast quantity of amphibian body parts that we tend to assume, perhaps deserves a deeper inquiry.

As far as frogs are concerned, the association between the French and jumping amphibians goes back into the mists of time. It probably originated with the heraldic device of the ancient kings of France, which was 'three toads erect, saltant' (Guillim's *Display of Heraldrie*, 1611). Ironically, the first recorded references to the French as 'frogs' seem to have come from the French themselves: as early as the sixteenth century the French apothecary and putative seer Nostradamus referred to the French as *crapauds*, or toads, declaring in a typically elliptical statement, that *les anciens crapauds prenderont Sara*. (As 'Sara' is the word 'Aras' reversed, when the French under Louis XIV took Arras from the Spaniards, this verse was quoted as prophecy.) The term 'frogs' was widely used of the Parisians when much of Paris was a quagmire or *marais* – *Qu'en disent les grenouilles?* ('What will the frogs say about it?') was in the 1700s a common phrase at the royal court in Versailles.[17] In England, however, 'frog' was originally used to denote the inhabitants of the marshy Fens of East

Il pleut, il mouille,
c'est la fête à la grenouille,
Il pleut, il fait pas beau,
c'est la fête à l'escargot.

It's raining, there's a fog,
it's the party of the frog,
It's raining, there's a gale,
it's the party of the snail.
FRENCH CHILDREN'S RHYME

Anglia and swampy flatlands of Holland; 'Nic Frog' was once a nickname for a Dutchman. The transference of the amphibious appellation to the French took place in the mid-seventeenth century, fuelled at the turn of the eighteenth century by the Napoleonic Wars.[18] The image was reinforced in subsequent years by the known penchant of the French for frogs' legs as a culinary delicacy. In his *Grand Dictionnaire de cuisine* (1873), Alexandre Dumas remarks that the English, who had a horror of frogs' legs, had for some 'sixty years' been drawing caricatures of French people consuming them.

As for the term *Rosbifs* or 'roast beefs', used by the French to refer to the English, this originated from the supposed dish of preference of His (or Her) Majesty's subjects.* The English were historically associated with the colour red, presumably from the uniforms worn by Wellington's 'redcoats' at Waterloo.[19] For the same reason they were also referred to at this time as *homards*, or lobsters.[20] Some uncharitable French commentators have also explained the terms *Rosbif* and *homard* as allusions to the colour of your average Englishman after exposure to the sun. French appellations of an unkind nature relating to the typical complexion of the average Englishman are legion, and include the fetching term *têtes d'endives*, or 'chicory heads' (chicory is cultivated in the dark to preserve the whiteness of the leaves).

Are the French the voracious eaters of cold-blooded amphibians that we think they are? It seems that they are not. In reality, the French don't eat nearly as many frogs' legs as one might expect. The biggest European importer of frogs' legs is not France but little Belgium, which imported a weighty 24,696 tons in the period from 1999 to 2009. Frogland itself trailed with a mere 10,453 tons. Nor do the Americans appear to be as frog-shy as one might expect: in the last decade, 21,491 tons of frogs' legs were imported into the USA.[21] Frogs' legs, in fact, are considered a delicacy in many parts of the world. In the Far East they are found in soups, or caramelized in sticky piles with sesame seeds. In the southern states of the USA they form an integral

* Now out of date for, as we all know, today's ubiquitous English national dish is curry.

part of Cajun cuisine, either coated in breadcrumbs or skewered on a barbecue. There are many in Texas who fondly remember frog giggin' (i.e. frog hunting) in their younger days, and grilled frogs' legs with cornbread and purple hull peas is still considered a classic summer dish in the Lone Star State. In France, on the other hand, frogs' legs are increasingly seen as a somewhat eccentric dish with the retro appeal of traditional cuisine at its most earthy, rooted in the regions or *le terroir*. If you see them at all, they will generally be drowned in butter, garlic and parsley. They are – allegedly – delicious, and as Hannibal Lecter said of the French themselves, supposedly taste like chicken. But a word to the wise: before attempting to cook them, you should be aware that fresh frogs' legs apparently deal with *rigor mortis* in a very different way from chicken. It's no coincidence that Italian scientist Luigi Galvani used dead frogs for his pioneering investigations of bioelectricity in the 1780s: the legs will likely twitch in the pan when placed in direct contact with the heat.

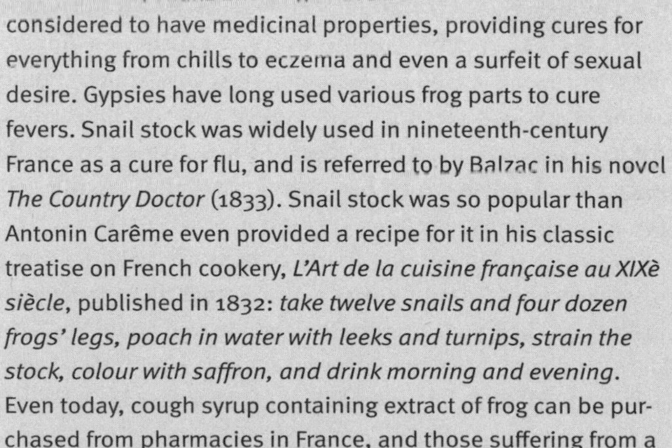

CURES FOR A FROG IN THE THROAT

For centuries, snails and frogs have been considered to have medicinal properties, providing cures for everything from chills to eczema and even a surfeit of sexual desire. Gypsies have long used various frog parts to cure fevers. Snail stock was widely used in nineteenth-century France as a cure for flu, and is referred to by Balzac in his novel *The Country Doctor* (1833). Snail stock was so popular than Antonin Carême even provided a recipe for it in his classic treatise on French cookery, *L'Art de la cuisine française au XIXè siècle*, published in 1832: *take twelve snails and four dozen frogs' legs, poach in water with leeks and turnips, strain the stock, colour with saffron, and drink morning and evening.* Even today, cough syrup containing extract of frog can be purchased from pharmacies in France, and those suffering from a surfeit of sexual desire can try toad poison in the form of the homeopathic remedy *Rana Bufo 5CH*.

Nobody is sure how this got started. Probably a couple of French master chefs were standing around one day, and they found a snail, and one of them said: 'I bet that if we called this something like "escargot", tourists would eat it.' Then they had a hearty laugh, because 'escargot' is the French word for 'fat crawling bag of phlegm'.

DAVE BARRY'S ONLY TRAVEL GUIDE YOU'LL EVER NEED (1991)

Rest assured, though, they really are dead.

Which brings us to the sticky subject of snails. Unlike frogs' legs, snails *are* eaten in vast quantities in France, the French being the largest world consumers of gastropods, at close to a billion snails eaten every year.[22] The snail is a part of French folklore, the subject of endless stories, legends and *comptines* (children's songs). Every French region has its own name for the humble creature: *cagouilles* in Saintonge, *carago* in Provence, *carnar* in Lorraine, *schnacka* in Alsace, *lumas* in Poitou, *caracol* in Flanders, *carcalauda* in Roussillon, and *cantaleu* in Nice. French gastronomy and the gastropod are as intimately linked as a snail to its shell: one of the signature dishes of French cuisine is *escargots de Bourgogne*, or snails stuffed with garlic butter and parsley.* The very creation of the dish *escargots de Bourgogne* is the stuff of legend. According to the story, in 1814 the great French politician and diplomat Charles-Maurice de Talleyrand-Périgord (commonly known simply as 'Talleyrand') asked his chef, Antonin Carême, to create a dish for a dinner in honour of Tsar Alexander I. Carême, who came from Burgundy, conjured up the buttery, garlicky confection, which became an instant classic, as integral to the French festive season as that other French fetish which has been known to discomfit some foreign visitors, *foie gras*.

In days gone by, the *chasse aux escargots* or snail hunt used to be as popular a family pastime in France after a shower of rain as blackberry picking in England, or frog giggin' in Texas. Many an ageing Frenchman's eyes will mist over in fond recollection of childhood days spent poking about under bushes for

* Like frogs' legs. For some reason, things that might be considered somewhat icky tend to be slathered in butter, garlic and parsley in French cuisine. Perhaps because virtually anything tastes good with this sublime accompaniment.

choicely glutinous specimens, which once caught would be fattened up on a diet of thyme leaves, prepared for cooking with a generous covering of salt, washed several times to get rid of the slime, and then plunged into boiling water. The classic Burgundy snail used to feed on the famous vineyards of its original home, to be collected by peasants and sent in baskets by train to the chic restaurants of Paris. But today the Burgundy snail is virtually extinct, and there are tough restrictions on snail-gathering in the wild. To satisfy the massive demand for *escargots de Bourgogne*, the French *escargotiers* now import vast numbers of snails from Central and Eastern Europe, where they are gathered in the wild by local villagers. In fact, if you order *escargots de Bourgogne* in a French bistro, the snails will most likely have come from Turkey, Poland, Hungary, Romania or Ukraine. The one place they are more or less certain *not* to have come from is Burgundy.

Everyone is delighted by the tree-shaded terrace, but when the menu arrives a shiver runs through the group.

FRENCHMAN DESCRIBING AMERICAN EXPRESS TRIP TO VERSAILLES, QUOTED IN RENÉE-PIERRE GOSSET, *LES TOURISTES À PARIS*, 1950

There is much confusion among the French, as well as everybody else, over the term *escargots de Bourgogne*. This may refer to the actual Burgundy snail, but most often it refers to the celebrated dish that is cooked *à la Bourguignonne* – i.e. 'in the Burgundy fashion' (the culinary myth attributed to Carême). The Burgundy snail is defined as the species *Helix pomatia* and is not specific to Burgundy – hence it can, and usually does, nowadays come from Eastern Europe. The species *Helix lucorum* comes from Turkey and is often passed off either as the actual Burgundy snail, or as a dish cooked in the fashion of *escargots de Bourgogne*. Snail farms in France produce the *Cornu aspersum* or *gros/petit gris*, which is the only variety you can safely be assured is well and truly French. Unfortunately, real French snails are rare these days.

Does it matter that a Burgundy snail is no longer a snail from Burgundy? Surely all snails are created equal? Not quite. The hitch is that gastropods have a high rate of retention of toxic metals and other substances from the soil (including cadmium, lead, zinc, copper, mercury, arsenic, and radon). So, along with all that garlic and butter that accompanies your Polish/Romanian/Ukrainian snail, you could in theory also be ingesting Chernobyl fallout. Not to mention the fact that certain unscrupulous dealers have been known to chop up the giant African snail, or *achatine*, and try to pass it off as the genuine thing (unfortunate, as it can play host to a parasitic worm that causes a type of meningitis). Better to stick with the home-grown French molluscs: at least you know what they (and consequently you) have eaten. Best of all, you will definitely put a frog in the throat of that snooty Parisian waiter if you ask, before you order the *escargots de Bourgogne*, whether it's *Helix pomatia, Helix lucorum*, or *Cornu aspersum* on the menu. He'll never think of the *Rosbifs* in the same way again.

Myth Evaluation: *Partly true. The French aren't as partial to frogs' legs as everybody thinks, but they are avid consumers of snails.*

The French are the world's no. 1 consumers of cheese

A dessert without cheese is like a beautiful woman with only one eye.
JEAN-ANTHELME BRILLAT-SAVARIN (1755–1826)

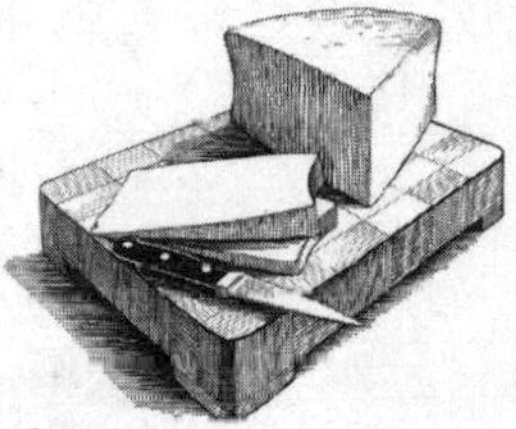

The French: a nation of 'cheese-eating surrender monkeys', as Groundskeeper Willie infamously said in an episode of the animated TV series *The Simpsons*. While the allegation of simian affiliation is contentious, to say the least, and cowardliness the subject of another chapter (see page 202), cheese eating is incontrovertibly something that the French do a lot of. Cheese is to France what the hamburger is to America, or chicken tikka masala now is to Britain: part of the national heritage. In fact, the average Frenchman eats around 26 kg of cheese a year (compared to 15 kg for the average American, and 11kg for the average Briton).[23] 'How can one be expected to govern a country with 246 different cheeses?' General de Gaulle once complained. By introducing 246 protection orders, of course. Actually, de Gaulle underestimated quite badly the number of cheeses produced in France. The real total is closer to 1,000. Many are produced in the French regions by local craftsmen or artisans from raw cow's milk, and are now protected under European law by the *AOP* label (*Appellation d'origine protégée*, formerly the *AOC* label or *Appellation d'origine contrôlée*).[24] Cheese, more than anything produced in France (wine excepted), embodies the French concept of *terroir*: that is, the idea that the food we eat is not an anonymous, factory-made product but rather a living, breathing entity with a personality according to what it is, where it comes from, and what has been done to it. 'Good cooking', the renowned French food critic known as Curnonsky (in real life Maurice Edmond Sailland; see page 43) once wrote, 'is when things taste of what they are.'

The *AOP* label is designed to protect this concept. Thus, the cheese that for many is the king of French cheeses – the *AOP* blue cheese Roquefort – can only be made from the raw milk of the Laucane sheep, fed on pastures within a pre-defined zone of the Aveyron *département* and surrounding regions, ripened with the mould of the genus *Penicillium roqueforti,* and aged in the damp, cool caves of the town of Roquefort-sur-Soulzon. Roquefort has been made in the caves of this town on the hills of the southern part of the Massif Central since time immemorial. The story goes that a local shepherd, spotting a beautiful shepherdess in the distance, was in such a hurry to pursue her that he left his lunch in the cave. Returning much later to retrieve it, he saw that the bread and cheese had gone mouldy. He tasted the cheese, and a pungent legend was born: in the words of Curnonsky, 'the genius of Roquefort', which 'brings with it the powerful scent of the earth and the fragrance of the prairies; whose presence seems to open a window onto the horizons of far-flung landscapes'.[25]

If life was once blessed for the French cheese-makers, however, it is tough for them nowadays. Sneaky EU legislation restricting the use of raw or unpasteurized milk (the key ingredient of artisanal cheese, and the only true milk for connoisseurs) has nibbled away at regional French cheese production, as has *listeria* hysteria fanned by the international press. For real cheese enthusiasts, pasteurization is a nuclear bomb that annihilates every organism in the milk, good or bad, including not only bacteria, but also friendly gut flora.*

* Despite the bad press surrounding raw milk, a 2008 study by the French agricultural research institute INRA (*Institut national de la recherche agronomique*) entitled *Qu'est-ce que le lait cru?* stated that *Listeria monocytogenes* had been more frequently detected in pasteurized milk than raw milk.

THE BIG CHEESE OF FRENCH FOOD CRITICS

Maurice Edmond Sailland (1872–1956), a.k.a. 'Curnonsky' or the '*Prince des Gastronomes*', was France's most celebrated food critic of the early twentieth century. He was the poet, or rather conductor, of French cheese: according to him, the northern French cheese Maroilles was 'the sound of the saxophone in the symphony of French cheeses'. Sadly, he did not assign instruments to the other cheeses of the French orchestra, so the musical qualities of Camembert, Brie and Comté remain a subject of speculation.

Curnonsky had a passionate dislike of cheese boards, considering that a meal should be finished on a single note rather than a cacophony of different flavours. He also took the French notion of *terroir*, or the connection between the thing eaten and its environment, to uncharted lengths. He went so far as to advise '... never eat the left leg of a partridge, for that is the leg it sits on, which makes the circulation sluggish'. He was also partial to asking for his beef to be cooked 'pink as a baby's bottom', and referred to French fries as 'the most spiritual creation of Parisian genius'. Gertrude Stein wrote that Curnonsky resembled a 'physically amorphous creature, not dissimilar to an unfinished tub of butter'. Restaurant owners quaked in their shoes to see him waiting to be served at one of their tables, his crisp white napkin tied under his many chins. He died falling out of the window of his Parisian apartment, reputedly because he felt faint from being obliged to follow a diet.

Pasteurized milk is no longer a living organism, bursting with unseen life and the feral flavours of the beast from which it came, but a mere white liquid containing proteins, fats and lactose, produced by the mammary glands of female mammals. Similarly, pasteurized blue cheese is no longer milk's leap to immortality, but a dead substance streaked with visible fungal mycelia.*

* With pasteurization, the *bête noire* of French artisanal cheese, the French have been hoist with their own petard. It was a Frenchman, the chemist and

Raw milk cheese made up only 15 per cent of French cheese production in 2011, and the number of local cheese shops or *fromageries* reduced by three-quarters in the thirty-odd years from 1966 to 1998.[26] For the big beasts among the French industrial dairy producers, cheese is France's money-spinning 'white oil'. But for small artisanal cheese-makers, it's a different story. According to the *Association Fromages de Terroirs* (Association for Regional Cheeses), more than fifty regional cheeses in France have died out in the last thirty years. This has not been helped by the refusal of ageing peasant farmers to pass on their trade secrets. The Lyonnaise cheese known as *la galette des Monts-d'Or*, for example, which had been produced for 400 years, died out in the 2000s following the death of the last producer, who refused to divulge the secret recipe.[27] Other regional cheeses are in danger as we speak: only three producers in the Loire, for example, continue to produce the bright, orange-rinded *Fourme de Montbrison*, made out of milk from the cows of the Haut-Forez. *Où sont les neiges d'antan?* the famous French *chansonnier* Georges Brassens once sang, quoting the medieval poet François Villon. Gallic cheese lovers might do well to respond, *Mais où sont les fromages d'antan?*

The French press has been busy lamenting the fact that French people today seem more interested in spending their money on mobile phones and fast cars than the traditional Gallic priority of fine food. Television interviews, conducted in the street by the French state broadcaster *France* 5 in January 2012, revealed that many French people did not know the difference between 'raw' and 'pasteurized' milk.* They bought cheese in bulk and put it in the freezer. They did not even know the difference between any old Camembert and a *Camembert de Normandie AOP*. Few people do. The difference arises from the fact that the villagers of Camembert in Normandy lost an attempt to have their cheese protected in 1926. Therefore, Camembert can come

---

microbiologist Louis Pasteur, who invented the technique that is coming back to haunt them.

* 29 January 2012, France 5, *La Guerre des fromages qui puent*. Gilles Capelle / Galaxie Presse / France Télévision.

Roquefort should be eaten only on one's knees.
ALEXANDRE BALTHAZAR LAURENT GRIMOD DE LA REYNIÈRE (1758–1837)

from virtually anywhere these days – Egypt, Tasmania, Ecuador or even Thailand. Camembert made in the traditional way in its original home is, however, protected, under the name *Camembert de Normandie AOP*. It is hard to find this even in French supermarkets – you have a better chance at the local *fromagerie,* if it still exists. The aroma of a true Camembert – should you ever be lucky enough to find one – has been compared to the whiff of God's feet, and divinely odoriferous it is indeed. The French, it is feared, are losing their *savoir-faire*, traditionally handed down through the generations. Their tastes are changing. The palate of the new generation no longer favours the pungent, feral bouquets of the cheeses of *le terroir*, preferring instead the processed blandness of *Babybel* or *La Vache qui rit* (The Laughing Cow).

But France's position as top cheese nation faces yet greater threats than growing domestic indifference and ignorance. For, while the French are deserting *Fourme d'Ambert* for *Squizzi the liquid cheese in a tube*, foreigners such as the Americans are discovering the hallowed French concept of *terroir*. In the 1980s, germophobic Britain and the United States elevated pasteurization to an Eleventh Commandment. Now, cheesed off with the blandness of factory food, the nation that invented Cheez Whizz has taken artisan cheese to its bosom with all the zeal of a convert. Stinky cheeses are suddenly all the rage in the USA, 'mold-ripened' the new 'rotten'. In recent years, the production of raw-milk cheese in the USA has multiplied by thousands. Artisanal cheese-makers are springing up everywhere: New York, Vermont, Los Angeles, Wisconsin. *Le terroir* – a concept unknown to the English language until a few years ago – is the buzzword on the lips of every new graduate of food technology. In New York, artisanal cheese from the *Broadway terroir* is even produced in a skyscraper in the city centre.* In Vermont, a for-

* It is intriguing to speculate on the defining characteristics of the *Broadway terroir*, if it were ever to be granted an *AOP*. Carbon dioxide, photochemical smog, and emissions from motor vehicles spring to mind.

mer financier who quit Wall Street for a life of artisanal cheese-making blasted a dozen caves into a hillside when he found that he lacked the right conditions in which to mature his crop. Already, Michelin-starred restaurants in New York offer half-French, half-American artisan cheeses on their cheese boards (a few years ago, it would have been 100 per cent French). As the ultimate insult, an advertisement in 2011 by the Québec government agency funding new business projects, *Investissement Québec*, featured a Québecquois farmer herding his sheep across the fields, with the strapline: 'Soon it will be the French who are eating *my* cheese.' French cheese loyalists are in despair. How long will it be before French cheese goes the same way as French wine? Just as the Old World châteaux *grands crus* have been ousted by New World upstarts such as Jacob's Creek and Oyster Bay, it is surely only a matter of time before classic Gallic cheeses such as *Crottin de Chavignol*, *Pont-l'Évêque*, and *Picodon de l'Ardèche* are replaced by Twig Farm, Slyboro, Redwood Hill or Cowgirl Creamery.

Worse still, not only are the French turning away from their own artisanal cheeses, but they are not even the number one cheese consumers in the world today. The global cheese-eating champions are – perhaps surprisingly – the feta-loving Greeks, who consume an impressive 31 kg of cheese per person per year.[28] The *Association Fromages de Terroirs* considers the issue a deadly serious one, and has even launched a cheesy calendar featuring scantily clad women with names like *Mademoiselle Cantal* and *Mademoiselle Gruyère* posing astride cheese wheels, in a bid to sex up the image of the dowdy *fromages régionaux*. There is now a *Diplôme Universitaire Fromage et Patrimoine* (University Diploma in Cheese and Patrimony), offered by selected French universities in collaboration with cheese industry specialists, in an attempt to transmit ancient cheese-making *savoir-faire* to the lacklustre younger generation.

If you believe what you read in the French press, there's a New World conspiracy out there to stamp out the glorious heritage of Gallic cheese. But – much as the French like to blame everybody else for their regional cheese crisis – the problem really lies at home rather than abroad. The French need to rediscover pride in their second-biggest olfactory legacy after perfume. They need to stop scoffing the processed stuff, and buy their own regional cheese. Now, that would really wipe the smile off the face of the laughing cow.

Myth Evaluation: *Not true. The laurels for the cheese-eating champions of the world go to the Greeks.*

The French consume a very great deal of garlic

There are five elements: earth, air, fire, water and garlic.
LOUIS FELIX DIAT, FRENCH CHEF (1885–1957)

Since time immemorial, people have praised and vilified the humble *Allium sativum* in equal measure. Garlic – the poor relation of the alliums, a family of loftier legumes that also includes the leek, shallot, onion and chive – has traditionally enjoyed a quasi-mystical status for its culinary, medicinal and vampire-exorcizing qualities. The French chef and restaurateur Marcel Boulestin, *patron* of London's prestigious Restaurant Français in the late 1920s, is reputed to have said, 'It is not really an exaggeration to say that peace and happiness begin, geographically, where garlic is used in cooking.' Famed for its medicinal properties, garlic was used as an antiseptic on wounds by shepherds long before Joseph Lister was born or Louis Pasteur confirmed its antibiotic properties; and as late as the First World War, the British government appealed to the public to donate their home-grown garlic for the wounded. Indeed, garlic was so widely used to treat battlefield injuries that it was known as 'Russian penicillin'.[29] Henri of Navarre, later King Henri IV of France (1589–1610), had a clove of garlic rubbed into his lips as a baby to protect him against evil and remained faithful to the herb all his life, consuming a clove a day for its alleged aphrodisiacal properties. He was said to have 'breath that would knock a bull flat from twenty paces away'.[30]

On the other hand, the pungent perfume that inevitably lingers on the breath after garlic consumption has earned the 'stinking rose' as much opprobrium in history as its medicinal qualities have earned it praise. Thus in Ancient Greece, those who had consumed garlic were forbidden to enter into the Temple of Cybele; and in the Middle Ages, King Alfonso of Castile ordered that any of his knights who ate onion or garlic were forbidden to come to court for a month.[31] Garlic, so goes an old

Indian saying, *is as good as ten mothers… for sending the girls away.*

Eat garlic. It revives your body and keeps importunate folk away.
ALEXANDRE VIALATTE, FRENCH WRITER (1901–71)

More than any other herb (with the possible exception of basil and oregano in Italy), garlic has long been associated with Continental cuisine – and, consequently, its pungent odour with dubious Continental exhalations. Thus American slang terms for garlic in the 1920s included 'Italian perfume', 'halitosis', and 'Bronx vanilla'. Alexandre Dumas, in his *Grand dictionnaire de cuisine* (1873), observed that 'everybody recognizes the smell of garlick, except the person who has eaten it, and cannot therefore understand why all turn away at his approach'. He also noted that the cuisine of Provence in particular is 'based on garlick', and that the air of Provence is 'impregnated with the perfume of this herb'. Without garlic, French cuisine would be lacking in countless signature dishes: *aïoli* (a Provençal garlic mayonnaise, traditionally served with the croutons that top the classic fish soup or *bouillabaisse*), *moules à la crème*, *fondue*, and of course the celebrated Burgundy snails or *escargots de Bourgogne*, typically served wallowing in a garlicky, buttery pool. Garlic is also a vital ingredient in some French cheeses, most notably perhaps in the case of *Boursin*, the squidgy garlicky spread that has travelled to the shelves of most of the world's supermarkets.

Although there are over 300 types of garlic grown in the world, garlic in England and the United States is usually divided into two broad categories – the 'soft-necked' or common-or-garden variety, most commonly found in supermarkets, and the 'hard-necked' variety with a stalk, considered the connoisseur's version. In France, a distinction is drawn not so much between soft-necked and hard-necked varieties, but rather according to colour and time of harvesting: the small, hard heads of 'white' garlic are generally seen in street markets in the winter, and therefore known as *l'ail d'automne*, whereas the more luscious, rosy heads of 'pink' garlic usually appear in the spring, and are consequently known as *l'ail de printemps*. (The French word for an old-fashioned heavy-knit jumper – *le chandail* – actually comes from an abbreviation of *marchand d'ail*, or garlic-seller, and derives from the jerseys that were worn by garlic-sellers in the old fruit and vegetable market at Les Halles in Paris at the turn of the last century).[32] Three varieties of French garlic have been granted protected geographical status: the white garlic harvested in the regions of Lomagne (Tarn-et-Garonne) and the Drôme, and the pink garlic of Lautrec (Tarn). Of these, the most luxurious is the rich and oozingly odoriferous Pink Rose of Lautrec. Farmed in the region for centuries, according to legend it arrived there in the Middle Ages, when a travelling merchant was unable to pay his hotel bill, and paid instead with a few bulbs of this potent specimen. Planted in the ground, the bulbs gave birth to a powerfully pungent variety that, hand-picked and trussed in a traditional bunch or *manouille*, now finds its way to restaurants around the globe.

All in all, garlic is to traditional French cuisine what the beret is to the Basque Country: the one is unimaginable without the other. And just as garlic is indissolubly linked to French cuisine, so, in the popular imagination, is garlic breath linked to the Frenchman. Only a few decades ago, a voyage on the Paris Métro necessitated plunging into a malodorous miasma of garlic, Gitanes and cheap perfume – a fact attested by a US military pamphlet issued in 1945 to address complaints about the French made by disgruntled American servicemen stationed in France during the Second World War. Entitled *112 Gripes about the French*, the pamphlet attempts to answer the GIs' grievances with reasoned responses. One of the commonest gripes listed is the fact that 'you ride on the subway and the smell almost knocks you out, Garlic, sweat – and perfume!' In response, the pamphlet authors concede that 'French subways today are overcrowded, hot, untidy, and smell bad.' But, they argue, 'You smell garlic because the French, who are superb cooks, use more of it than we do.'[33]

Such subterranean odours, however, are now scents of the past. The Paris underground no longer oozes with the juices of the stinking rose (although it does have plenty of other nasty niffs – more about which in a later chapter). These days, it would appear that the French are (statistically at least) no longer the champion garlic-munchers of national stereotype. The biggest world consumers of garlic today are not the French – or even the Italians – but the South Koreans, who eat a startling 10 kilos of the stuff per capita annually.[34] Nor are the French even in the top rank of world garlic producers. The global garlic production league is in fact headed by China, which produces 75 per cent of the world's garlic (a stinking 12.5 million tons), followed by India and South Korea.[35] The French garlic industry, in fact, is a mere drop in the ocean of garlic production. If you buy your garlic in England or France, chances are that it will have come from Spain, Argentina, China or Egypt: in 2006 alone, the UK imported some 25,000 tons of fresh

A PUNGENT REVOLUTION

A curious feature of French garlic is that the varieties are named after some of the months in the French Revolutionary Calendar, a bizarre experiment in timekeeping introduced by the Revolutionary government, which lasted for twelve years, from 1793 to 1805, before it was wisely abandoned. French varieties of garlic thus have such exotic names as 'Germidour' (from *Germinal*, the first month of spring), 'Messidrome' (from *Messidor*, the first month of summer) and 'Fructidor' (the final summer month). The principal aim of the Revolutionary calendar was to rationalize and remove all trace of religion from timekeeping. Time began from the date of the Revolution, the twelve months had their traditional names replaced with 'poetic' French equivalents evoking the weather around Paris, and saints' days were replaced with patriotic days dedicated to French flora and fauna, crops and proletarian tools. French citizens of the new Republic found themselves celebrating the day of the Plough, Pickaxe, Grub-Hoe, Parsnip, Cauliflower and, of course, Garlic. Relics of the Revolutionary Calendar live on in French nomenclature to this day, including the famous dish 'Lobster Thermidor', and the ships of the 'Floréal' class in the French Navy.

He added that a Frenchman in the train had given him a great sandwich that so stank of garlic that he had been inclined to throw it at the fellow's head.
FORD MADOX FORD,
ENGLISH NOVELIST (1873–1939),
PROVENCE

garlic from China. Garlic is even being farmed commercially (albeit on a relatively small scale) on the Isle of Wight.

The reality is that garlic consumption in France has taken a nosedive in recent years. This is particularly the case with the younger generation, who are keener on hamburgers and sushi than on *bouillabaisse* with *aioli* or gastropods swimming in garlicky butter. Recent figures show that the biggest consumers of garlic in France today are the elderly and middle-aged, with younger people and families with young children at the bottom of the consumption ladder.[36] Conversely, the market in garlic in the USA has increased: Americans eat three times as much of it as they did in the 1980s. Doubtless some of this rise is explained by the Anglo-Saxons rediscovering the near-magical health-promoting properties of this most aromatic of the alliums.[37]

Could garlic be quietly going the same way as French regional *fromages*, and if so, why hasn't there been more of an outcry? Perhaps because there are simply too many French food wars being waged right now. In the heat of the bloodier battles to save French cheese and wine, another pungent Gallic tradition seems to be drawing its last breath, without anyone even kicking up a stink about it…

Myth Evaluation: *Partly true. French people have traditionally eaten a lot of garlic, but the quantity they consume annually is decreasing, and comes nowhere near the amount eaten by the world's greatest garlic consumers, the South Koreans.*

The French don't eat fast food

Fast food is a perverse pleasure. Firstly, an intellectual ecstasy: the indulgence of wallowing in political incorrectness.
PHILIPPE DELERM, *DICKENS, BARBE À PAPA ET AUTRES NOURRITURES DELECTABLES* (2005)

The French *never* eat fast food. Of course they don't. For the average French person, lunch is a leisurely meal partaken with a carafe of wine and good company, on a sunny bistro terrace. Children enjoy four-course lunches prepared by their school canteen and showcasing France's finest foods, featuring *foie gras* and a rotating cheese course. The French do not grab a wilting sandwich filled with plastic cheese or nitrate-soaked ham and wolf it down at their desk while trying desperately to finish yesterday's target product profile, answer the telephone and fix an appointment for their child with the behavioural psychologist. The French don't do fast food. *Jamais!*

To understand the position of fast food in France today, one has to look at recent history. The French have coined a special word for fast food: *malbouffe*. And, France being a nation of Cartesian dualisms, *malbouffe* naturally has its opposite – *bonne bouffe*. The battle of the good and bad *bouffes* for French stomachs has swung this way and that over the years. The first blow was landed by a group of French farmers led by a certain José Bové in 1999, who drove their tractors through an early McDonald's restaurant then being built in Millau, in the Midi-Pyrénées. The farmers were protesting against US restrictions on the importation of Roquefort cheese: consequently, they took revenge on the Temple of the Plastic Slice by throwing bricks through the windows and handing out Roquefort to the crowd of gathered onlookers. Martyred by a jail sentence, Bové became a cult figure for French resistance against the American-led invasion of *malbouffe*: a diminutive firebrand with a handlebar moustache, he provided the land of Astérix with a real-life, plucky Gallic defender against McDomination. After

Millau, there was a rash of McDonald's 'incidents' in France, including the dumping of manure and rotten apples in McDonald's restaurants and the kidnapping of Ronald McDonald effigies by sundry eco-warriors, one of whom accused the clown of being 'the subliminal ambassador of mercantile empires of standardization and conformism'.[38]

The response of McDonald's France was quickly (and smartly) to change the subliminal messages it was sending. Out went the massive telegraph poles surmounted by golden arches that signalled the conquest of the French countryside by Uncle Sam, along with the neon lighting and garish red and yellow American diner fittings. In came ambient lounge music, plush velvet sofas and armchairs, and discreet arches set against a green forest background. Burgers were offered with a choice of AOP cheeses from Cantal to Camembert, while wholegrain French mustard was an optional extra. The *McBaguette* was born, along with the *McCroque-Monsieur* and *Le Charolais*.* *McCafés* were added to the existing McDonald's restaurants, offering opulent coffees, macaroons from the luxury French chain Ladurée, and even waiter service. The message was clear: McDonald's France might be Born in the USA, but it was Made in France. And the strategy worked. Today, France is the second-biggest market in the world for McDonald's, after America.[39] Every day, 1.7 million French people eat at McDonald's; and the chain turns over €4.2 billion a year.[40] Four out of five French people know the famous McDonald's French slogan, *venez comme vous êtes* ('come as you are'). The French are clearly lovin' it. Burger King (which, when McDonald's entered the market, was one of its major competitors) made the fatal mistake of selling the American dining experience, rather than cannily going native. It didn't stand a chance. The Whopper was shown the door by the Big Mac, and today there's no doubt who's the boss. (McDonald's sole com-

---

* *Charolais* is the name of the ancient, distinctive breed of white beef cattle reared in Burgundy since the seventeenth century. McDonald's introduced the *Le Charolais* burger in its restaurants in 2011, made of meat from French livestock. It was the first time that a McDonald's burger in France had been named after the origins of the beef it contained.

petitor in the French hamburger market now is the Belgian chain Quick, although KFC has a big presence, along with Subway. After fifteen years' absence Burger King returned to France in December 2012, but it faced a tough road ahead competing with the Golden Arches.)

The most spectacularly daring marketing ploy of all was when McDonald's France first took a stand at Paris' massive agricultural fair, or *Salon d'agriculture*, in 2001. The *Salon d'agriculture* is Paris' annual encounter with rural France, the place where politicians come to be photographed shaking hands with farmers of *la France profonde* and bourgeois Parisian families come to goggle at the amount of poo that can exit the back end of a pig. Nobody could believe it when McDonald's announced it was entering the dragon's den. However, dire predictions of a repeat of the Millau bloodbath were not borne out. The McDonald's stand was a resounding success, and was even described as 'exemplary'. And why would anyone want to complain, anyway? McDonald's buys hundreds of thousands of tons of meat and potatoes from French farmers every year. It is, in fact, one of the principal purchasers of French beef.[41] Nobody in their right mind throws a brick at their best client. Not even José Bové. Indeed, Bové could be said to have done McDonald's a favour: he goaded Ronald McDonald into learning to speak French, thus winning the hearts (and the stomachs) of the French populace.

Since the furore over McDomination in the 1990s and Ronald McDonald's subsequent acceptance, the consumption of fast food in France has skyrocketed. By 2010, fast food accounted for 7 out of 10 meals eaten outside the French home, and the length of the average French meal had gone down to 31 minutes, from 1 hour 38 minutes in 1975.[42] The French are now the second-largest consumers of hamburgers in Europe, still lagging some way behind the British, but way ahead of the Germans, Spanish and Italians.[43] And as the nation's fast-food industry has ballooned, so has its waistline: a 2007 study by the French government statistics and research institute INSEE (*Institut national de la statistique et des études économiques*) found that over a third of French people were overweight, including 16 per cent of young people.[44] The figures are as yet party-balloon size compared with the hot-air balloon statistics coming from the USA and UK, but they are set to match them by 2025. Anxious about a future generation of Obélixes gobbling up the country's resources and health service, the French government has introduced legislation to ban machines dispensing colas and crisps at school and the advertising of sugary snacks during children's television. In October 2011, in the Val d'Oise town of Franconville – an area with a historically high child obesity rate – parents presented a petition to stop a McDonald's being built strategically at the intersection of local schools and the town's sports and leisure centre. Even France's answer to Jamie Oliver – the television chef Cyril Lignac – has descended on schools in the *banlieues* (the deprived suburbs on the outskirts of major cities) to try to persuade recalcitrant French teenagers to abandon KFC and return to the school canteen.*

Not everybody in France is hatin' it, though. The fast-food industry does have some surprising apologists – not least a coterie of French intellectuals. For example, in 2010 François Simon – France's most feared restaurant critic – went 'undercover' in a McDonald's restaurant to check out a Big Tasty for the television channel ARTE,† and came out with the surprising verdict that, although the 'field of flavours' was 'quite restricted', it wasn't too bad. And he reserved the highest praise for the Caramel McFlurry topped with crispy nougatine. In characteristically laconic and blackly humorous style, he summed up his opinion thus: 'At McDonald's, you can slum it. There are no words to describe it – it's pure emotion, the ultimate in junk food. For me, an ice-cream should have a perversely seductive side, in the ways it sickens you and sets you off on an internal monologue

---

* Cyril Lignac – a suave thirty-something whose flick and designer stubble are the stuff of bourgeois housewives' dreams – hates being compared to Jamie Oliver. In fact, he was accused of disparaging Mr Oliver as a cook who makes 'nosh', as opposed to himself, a chef trained in the highest gastronomic tradition (an allegation that he subsequently denied).

† *McDo, une passion française*, documentary by Stanislas Kraland, broadcast 29 December 2010 (ARTE France/Doc en Stock).

A PRINCE OF GASTRONOMES FOR THE FAST FOOD AGE

François Simon (b.1953) is one of the most feared and venerated French food critics writing today. French restaurateurs quake in their shoes to read his waspish reviews in the French newspaper *Le Figaro*, and it has been whispered that he was the inspiration for the exacting food critic Anton Ego in the 2007 Pixar film *Ratatouille*.

Simon once described a meal at the Michelin restaurant Guy Savoy as 'a three star crucifixion', lambasting M. Savoy for serving his signature artichoke and truffle soup out of season. He described the chef Marc Veyrat, who achieved the feat of a perfect 20/20 score in the Gault-Millau guide, as a 'fake peasant' with megalomaniac tendencies. Simon has the peculiar distinction of never revealing his face fully in the media, to enable him to preserve his anonymity for the purposes of restaurant reviews.

He is said to be able to cook a chicken in two hundred different ways, including in Coca-Cola, which he is alleged to have served at his wedding feast – surely an endorsement of the culinary potential of fast food at the highest level.

of the soul… ' Not without a soupçon of irony, he acknowledged that 'there is in the depths of my soul a moron who adores this stuff; I must feed this moron regularly, and obey his commands.'

For the sophisticated Parisian intelligentsia, McDonald's represents an intriguing social phenomenon: a dark rebellion against the social *Zeitgeist*, a transgression of the sacred French rules relating to family meals and dining out. And it's not just French intellectuals who are interested in the socio-economic effects of fast food. Top French chefs like Alain Ducasse have spotted the economic potential of France's desertion of the long lunch in favour of the quick snack. All over Paris and other major French towns, posh sandwich chains are mushrooming. Gone are the days when the standard Parisian worker's lunch was a *steak au poivre* and a half-carafe of tepid wine in a local bistro. These days, it could just as well be a *croque-monsieur* with shavings of Cantal, a *brioche* with *foie gras* and wasabi dressing, or even sushi (France is now Europe's biggest sushi consumer). Critics like François Simon take a laid-back view of the matter. 'When a food culture is strong,' he observed during his secretly filmed foray into *McDo*, 'you can allow a mixing of influences and accept foreign imports such as hamburgers, sushi, pizza and the like. There's nothing to get in a flap about.'

Even if they might have the occasional secret fling with a Royal Deluxe or a McFlurry, the French will always come back to the *potage bonne femme* of hearth and home. Cuisine simply runs in the Gallic blood, as visceral a reflex as hitting the street, or queuing on the motorway in August. And what is a burger and fries anyway, if not a variation on the traditional *steak-frites*?

Myth Evaluation: *False.*

The French drink wine with every meal

Burgundy makes you think of silly things, Bordeaux makes you talk of them and Champagne makes you do them.
JEAN-ANTHELME BRILLAT-SAVARIN (1755–1826)

André Simon, a French-born gourmet and wine merchant who dominated the British wine scene for much of the early twentieth century, once observed that 'food without wine is a corpse; wine without food is a ghost; united and well-matched they are as body and soul, living partners.' A few decades ago, a French meal without wine would have been gastronomic heresy. Gingham checked bistro tables in Paris and the regions came ready-dressed at lunchtime with a carafe of the local libation; dinner involved at least three or four glasses of *vin de table*; even at breakfast, barflies in the local café would customarily start the day with *un express* and a *p'tit rouge* to accompany their daily croissant. Those who abstained from wine were regarded with the deepest suspicion. 'People who never drink wine are imbeciles or hypocrites,' the poet Charles Baudelaire observed. 'A man who only drinks water has a secret to hide from his peers.'[45] The French, in fact, lived off wine in the way other people live off water; and the medieval custom of drinking wine because it was safer than water persisted well into the age of sanitation.

For a gourmet wine is not a drink but a condiment, provided that your host has chosen correctly.
ÉDOUARD DE POMAINE, FRENCH SCIENTIST AND BROADCASTER (1875–1964)

But things seem finally to be changing. Nowadays, France is still the world's biggest wine producer (followed by Italy and Spain).[46] The French are also fourth in the league of wine consumers, drinking 46 litres per person a year, or almost three bottles per person a month.* Yet while in terms of world wine

* Oddly enough, the leader in world wine consumption is the Vatican City State, whose 800 faithful manage to down an impressive 55 litres per head

consumption the French figures may seem as buoyant as a cork, the reality is that the nation's wine drinking has plummeted in the last thirty years, decreasing from 50 billion litres in 1980 to 32 billion litres in 2008.[47] In two generations, the number of bottles of wine downed annually by the French has dropped from seven to four billion bottles – the equivalent of losing one bottle a week for every adult. And whereas in 1970 the French drank over twice as much alcohol as mineral water or fruit juice, that situation has now been reversed: by 2002, they were drinking twice as much water as alcohol.[48]

What accounts for this oddly reversed transubstantiation of wine into water? It seems that the explanation lies in a profound generational shift of French attitudes to the vine. A 2011 study by researchers at the University of Toulouse[49] into wine-drinking practices across three generations of French people – those aged over 65, those aged 30–40, and those under 30 – found that only the oldest generation were daily wine drinkers. For them, wine had a sacred status as a symbol of French family life and conviviality. This was the group that recalled stories of Henri IV being baptized in Jurançon wine and had memories of swilling a cup of *troussepinette** when sweating in the fields, or the daily 'beaker of wine' that was the standard army ration. For this generation, lunch without a bottle of the local wine was unthinkable. The 30–40 year olds, on the other hand, had only the most basic knowledge of wine, namely that it involved different types of grape, vintage and complicated labelling. They were aware that top-rated French *AOC* wines carried huge prestige, and so provided an opportunity to show off to bosses and col-

I drink champagne when I win, to celebrate… and I drink champagne when I lose, to console myself.
NAPOLÉON BONAPARTE (1769–1821)

annually. Second comes the minuscule Pacific enclave of Norfolk Island, whose 2,300 residents – claiming a mixture of British and Tahitian descent going back to the mutiny on the *Bounty* – drink an average of 54.5 litres per head a year. Third comes the tiny state of Luxembourg, with a per capita figure of 52 litres.

* A form of sloe wine, produced in the Vendée in the region of the Loire.

leagues by ordering the very best. Yet in their eyes, wine was no longer an essential accompaniment to the family's daily meal, but rather something to drink in significant quantities once a week or so, with friends or colleagues. Finally, for the youngest generation – the hard-wired, social-networking under-30s – wine was almost never consumed outside of family occasions with older people.* Outside a small group of ardent young enthusiasts born into regional wine families, knowledge of wine in France's Generation Y† was practically non-existent. While they appreciated that wine was of enormous national and cultural significance, their prevailing attitude to the libation of Bacchus was one of mystification, of disconnection from an arcane and somewhat sinister Sphinx presiding over a bygone age.

And so it seems that the Anglo-Saxon myth of the French as a nation of quotidian wine-bibbers applies mainly to an older segment of the population. Across the younger French cohorts,

* Not that this means that alcohol is not consumed within this group, as we shall see in the next chapter.

† The term *Generation Y* is used primarily to refer to the generation born from the 1980s onwards. Sometimes also referred to as the *Facebook* or *Millennial Generation*, members of this cohort are typically perceived as increasingly familiar with digital and electronic technology.

drinking patterns appear to be converging with the Anglo-Saxon norm. For the French wine industry, this state of affairs has been hard to swallow. And the home market is not the only place where beleaguered Gallic winemakers are taking a drubbing. For over thirty-five years, a global war has been raging between Old and New World wines for conquest of the planet's palate. On 24 May 1976, there took place in the French capital a seminal event that has come to be known as the 'Judgement of Paris', in which celebrated wine critics carried out blind-tasting comparisons of Old and New World wines (Chardonnays and red wines). To the surprise of Steven Spurrier, the Francophile British wine merchant who had arranged the tasting, and to the lasting mortification of the French, Californian wines were judged to be the best across the board. The Judgement launched a thousand New World wines onto a market hitherto dominated by the Old. The war of the wine worlds has been raging ever since. The world's biggest importer of wine is the UK, and while French wines traditionally dominated UK wine imports, by 2012 that list was headed by Australia, followed hot on its heels by Italy,* with France trailing a poor third.[50] Although Champagne and the French *AOC* wines are still going strong, it is the French regional wines that have retreated in the face of the onslaught by the likes of Jacob's Creek (at the lower end of the market) and Penfolds Grange (at the upper).

Every year, while the vineyards of Europe stagnate, hundreds of hectares of vines spring up in the New World (the most spectacular increases are in Australia and Chile).[51] But the battle between Old and New World wines is far more than a matter of simple geography. It is a conceptual battle over what, ultimately, wine actually is. For the French, wine is identified not so much by the type of grape (virtually all red Burgundy wines come from the Pinot Noir grape, and all white Burgundies from

* While Italian wine imports came second to Australia in 2012, Italian wine is the fastest growing wine on the British market. This is partly due to the 'Pinot Grigio effect' (Pinot Grigio swiftly replacing Chardonnay and Sauvignon Blanc as the 'standard' white wine), but also to the relentless rise of Prosecco as an alternative to the pricey Champagne.

the Chardonnay). Rather, wine is intimately bound up with the concept of *terroir*: the wine produced from *this* grape, in *this* vineyard, on *this* slope, in *this* subsoil, aged in *these* barrels, in *this* cellar, in *this* particular year. It follows, therefore, that characterizing a wine by grape type alone – say, a Merlot – is strictly meaningless in French terms, as a wine produced from Merlot grapes grown in the Limari Valley in Chile will be a completely different wine from one produced by Merlot grapes in Valeyrac in the Médoc. It is the way in which wine from a particular vineyard gives 'expression' to the Merlot grape that matters. It is this reasoning that underlies the unfathomable complexity of French wine labels. There will inevitably be the region (say, *Mâcon-Villages*), estate (*Domaine de Champ Brûlé*), producer (*Vincent*), date and *AOC* statement, but no obvious reference to the grape variety (which, clearly, you will know already thanks to your intimate knowledge of the wine map of France). In contrast, New World wine labels do not assume a PhD in oenology. Indeed, they jump out at you with the enthusiasm of a waitress in a Californian diner: 'Hi, I'm Chardonnay from the Blackstone Winery, Monterey County, can I get you a drink?'*

The New World winemakers' technique of prominently identifying particular brands of wine by grape variety has had so great a success that many people believe that, for example, Chardonnay is a wine produced by Jacob's Creek, not a grape variety of which some of the most classic expressions hail from Burgundy. It is as though the grape variety known as Chardonnay – and consequently the wine produced from it – has been appropriated by certain brands of New World wines. At the same time, Chardonnay is strongly identified by evocative wine labels and advertising slogans with the sunny climes of America, South Africa, or the Antipodes: as the Australian slogan put it, Chardonnay is 'sunshine in a bottle'.

* The labelling of wines by grape variety rather than vineyard was pioneered by one of the founding fathers of the Napa Valley, Robert Mondavi, and is now followed by most New World wines. It doesn't tell you much more about the wine, but it is easier to remember.

The French for their part will swear that New World wines taste different from those of the Old World: big, buxom fruit bombs with artificial enhancements like oak chips – more Pamela Anderson than Emmanuelle Béart. A perennial French complaint against New World wines is their alleged masking of natural flavours with additives, which imposes a fruity, smoky uniformity across the wine spectrum. The man accused of diffusing this monotaste is the American wine critic Robert Parker, whose newsletter, *The Wine Advocate*, publishes ratings out of 100 for wine (it is said that a positive or negative rating after a Parker tasting can add or substract up to £5 million from the value of a wine). Infuriated by the complexity and class-ridden structures of the French wine system, Parker set out in the late 1970s as an oenophile Lone Ranger, the only person with the bottle to face the mighty Gallic wine establishment. He once said: 'What I've brought is a democratic view. I don't give a shit that your family goes back to pre-Revolution and you've got more wealth than I could imagine. If this wine's no good, I'm gonna say so.'[52] He also decreed that Penfolds Grange, Australia's most famous wine, 'has replaced Bordeaux's Pétrus as the world's most exotic and concentrated wine.' His 100-point rating system for wine was a boon for wealthy clients, who wanted the best but didn't have time to figure out what that was. The chances are, if a Texan millionaire tells you he has a '93 Bordeaux', he's talking Parker points, not vintage.*

And a new threat to French viticulture is approaching from further afield. The Chinese thirst for French wine, in par-

* In the 2004 French documentary film *Mondovino* – a lyrical elegy to small French wine producers and a vitriolic attack against the forces of globalization – Parker is pictured grinning in front of a massive, neon-lit advertisement for Burger King. *Mondovino* was one of the very few documentary films ever to be nominated for the *Palme d'Or* at Cannes.

ticular Bordeaux, seems insatiable: China is now the number one buyer of Bordeaux wines.[53] However, the Chinese are not content just to drink wines from the Gironde – they seem to want to produce them, too. Over the past five years, around twenty Bordeaux wine châteaux have been bought by the Chinese; and in 2012, ripples were sent through the French winemaking world when a Chinese buyer acquired an ancient estate in Burgundy, the Château de Gevrey-Chambertin, for €8 million. (One of the reasons why the Chinese purchase in Burgundy caused such a storm was because it was some €6 million above the original asking price for the estate, and a consortium of local French winemakers had already unsuccessfully tried to bid to keep the vineyard in the French family.)

I have never drunk a drop of alcohol in my life. In France! And the French still elected me president.

NICOLAS SARKOZY, 23RD PRESIDENT OF FRANCE (2007–12)

What is the future of French wine? At the moment, it would appear to be murky rather than *rosé*. But it's promising that the notion of *terroir* is increasingly taking root around the world, with a return to wines that taste of the sun and soil, as opposed to a chemistry lab. The wine from that family run château in Bordeaux might be more spit and miss than the identikit throughput from a 40,000-acre estate in the Napa Valley, but at least you can be sure that God (and not some micro-oxygenating manipulator) made the ingredients. But don't, for goodness' sake, fall for one of the most time-honoured excuses of the French waiter for a below-par bottle of wine – yes it is corked, and no it's not the *terroir*.

Myth Evaluation: *False. French people over 65 drink wine with every meal; French people under 65 prefer Evian, Badoit or fruit juice.*

The French don't get drunk

It is not necessary to be drunk in order to be immortal.
VICTOR HUGO, *LES MISÉRABLES* (1862)

'An Englishman is a drunkard,' according to an old Spanish saying. Most Europeans would echo that view. From boozy Brits terrorizing Alpine ski resorts on rowdy stag weekends to the violence of English football hooligans, the image of the Englishman abroad has become synonymous with alcoholic excess. Nor is the association between the English and drunkenness anything new. In the mid-nineteenth century, the French poet Paul Verlaine, arriving in London to scratch a living as a French teacher, recalled the city as a reeling centre of drunken, proselytizing hypocrisy:

'London, black as crows and noisy as ducks, prudish with all the vices in evidence, everlastingly drunk, in spite of ludicrous laws about drunkenness, immense, though it is really in essence just a collection of scandal-mongering boroughs, vying with each other, ugly and flat, without any monuments except interminable docks.'[54]

Naturally, the French pride themselves on not getting drunk in the way the English do. The French, so the saying goes (and as they themselves like to believe), drink in a civilized fashion, *en famille* at lunch and at dinner. They do not binge-drink on a Friday night in pubs and clubs and end up vomiting on the pavement, like the British or the Irish. As the French philosopher Roland Barthes remarked, ever-observant until he was knocked down by a laundry van in the streets of Paris: 'Other countries drink to get drunk, and this is accepted by everyone; in France, drunkenness is a consequence, never an intention. A drink is felt as the spinning out of a pleasure, not as the necessary cause of an effect which is sought: wine is not only a philtre, it is also the leisurely act of drinking.'[55]

THE ART OF DRINKING WITHOUT GETTING DRUNK

Jean-Anthelme Brillat-Savarin (1755–1826) was a leading French gastronome and food writer. His masterpiece, *La Physiologie du goût* ('The Physiology of Taste'), a collection of essays and *bon-mots* relating to the pleasures of the table, has been continuously in print since 1825 (see page 22), and has become a classic of gastronomic literature. Brillat-Savarin was a well-travelled man, with idiosyncratic views on the peoples he visited. He dismissed the Swiss as 'eminently civilized, but fools because they have no time for pleasure'. Other nations fared even worse: he thought the English were 'snobs with no appreciation for the finer things in life', and found the Americans to be 'charming barbarians'.

Together with Alexandre Grimod de la Reynière, Brillat-Savarin is credited with founding the genre of the food essay. A character featured in the *Physiologie* is the bibulous General Bisson, who like the mythical Frenchman appears to imbibe great quantities of wine, without ever actually showing signs of inebriation:

'General Bisson... drank eight bottles of wine at dinner every day, and... never appeared the worse for it. He had a glass larger than usual and emptied it oftener. He did not care for that though, for after having swallowed six ounces of fluids he could jest and give his orders as if he had only swallowed a thimbleful.'

It is certainly true to state that, for the traditional French upper-middle classes or bourgeoisie, it is considered the height of impropriety to be seen drunk in a public place. The French rules of *savoir-vivre* – that highly complex and codified set of formal 'manners' devised in the nineteenth century to distinguish the bourgeoisie from the rabble – place enormous emphasis on *le maintien*, that is, giving the impression of always being in control of one's body, emotions and language.*[56] It follows

* *Savoir-vivre* is a concept that is indispensable to an understanding of

that staggering about, declaring undying love for one's boss in slurred tones, or collapsing on the floor in a stupor at the office Christmas party, is utterly beyond the pale of acceptable behaviour in such circles. On the other hand, the rules of *savoir-vivre* are closely linked to place, with a strict demarcation between public spaces such as restaurants (where discretion and self-control are *de rigueur*) and private spaces such as a drinks party among one's peers (where guests will have been preselected and therefore less likely to include the dreaded riff-raff).[57] Therefore, it may be permissible in such select milieux to let your self-control go a little. A typical example of this type of event is the lengthy *apéro* or pre-dinner drinks session of which the French are inordinately fond, where copious amounts of wine and champagne are served with fiddly little canapés of tenuous ethanol-absorbing capacity, and where it is not uncommon to see grown men blind drunk but cleverly disguising the fact. This slight flexion of the drunkenness rule, naturally, strictly applies to men only. For a woman to be seen drunk in a public space is a mortal sin of French etiquette, and in fact it is generally assumed that any such woman is probably English. As the author of the leading French book on etiquette – written in the 1890s but still an authority today – notes, a lady should never drink 'neat wine', and certainly not hard liquor, if she wishes to maintain her beauty and decorum.[58]

The man who likes good wine is never a drunkard; his pleasure is the appreciation of quality, not the consumption of quantity, which lowers a human being to the level of a brute.
MARCEL BOULESTIN, FRENCH CHEF (1878–1943)

So much for the ageing ranks of that endangered species, the traditional French bourgeoisie. But what about the generation of tomorrow? There, alas, we find that – whereas their grandfathers are downing civilized quantities of Burgundy while discussing the merits of Molière versus Racine – their grandchildren will most likely be following their Anglo-American counterparts in tequila-slamming the night away. For while (as

the French bourgeoisie and is discussed in depth in the chapters on French women and manners.

we saw in the previous chapter) daily wine consumption across all age groups has fallen considerably in France, binge-drinking among the nation's youth has dramatically increased since 2007. In fact, '*le binge-drinking*' has now entered the French language as a new piece of *Franglais* (the official term, as sanctioned by the *Académie française*, is the rather less catchy *biture express* – literally 'high-speed drunkenness'). Between 2005 and 2007 there was a 50 per cent increase in young people hospitalized for excessive drinking, which has become the principal cause of death among French youth, claiming three victims a day.[59] Although the rate of road accidents overall in France has dropped dramatically, there is still a high rate of drink-driving accidents among the nation's youth, with many a fatality caused by out-of-control cars smashing into the plane trees that characteristically line roads throughout the French countryside (the French, typically, have responded to this problem by chopping down the trees).* In addition, several major French cities – such

* Perhaps more sensibly, a 'zero alcohol' limit has been in force since April 2012 for drivers under 21 years old.

as Lyons, the second city of France – have announced that all shops selling alcohol are to be closed by 10 p.m.

The French, of course, blame the English for exporting *le binge-drinking* to France. In a 2011 survey of European youth by the pan-European agency ESPAD,[60] 44 per cent of French youngsters aged 15–16 years admitted to having binge-drunk in the past month. This is above the European average, but well below the British level (52 per cent). On the other hand, though British students drink their French counterparts under the table, the latter easily outstrip the British where tobacco smoking, consumption of non-prescription tranquillizers, and cannabis usage are concerned. Indeed, French students are the heaviest cannabis smokers in the whole of Europe: their reported lifetime use of the drug is over twice the European average. When use and abuse of the whole gamut of illicit substances (i.e. cigarettes, alcohol, barbiturates and other drugs) is compared, French students are in fact ahead of the British. The scale of cannabis use in France, across all age groups, is quite literally mind-blowing. Hardly a day goes by without a news item on a crop of the wrong sort of grass having been discovered growing in the walled garden of a seemingly innocuous rural farmhouse, or even in a prison allotment. And when French kids do drink, it's not wine that is their favourite tipple: rather, alcopops, hard liquor (especially whisky, currently all the rage with French youth) and cocktails are the big hitters.

The image of the archetypal French teenage party has undergone a radical change in recent years. No longer is this an innocent affair of smooching under a disco ball, as in the celebrated 1980 French teen movie *La Boum*, which shot 13-year-old Sophie Marceau to stardom. The gritty British teen television series *Skins*, broadcast in France since 2007, first by Canal + and then by the teen channel June, was a massive hit with French teenagers, inspiring a rash of copycat *Skins* parties across the country. For a couple of years, French teenage girls wrapped themselves in clingfilm for the benefit of their male classmates, who filmed it all on their iPhones at 'secret' parties, the location of which would be revealed on Facebook a few hours beforehand.

Then *Skins* parties became institutionalized and taken over by the events industry, turning into little more than mildly risqué fancy-dress occasions. The 'cool' scene moved on, this time inspired by another teen film with more grit than schmaltz: the 2012 American movie *Project X*, which features a massive party that gets out of control. Copycat *Project X* events began popping up over France, including one in the summer of 2012 on the Riviera near Fréjus, where 400 teenagers descended on and wrecked an unoccupied villa. *Project X* parties are now subject to strict surveillance by the French police, who expend a great deal of time and manpower searching for them on Facebook and warning the organizers to remove them from the site.

More significant than any of the actual parties themselves is the after-party twittering, tweeting and skyping that goes on via Facebook, Myspace, and a dozen other social media sites. In essence, this is no different from what is happening with teenagers everywhere, but in France the public broadcasting by the younger generation of their not-so-private lives has resulted in a realization of the ultimate French nightmare: a breach of etiquette. The sacred Gallic demarcation between public and private space – each with their respective codes of behaviour – becomes hard to enforce when faced with this new Millennial Generation, determined to expose their love bites, high heels, and much in-between to an audience of 2.3 billion users of the World Wide Web. Have the sacred principles of *savoir-vivre* gone to pot? Hard to tell if the spaced-out new generation of French is going to come back to Earth and reconnect with the disciplined and self-controlled past. If it doesn't, their grandparents may just have to… put that in their pipe and smoke it.

Myth Evaluation: *False. Older French people get drunk and hide it. Younger French people get drunk and high and post pictures of themselves in all states of inebriation and undress on social networking sites.*

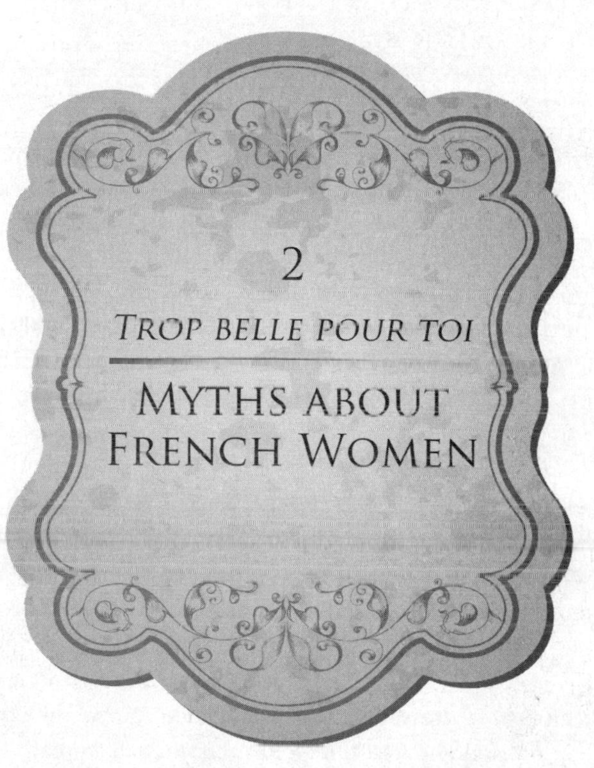

2

Trop belle pour toi

Myths about French Women

French women are the most stylish in the world

Fashion is to France what gold mines are to Peru.
JEAN-BAPTISTE COLBERT, FINANCE MINISTER TO LOUIS XIV (1619–83)

The French woman's sense of style is legendary. According to popular belief, Gallic women have a mysterious ability to look classy and glamorous, even if they actually have a face like a dog's breakfast (the French have even enshrined the notion that a plain woman may still have something ineffably attractive about her in the oxymoronic term *belle-laide*). Somehow, though, you just don't notice the effortless stylishness, because of some mysterious *je ne sais quoi*. It is a look perhaps most famously epitomized by the legendary Coco Chanel and her eponymous suit: classy, chic and polished down to the coordinated jacket and gleaming stilettos. So powerful is the image that there is a veritable mini-industry of books giving guidance to English and American women on how to dress, accessorize and style yourself like the French: in short, on how to 'find your inner French woman'.

If a woman is badly dressed you notice her frock, but if she is impeccably clothed, you notice her.
COCO CHANEL (1883–1971)

In truth, there is no great 'mystery' to the bourgeois French woman's sense of style. (Note: we are talking here about the style of bourgeois women, generally in Paris and the Île de France, along with a few other exclusive areas, not French women as a whole. As usual, Froglit* authors extrapolate from a limited sample of metropolitan women to draw sweeping conclusions

* Froglit, *n.*: a highly commercialized and formulaic genre of lightly humorous fiction or non-fiction, generally written by Anglo-American expats living in France and usually with an autobiographical bias, dedicated to eulogizing, elucidating, satirizing or otherwise promulgating stereotypical ideas about the French.

about the whole of France.) Like so many aspects of the Parisian French that foreigners marvel at, bourgeois French female style derives ultimately from the rules of *savoir-vivre*, examined in detail below.* These rules still apply to many upper-middle-class French today.

Savoir-vivre consists of a body of rules with certain distinct objectives. Firstly, it exists to mark out those people of manners and taste from the riff-raff. Secondly, it is there to maintain boundaries and hierarchies. Thirdly and above all, its purpose is to maintain the social status quo. The rules of *savoir-vivre* are much more than a matter of 'etiquette' in the narrow sense – such as how to greet somebody, or set a table (although they do cover these things). They are really a way of life – which is why they are called *les règles de savoir-vivre* ('rules of how to live'), rather than mere *savoir-faire* (how to do something). According to the rules of *savoir-vivre*, the presentation of oneself to the world is of cardinal importance. Personal appearance, in fact, is an aspect of politeness and respect to others. Key rules include:[1]

Grooming ('*le soin*'). This means paying careful attention to all the minutiae of personal care and dress – no unclipped fingernails, uncombed hair, dirty shoes or missing buttons. Nipping to the corner shop in one's pyjamas is definitely not an option. Ditto collecting the kids from school with yesterday's baby spit-up on one's coat.

Harmony ('*l'harmonie*'). This means coordinating one's clothes and accessories (i.e. no clashing colours), but it also means coordinating one's appearance with one's location and status in the world. So, for example, a bohemian artist-type might be permitted a smattering of designer stubble or a scarlet cravat, but these would obviously be completely out of the question in the office environment. A professional woman who entertains clients to lunch during her working day orders the wine and settles the bill; when she dines at a restaurant with husband and friends in the evening, however, etiquette dictates that she cedes these functions to the men.

---

* The rules of *savoir-vivre* are further considered on pages 156 to 162.

THE DISCREET CHARM OF THE BOURGEOIS DÉCOLLETÉ

Traditional French female style places great emphasis on discretion, on hinting at what lies beneath rather than letting it all hang out. Here, for example, is the advice of Baronne Staffe, a nineteenth-century writer on etiquette, relating to the vexed question of the *décolleté*:

'There are three styles of "décolleté" from which one can choose, depending on the shape of a woman. They were classified as follows during the period of the Second Empire: "full décolleté", "half décolleté", and "quarter décolleté". Those with alluring, shapely shoulders adopted the "full décolleté"; those with white skin the "half décolleté", or décolleté with a square neckline; and those who had only an attractive neck, the "quarter décolleté", a very restrained affair with a pointed neckline before and behind...

'If one is obliged – from necessity – to wear a low neckline, why not veil with tulle or lace what is, after all, a tactless sight to reveal to spiteful onlookers? It is charming to see emerging from a low neckline a bust and arms whose imperfections are masked by a transparent cloud, which doesn't completely hide the skin. All things concealed have a profound air of mystery, of the unknown, and allow one to imagine that true beauty lies beneath.'

From *Mes Secrets pour plaire et pour être aimée*, 1896.

Discretion (*'la discretion'*). In the words of the celebrated nineteenth-century authority on etiquette, Baronne Staffe, 'a woman does not truly have charm unless by her manners and toilette, she seeks to go past unnoticed.' Even to this day, French people in a pan-European poll were the ones who most frequently declared that 'it's important not to be noticed too much.'[2] The obsession of the French bourgeoisie with discretion approaches fanaticism. Why this should be the case is not entirely clear: perhaps because they are petrified of being hammered by the post-Revolutionary mob for wealth tax if they even hint, by the very presence of a flashy jewel, that there may be secret stashes of

dosh in a tax-free haven somewhere in the DOM-TOMs.* It follows that fluorescent colours, in fact anything too colourful or eccentric, are completely out. So too are showy designer labels, the sure-fire indicator of the vulgar social upstart or parvenu (the most unforgivable of French social sins). Most bourgeois French women's wardrobes, if not their libraries, will contain at least fifty shades of grey.

Decorum ('*le maintien*'). One must always behave with discipline and decorum. This means one does not plonk down heavily into a chair, but lightly and gracefully; one walks with elegant and measured steps; one does not grin or express any excessive emotion whatsoever unless one is in private (and even then, the degree of emotion expressed depends on the circumstances). The whole of life, in fact, becomes a piece of theatre

* DOM-TOMS: *Départements et territoires d'outre-mer*. That is, French-administered overseas departments and territories outside Europe.

It's in Paris that you see the most attractive faces with real beauty: women of forty-odd years old, who have kept their fine noses, their doe eyes, and who allow themselves to be looked at with pleasure.
COLETTE, FRENCH NOVELIST (1873–1954), *CLAUDINE EN MÉNAGE*, 1902

in which every act and scene has an appropriate role that must be played, a script that must be recited. Reading the French guides to *savoir-vivre*, one wonders when (if at all) the role-playing stops. Is there a scene of life without an appropriate script?

The discreet, polished, yet self-effacing elegance of a certain sector of the French female *haute-bourgeoisie* makes complete sense when read in the light of these rules. It's a good look for many, perhaps even the majority, of women: classic, tailored elegance that maintains a discreetly charming presence but never screams its existence. It allows women with less than perfect figures discreetly to conceal what lies beneath (a bourgeois French woman will never reveal any part of her body unless it is perfect, which spares one some unsightly spectacles on public transport in central Paris). It is a look that also allows women to age gracefully, without resorting to nips, tucks, lifts or plastic inserts in their breast tissue. Special reverence, in fact, is devoted in the etiquette tomes to women who reach the twilight of their years well-preserved, rather than pickled, by time. '*Personne n'est jeune après quarante ans, mais on peut être irrésistible à tout âge*,' the eternally elegant Coco Chanel once observed ('Nobody is young after forty, but one can be irresistible at any age').

On the other hand, discreet, tailored elegance is not necessarily a good look for the young and free-spirited, or for sartorial rebels. In fact, judging by the number of tattoos, nose rings, eyebrow piercings, fluorescent colours and exposed bra straps sported by younger French women nowadays, classic French bourgeois style is associated very much with an older generation. French teenage girls' discussion forums seem a lot more concerned these days with figuring out where to get boots in the Gothic punk style of Effy from the British teen series *Skins*, than whether it is a social *faux pas* to combine a *décolleté* with a mini skirt. (The advice from fellow French teenage *internautes* on where to get clothes in *le style Effy* is inevitably to try those

RIPENED NOT RAVAGED BY TIME

In late 2004, the French polling agency Ipsos conducted a survey of 1,002 French people to find out which women the French considered the most beautiful in the world. The results were somewhat surprising. The two women who came out top (the actresses Monica Bellucci and Isabelle Adjani), although French-speaking, are of Italian and Algerian origin respectively, suggesting a certain exotic leaning in French taste. The results also suggest that the French take a similar view towards women as they do towards wine – that is, that a great specimen improves with age.

Over half the women on the list were, at the time of the survey, on the 'wrong' side of 40. In fact, apart from the predictable inclusion of the national treasure Catherine Deneuve – at that point a venerable 61 years old – five of the women featured were then in their late forties: the movie star Isabelle Adjani, the elegant actress Corinne Touzet (little known outside France), the newsreader Claire Chazal, and the actresses Carole Bouquet and Sharon Stone. The youngest woman on the list (Julia Roberts) was then a mature 37. Women over forty can take comfort in the fact that, in French terms at least, they are in their prime.

1. *Monica Bellucci*
2. *Isabelle Adjani*
3. *Corinne Touzet*
4. *Julia Roberts*
5. *Sophie Marceau*
6. *Claire Chazal*
7. *Carole Bouquet*
8. *Catherine Deneuve*
9. *Emmanuelle Béart*
10. *Sharon Stone*

Source: Ipsos/Coyote, 'Les Français élisent la plus belle femme du monde', 10 November 2004.

oh-so-French outlets Zara or Top Shop online, or – best of all – head to Camden Market, the new sartorial Mecca for the French teenager.) French teenage girls today are taller, bigger and heavier than their mothers;* and in the regional town near which I live, many is the time I have spied a delicate, bird-like forty-year-old in a Chanel suit hopping daintily beside her much taller, heftier and generously proportioned eighteen-year-old daughter, with punk hairdo, tattoos and a liberal sprinkling of piercings. They make an odd couple.

Fashion fades, only style remains the same.
COCO CHANEL (1883–1971)

'A woman who lacks beauty,' observed Louis XIV's mistress Madame de Maintenon, 'has only half a life.' Under the traditional rules of French etiquette, women have a social duty to brighten the grey world of men with a decorative, discreetly coquettish, harmonious, seductive and elegant presence... but not to affront, challenge or set the world alight. Perhaps the new generation of young French women – loud and proud with their added height, bold and confident fluorescent T-shirts, nose rings and tattoos – have picked up the torch.

Myth Evaluation: *The truth of this myth is hard to evaluate because of the innately subjective nature of what constitutes 'style'. But it remains a fact that certain, mainly middle-class and older, French women, achieve what many would consider to be exalted levels of sartorial elegance and stylishness of appearance.*

* The *Campagne de mensuration* of 2006, a nationwide survey of the vital statistics of French men and women, found that a new group of 'very tall women' had emerged in France since the 1970s, reaching a maximum of 190 cm (6 feet 2 inches) in height.

French women don't get fat

I never wanted to weigh more heavily on a man than a bird.
COCO CHANEL, CELEBRATED HAUTE-COUTURIÈRE (1883–1971)

This myth is the only one in this book that is a registered trademark (the phrase *French Women Don't Get Fat* ® was registered as a patented commercial product with the US patent office by the Franco-American author Mireille Guiliano, after the appearance of her eponymous 2006 guide to the secrets of the French woman's allegedly enviable silhouette). Since the appearance of Guiliano's book, many others have leaped on the gravy train, and there is now a veritable deluge of guides laying bare the mysteries of the so-called 'French Paradox': that is, how French women – while still indulging in red wine, cheese and croissants – somehow manage to retain a figure to die for. Here, for example, is a typical entry in an American blog after a visit to Paris: 'French women are known for being beautiful, sexy and slim. Women in France walk around in mini-skirts* looking graceful and lean, all while enjoying the greatest pleasures in life. They eat full-fat dairy, butter, real cheese, desserts, red meats, pastas, gourmet breads and top it off with a glass of wine or champagne, yet they continue to have a very low obesity rate.'

The use of the phrase '*Women in France*' in this extract is intriguing. Of the top tourist destinations in France, Paris and its surrounding region of the Île de France are by far the most popular destinations, followed by the French Riviera. The French women that the vast majority of Anglo-American tourists encounter, therefore, are those to be found in the

* This is patently incorrect. Most French women above the age of adolescence would consider mini-skirts vulgar. The description is closer to a gym-toned, Manhattanite ideal of beauty than anything French, which in fact is the case for many foreign eulogies of Gallic women. As usual, we insist on reading into the French distorted images of ourselves.

historic centre of Paris, and on the glamorous beaches of the Côte d'Azur. And yet, as many writers and commentators on France would have us believe, these well-heeled, stylishly svelte specimens represent the Women of France.

Do French women get fat? Considering the number of times I have found myself behind a large female bottom at a supermarket queue in a regional Carrefour, I would be tempted to say that at least some of them do. It is certainly true that France historically has had a very low obesity rate. But that position is changing. A three-yearly survey of obesity in the French population by the French pharmaceutical group Roche – the ObÉpi survey – found that in 2012, 47 per cent of the total French adult population was overweight or obese, including 42 per cent of French women. Obesity in France increased by 76 per cent over the period 1997–2012, with the largest recent recorded increase in women aged 18–25 years.[3]

The skinny cat and the fat woman are a household disgrace.
CORSICAN PROVERB

But how does the 'average' French woman compare physically to her cousin across the Channel? Two nationwide sizing surveys conducted in Britain and France, coincidentally at similar times, provide an intriguing (and surprising) answer. They are the UK National Sizing Survey, carried out in 2001–2 by the Department of Trade and Industry in collaboration with leading UK retailers, and the *Campagne nationale de mensuration*, or National Measuring Campaign,

PLUMPNESS – *QUELLE HORREUR!*

'A woman who is too fat cannot take a step without panting like a seal, or sweating like a river; she is as heavy as an elephant, her shape thick; the swaying of her massive hips gives her a vulgar look, however distinguished she may be by birth. Her overflowing cheeks and eyelids heavy with fat make a repulsive mask of her face. She loses beauty, form, and grace.' From Baronne Staffe, *Le Cabinet de Toilette*, 1897.

conducted in France in 2003–5 by the French textile industry. Both surveys used high-tech scanning techniques to measure thousands of men and women on either side of the Channel, collating the data to produce the vital statistics of the 'average' British and French woman respectively. And here they are (with the French metric stats imperialized):[4]

	HEIGHT	CHEST	WAIST	HIPS	WEIGHT
UK	5ft 3.5ins	38.5ins	34ins	40.5ins	10st 3.5lbs
FR.	5ft 3ins	37ins	31.5ins	39.5ins	9st 11.5lbs

The most striking thing about these statistics is their broad similarity. French women come out on average as half an inch shorter than English women (both being at the shapely end of the size spectrum), and there are a few inches between the other measurements (notably the waist). There is about half a stone difference between them. Are the differences between French and English women in terms of size large enough to justify the big fat fuss being made about it?

None of this alters the fact that, in Paris and the regions most exposed to tourists and expats at least, there do appear to be an awful lot of skinny and elegant bourgeois French women tottering about in high heels and coordinated bolero jackets. Several of the reports on obesity in France note the fact that the global averages conceal large discrepancies based on the geographic location, class and education of the French women concerned.[5] The highest rates of female obesity are in the North and East of the country – notably in the depressed region of Nord-Pas-de-Calais – versus the tourist-heavy Provence, Côte d'Azur and Loire valley, with the lowest obesity rates; while women without the *Baccalauréat* or other diploma are likely to weigh over half a stone more than their *Bac*-qualified compatriots.[6] An OECD report in 2011 observed that women with a poor education in France were almost three times more likely to be overweight than more educated women. This contrasted with a much lower 'inequality index' in the UK, where the likelihood of a poorly educated woman being overweight was about one and a half

The source of the deep evils suffered by humanity is the muffled war between thin and fat women.
RÉMY DE GOURMONT, FRENCH SYMBOLIST POET, NOVELIST AND CRITIC (1858–1915)

times that of her middle-class equivalent.[7]

Why are the Parisian female bourgeoisie the least likely to be fat out of everybody in France? Well, partly it's a matter of education, but it's also a matter of social pressure. The rules of *savoir-vivre* – the traditional, post-Revolutionary French code of etiquette – place enormous importance for women on *la bonne tenue*: that is, an elegant and self-disciplined presentation of oneself that includes sober attire and a moderate attitude to consumption.* As the celebrated author of manners Baronne Staffe noted in her hugely popular nineteenth-century manual of etiquette *Usages du monde*,† it is of particular importance for the young ladies of the bourgeoisie to 'avoid greediness, which ruins one's looks and denotes a poor education'.[8] Slimness for French women is, traditionally, one of the key means by which they demonstrate to the world that they belong to the affluent bourgeoisie or middle class.

The equation that slim female = bourgeois and that love handles = lower-class is one that runs deep in French psychology and culture. The vast majority of French women in public life – from television presenters to politicians – are impossibly slim and glamorous. Where, one wonders, are the women who do not look like Ségolène Royal, Carla Bruni or Valérie Trierweiler? After all, wasn't feminism invented so that all women could accede to positions of power, despite not looking like Marion Cotillard? The identification of the female sex with slimness and glamour in the French psyche means that the French have had particular difficulty in facing up to their nascent obesity crisis. The 2012 ObÉpi study was reported (with a certain smugness) in the British press, but the French media passed it over. Although much fuss has been made about child obesity in the French press recently, the issue of adult obesity has been much less

* For a detailed discussion of the rules of *savoir-vivre*, see the chapter on French women and style (page 75).

† First published in 1889, this bible of French etiquette went through more than twenty-four editions in the nineteenth century and is still in print today.

prominently featured. Even French women's clothes shops seem to have a problem admitting the new, shapelier proportions of their clientèle. Although French clothing sizes were revised upwards in the light of the 2006 industry sizing survey, looking at the clothes stocked by the average French clothing store, one could still be forgiven for getting the impression that all women in France are a maximum size 10. In the *Campagne de mensuration*, one in three female respondents to the survey claimed to have difficulty finding clothes that fitted them in the shops. The report blames *them* for being too fat or too thin – even though the majority of women who complained were within the normal range. The tone and content of the French sizing report, in fact, is at times nothing short of extraordinary. The average height of French women, for example, is compared to that of the average height of candidates for Miss World in 2006. French women were found to be 14 centimetres shorter. It seems somewhat odd, to say the least, for a quasi-official report to be using a beauty contest as a standard for the purposes of evaluating the physical attributes of a country's females.

With such a dearth of appropriately sized clothing in the shops, it is little wonder that the French clothes market for plus-sizes has gone viral. A French Google search of the terms '*habillement femme grande taille*' will throw up dozens of names of French and foreign stores doing a roaring Internet trade selling outsize clothes to French women: La Redoute, Dorothy Perkins, Kiabi, Evans, C&A… the list goes on. One of the French outsize Internet shopping sites observes: 'Sales of large size clothes for bigger women have become a fashion phenomenon, followed by a number of observers. Large-size clothes now have their own fashions. Fashion designers are offering complete collections, with oversize dresses, trousers and lingerie.' There is also a fast-growing number of specialized Internet dating agencies for curvy folk or *personnes rondes*, offering dating opportunities for people falling outside 'conventional beauty criteria', who with an ordinary dating agency might feel 'pressurized' into falsifying their body measurements or feel coy about posting a personal photo. Organizations have been formed to fight for the rights of *personnes rondes*, including against discrimination in the workplace.* In the meantime, the French government, while downplaying the adult obesity issue in public, has quietly swung into action to safeguard what amounts to one of France's greatest marketing assets: its worldwide reputation as the land of luxury, style and of slim and glamorous women. Propositions have been made to ban fattening palm oil in food products (the so-called 'Nutella amendment'), and even to provide gym sessions free on the national health service to pudgier French citizens.

All in all, France seems to be in deep denial of the reality of its new, curvaceous reflection in the mirror. This denial is not helped by the acres of garbage spewed by foreign visitors who spend a year or so 'assessing' the proportions of women in the exclusive *arrondissements* of central Paris or the beaches of the Côte d'Azur, sending back breathless eulogies of admiration and wonder about the mystical thinness of French women. Will there ever be an end to this flow of *merde*? Maybe one day, when the growing number of French women who do not conform to the bourgeois ideal finally have a voice. Maybe one day, when the fat French lady sings…

Myth Evaluation: *False: an increasing number of French women are running to fat.*

* Organizations fighting for the rights of *personnes rondes* have been formed throughout France and include: *Allegro Fortissimo* (Paris and regions), *Amitiés rondissimes* (Loire), *Gros* (Paris), *Grossomodo* (Gard), *Pakyna* (Oise), *Ronde Attitude* (Bouches-du-Rhône), *Rondeurs en plus*, and *Tout en rondeur* (Pas-de-Calais).

French women are kitchen goddesses

To cook is above all an act of love and a language which women have developed through the ages to express their feelings. In this field, they have absolute power.

FATÉMA HAL, MOROCCAN-FRENCH CHEF AND OWNER OF THE CELEBRATED PARISIAN RESTAURANT MANSOURIA, *FILLE DES FRONTIÈRES*, 2011

The image of the French woman as a kitchen goddess is an old one. We find it in depictions of the homely, traditional cuisine of the *bonne femme*: women like the diminutive, white-haired Madame Robertot, who in the late 1920s inspired a sixteen-year-old Elizabeth David, fresh from boarding school in England, to devote her life to proselytizing for French cooking. Madame Robertot ruled her kitchen with a rod of iron. Every week, she would trot to the huge, open market then located in central Paris – *Les Halles* – and stock up on the weekly provisions, her bag bursting with fresh fruit and vegetables. At her table were served not the pretentious creations of *haute cuisine*, but food that was 'lovely without being rich or grand'. In place of elaborate sauces and sensational puddings, there were simple salads of rice and fresh tomatoes; soups of coral, ivory or pale green, as 'delicately coloured as summer dresses'; and the rich delight of an apricot and chocolate soufflé.[9]

Inspired by the cooking of *bonnes femmes* like Madame Robertot, Elizabeth David breathed a waft of exotic life into a British cuisine that was old and war-weary. Decades later, her earthy depictions of the *bonne femme* were blended, by a new generation of Gallic heroine-worshippers, with the evolving image of the stereotypical French *Überwoman* as classy, skinny and seductive. Madame Robertot, as David describes her, was short, fat, and dumpy; the new breed of *bonne femme* was slim and deadly elegant. Thus the contemporary picture of the French woman in the kitchen – as painted by countless expat eulogies – is that of some impossible Gallic diva, who apparently picks up

Men become passionately attached to women who know how to cosset them with delicate titbits.
HONORÉ DE BALZAC, FRENCH NOVELIST (1799–1850)

her brood of five children from the crèche in the twinkling of a pair of tottering high heels, whisking them home and treating them to a welcoming *chicken julienne* with three different sauces that she just happens to have prepared earlier (in between holding down a high-powered job and having her perfectly pampered toes re-pedicured). Surely the image of the *bonne femme* and her cooking merits a somewhat deeper inquiry.

The first thing to note about the cooking of the *bonne femme* is that she was never rated in the French hierarchy as on a par with the chef. In France – to a much greater extent than in England – there has traditionally been a yawning divide between *haute cuisine* and *cuisine bourgeoise*, or *cuisine familiale*: that is, between chefs and cooks, the hallowed temples of refined gastronomy on the one hand, and plain, hearty family fare on the other. For most of French history, men have been the chefs and women the cooks. It is a law of most societies in the world that women lord it over the family kitchen, but that whenever a more socially prestigious or elaborate code of cuisine develops, it uncannily but invariably gets handed over to men.*[10] So it was that when French *haute cuisine* evolved from the seventeenth century onwards, the leading chefs of the day, such as Taillevent and La Varenne, invariably were men, often hailing from a military background where they had served as army cooks. After the Revolution, when most of their former employers were decapitated, this

A good cook is not necessarily a good woman with an even temper. Some allowance should be made for the artistic temperament.
MARCEL BOULESTIN, FRENCH CHEF (1878–1943)

* This discrimination between male 'chefs' and female 'cooks' has also reared its ugly head in England in the twenty-first century, with a coterie of male television celebrity chefs dominating the culinary scene. Tellingly, Jools Oliver, wife of Jamie, published a book (*Minus Nine to One: The Diary of an Honest Mum*, Penguin 2006) in which she included family and children's recipes; and the blurb to Tana Ramsay's book of recipes, *Family Kitchen* (HarperCollins, 2006), states that, while husband Gordon may be the restaurant chef, Tana is 'firmly in charge of the family's cooking'. *Plus ça change...*

army of chefs found work in the kitchens of the restaurants that were beginning to appear and in the homes of the expanding bourgeoisie. As before, the upper-crust sought male chefs for their kitchen brigades. Only the humblest resorted to the desperate measure of hiring that abomination of nature, the *female cook.*

At a meeting in Paris in 1893, the chefs' trade union voted to veto women from training as apprentice chefs in the kitchens of the great Parisian hotels and restaurants, on the basis that they wouldn't cut the mustard. Cookery as a branch of domes-

tic science, however, was clearly a very different kettle of fish, and was approved for the instruction of girls at school since 'the rules of hygiene, sewing, ironing and cooking' were considered an appropriate preparation for women, particularly of the lower classes, for future duties as keeper of hearth and home.[11] Women who wished to make their way in catering were directed to areas considered more suitable for the feminine disposition than the creative genius of the *chef-artiste*: hotel management

THE ART OF THE TART

Myths surrounding the genesis of *tarte tatin* – the world's most illustrious apple tart – are legion. The story goes that it was invented by mistake in the 1880s by one of the Tatin sisters, who kept a modest *auberge* in the town of Lamotte-Beuvron (Loir-et-Cher), when she put an apple tart in the oven and forgot to add the pastry topping. The singed, crispy confection that resulted subsequently became a house special, and was elevated to the heights of the best restaurants when the food critic Curnonsky (see page 43) published the recipe.

Louis Vaudable, the owner of the Parisian restaurant Maxim's, who helped make *tarte tatin* a household name, gives an account of his 'discovery' that perfectly mirrors the way in which the male chefs of *haute cuisine* typically appropriated and subsequently mythologized the recipes of their female colleagues in the inferior domain of bourgeoise cuisine. His account should be taken with a hefty pinch of salt:

'I used to hunt around Lamotte-Beuvron in my youth, and had discovered in a very small hotel run by elderly ladies a marvellous dessert listed on the menu under "tarte solognote". I questioned the kitchen staff about its recipe, but was sternly rebuffed. Undaunted, I got myself hired as a gardener. Three days later, I was fired when it became clear that I could hardly plant a cabbage. But I had the recipe, and it became "the tarte of the Tatin sisters".'

From J. Barbary de Langlade, *Maxim's: Cent ans de vie parisienne*, 1990.

(women being considered especially suitable for managing the humdrum and routine), or *pâtisserie*. It is no accident that many of the leading schools of hotel management in Europe were founded by women, and that even today, the *pâtisserie* brigade in the kitchens of high-end French restaurants will be the one most likely to be headed by a woman. Those women who did branch out into the restaurant trade tended to focus on cafés or the *auberges*, rustic hotels with a few rooms offering traditional fare and convivial company: less champagne and caviar than a succulent joint of roast pork followed by hearty *tarte aux pommes*. There were French women who made this type of cuisine famous: the *Mères Lyonnais*, who put the city of Lyons on the map for such hostels; the celebrated *Mère Poulard* of Mont St Michel (who is said to have invented the illustrious *Omelette Poulard*, a cross between an omelette and a soufflé, still served in the restaurant named after her in Mont St Michel); and of course the famous Tatin sisters, who according to legend created the eponymous upside-down apple tart, or *tarte tatin*.

Behind almost every grand French chef in history, in fact, are the aromas of inspiration from the kitchens of their grandmothers: the rustic, feminine raw material from which the alchemy of male genius creates sophistication and refinement. The culinary nomenclature is telling: while the great male chefs of French history were traditionally accorded the professional title of *Maître Cuisinier* ('Master Chef'), female cooks have traditionally been known by such homely names as *Mère, Soeur*, or *Tante*.

However, the modern world of French *haute cuisine* continues to be a tough nut for women to crack. As late as 2006, only 6 per cent of French chefs were women, in contrast to 20 per cent of English chefs.[12] The French state qualification for a chef – the 'C.A.P. de cuisine' – was only opened up to women in the 1980s. And even today *haute cuisine* remains a predominantly male calling, in which the prevailing attitude remains that too many female cooks spoil the broth. The leading industry body, the *Association des maîtres cuisiniers de France*, is virtually 100 per cent men, and large numbers of French chefs are alleged to be members of that ultimate old boys' club, the Masons. The

Association des maîtres cuisiniers de France caused a sensation in 2001, when it rejected the candidature of the female chef Anne-Sophie Pic – who subsequently went on to be granted three Michelin stars for her Maison Pic restaurant in Valence, was voted Chef of the Year in 2007, and awarded the Veuve Clicquot prize for Best Female Chef in the World in 2011.

French feminists have naturally cooked up a storm over such alleged discrimination. The masculine/neutral French word *chef* has now undergone an unofficial feminist gender-reassignment, with the coinage *cheffe*. In the last five years or so, a truculent posse of new *cheffes* has mushroomed on the French scene – presenting cookery programmes on television, managing high-profile restaurants, or winning some of the many television cookery contests. Alongside the illustrious Anne-Sophie Pic, the *crème de la crème* of French *cheffes*, there are also other kitchen divas such as Rougui Dia (an exotically beautiful *cheffe* of Senegalese extraction, who caused a stir in 2005 when she was appointed head of the kitchens at the distinguished Franco-Russian restaurant Petrossian 144), Hélène Darroze of the Connaught Hotel in London, or Anne Alassane (winner of French 'Masterchef' in 2010). Nevertheless, in the rarefied world of *haute cuisine*, women are still very much in the minority.

But what of the homelier space of the French domestic kitchen, where the cooking of *la bonne femme* has traditionally ruled the roost? The evidence suggests that, while they are still rarely chefs in restaurants, French women remain the cooks at home. According to a 2011 survey by the polling agency Ipsos, in the case of 72 per cent of French couples, it is the woman who does the cooking.[13] Quizzed on whether they could cook any one or more of sixteen 'great classics' of French cuisine, French women on average felt they could cook just over half (9.8 dishes): the top three dishes were *crêpes*, followed by *tarte aux pommes*, then *quiche lorraine* and *gratin dauphinois*. In this respect, French women seem to be doing better than British women, who can on average make only seven dishes from scratch, according to a 2011 survey of 2,000 British women commissioned by the Good Food Channel (the most common dishes cooked up in British

VIVE LES CRÊPES!

The percentages of French people (of both sexes) who declared they could cook sixteen dishes identified as 'classics of French cuisine' were as follows (although the presence of pizza and couscous in a list of 'classics of French cuisine' might strike some as rather peculiar):

Crêpes	80 per cent
Tarte aux pommes	73 per cent
Quiche lorraine	69 per cent
Gratin dauphinois	69 per cent
Pizza	63 per cent
Mayonnaise	63 per cent
Mousse au chocolat	62 per cent
Boeuf bourguignon	56 per cent
Blanquette de veau	51 per cent
Gigot d'agneau	51 per cent
Île flottante	44 per cent
Couscous	39 per cent
Sole meunière	35 per cent
Charlotte aux fraises	34 per cent
Cassoulet	30 per cent
Soupe de poissons	24 per cent

'Les Français et la cuisine', Ipsos/Logica Business Consulting, 21 September 2011.

kitchens were shepherd's pie, casserole and lasagne). In both the Ipsos and the Good Food Channel surveys, French and British women felt that they were less accomplished cooks than women of their mothers' generation. Intriguingly, though, it seems that French people of both sexes actually cook less than their British counterparts. An OECD survey of 29 member countries in 2011 found that 63 per cent of French people cooked on an average day (just under the OECD average of 64 per cent), as compared to 75 per cent of British people.[14] It appears, then, that while

French women have a greater culinary knowledge and expertise than their Anglo-Saxon cousins, they, along with their male peers, actually exercise it less. The reason for this state of affairs is not hard to surmise. With the highest birth rate in Europe and one of the highest percentages of women at work,*[15] France is a country where women are more and more pressed for time. Hence the continuing love affair of the French bourgeoisie for posh frozen food.†

So it seems that – contrary to popular wisdom – French women actually cook less at home than their British counterparts. Not only that, those who do want to earn their bread from their culinary skills struggle harder to break through the glass ceiling to the highest echelon of the profession. Which just goes to show that French women don't have their cake and eat it, whatever traditional Froglit authors would have you believe. But hey, why stop the gravy train? Let's continue to bask in the comforting glow of that myth of the rustled-up *chicken julienne.* In fact, I definitely feel like *poulet tonight...*

Myth Evaluation: *False. French women know more recipes than British women but French people cook less on average, and French women find it even harder than their British counterparts to break into the hallowed temples of haute cuisine.*

---

† To understand the French middle-class *folie* for frozen food, one needs to forget Iceland and think Picard, i.e. imagine something along the lines of Alain Ducasse on ice. Picard is one of the fastest-expanding of the French food giants, with a turnover of over €1.24 billion in 2008. Under the tutelage of a grand *maître cuisinier*, the chain specializes in high-quality frozen versions of classics of French cuisine. Their celebrated *moelleux au chocolat* – a gooey French hybrid between a chocolate mousse and sponge pudding – alone sells over 2 million units a year. Picard has, however – in common with other frozen food chains – suffered a blip as a result of the 'Horsegate' crisis.

French women don't shave

O soft women's beard, / Receive my verse like a kiss!
THÉOPHILE GAUTIER, FRENCH POET (1811-72),
'*MUSÉE SECRET*', 1864

The myth of the hairy French female is one of the most hoary of all Anglo-Saxon myths about the French. There are entire Internet sites where men debate whether French girls' armpits, legs and/or other body parts are smooth as silk or a shaggy-bear hangout to be avoided at all costs. The myth of the hairy French female sits oddly with the other characteristics of the mythic French woman, a creature preened and groomed to perfection. Like the myth of French women stripping off on public beaches with abandon (see pages 275–80), it illustrates the flipside of the ambiguous image of the Gallic female: cool, controlled and sophisticated on the one hand, but at the same time more 'natural' and 'liberated' than her puritanical sisters.

The controversy concerning the presence of hair on any part of the female body other than the head is nothing new, the 'hair versus bare' debate having raged unceasingly since ancient times. The ancient Romans had a horror of furry women: Ovid, in his lengthy treatise on the arts of love, *Ars Amatoria*, called on women to ensure there was 'no rankness of the wild goat under your armpits, no legs bristling with harsh hair!'[16] The removal of female body hair has long been a sacred Islamic rite, and noble Muslim women in the Arabian courts of old perfected the technique of a full-body wax followed by depilation with a double silken thread – secrets that were revealed to Gallic women via Alexis Piémontais' hugely popular and somewhat coyly entitled sixteenth-century tome *The Marvellous Secret of How the Great Moorish Ladies Ensure that their Daughters Do Not Have any Hair under their Arms or Other Places.* Western European art up to the nineteenth century almost invariably omitted any representation of female pubic hair, to such an extent that the art critic John Ruskin felt unable to consummate his marriage to his wife Effie on the grounds, *inter alia,* that her pudendum did not match that of the hairless female nudes of Michelangelo, and therefore was not correspondent with description nor fit for purpose.[17] The rare works of pre-twentieth-century European art that do depict the female genitalia in their hairy glory – or gory hairiness, depending on your point of view – still disturb us today. Take, for example, Gustave Courbet's *L'Origine du monde,* or 'Origin of the World': a shockingly realistic close-up depiction of a bristling female *mons pubis* which, when it was reproduced on a book cover in France in 1994, caused the police to raid several bookstores and summarily remove offending copies from the window on the grounds of indecency. A similar confiscation occurred in Portugal in 2009, when the painting was again featured on the cover of a book. The postcard of this painting is the second-bestselling after Renoir's *Bal du moulin de la Galette* in the souvenir shop at the Musée d'Orsay;[18] and it has the distinction of probably being the only work of art exhibited at a major art gallery that was censored by Facebook when somebody attempted to post it on the site.[*19]

On the other hand, reviled and vilified as female body hair has been in our history, cultures other than those of Western Europe have celebrated the bushy beauty of the female body in its unplucked splendour. In the countries of the former Yugoslavia, for example, hirsute ladies were traditionally held in great esteem, and until the Second World War, women of the Balkans were wont to snip off pieces of head hair to put in their stockings, to give the appearance of hairy legs.[20] The hippie movement in the 1960s and 1970s heralded a brief Age of Aquarius when, for a short while, women could party unashamed of their body hair. In the celebrated 1972 sex manual by Alex Comfort, *The Joy of Sex*, it was counselled that women's armpits (and indeed regions further south) should 'on no account be shaved', so as to preserve their natural eroticism, and that deodorant for both sexes was

* In February 2013, a sensation was caused by the discovery of a torso said to constitute the missing top half of *L'Origine du monde*, discovered by an art buff in a Paris antiques shop. Somehow, the painting seemed a lot less shocking when identifiable as an individual.

'banned absolutely'. (The primitive-looking lovers in the graphic charcoal illustrations to the original edition of this book could have come straight out of the caves of Lascaux in the Dordogne.) The modern preference for smooth pits came into being as a result of a marketing campaign by American manufacturers of depilatory creams and razors in the early twentieth century. Until then, the only hair that Western women (other than prostitutes and chorus girls) felt compelled to remove was, for an unlucky few, facial hair; most of the rest of a woman's body was discreetly concealed. In 1915, however, a landmark advertisement appeared in the May edition of the upper-class American women's magazine, *Harper's Bazaar*.[21] It featured a woman in a toga-like evening outfit raising one arm to reveal a perfectly smooth armpit, with the headline, *Summer Dress and Modern Dancing combine to make necessary the removal of objectionable hair*. Thus began what has been dubbed the 'underarm campaign' – a blitz of magazine advertisements over the ensuing years designed to convince women of a need that they didn't know they had, first in *Harper's Bazaar* and then filtering through to the more middle-brow *McCall's* by 1917. Women's razors and depilatory creams showed up for the first time in the Sears, Roebuck catalogue of 1922, the same year the company began offering dresses with sheer sleeves. By then, the battle of the pits had been won by the smoothies. The battle of the legs was to come later, with the rise in hemlines and invention of stockings in the 1930s – the occasion for women's magazine editors to declare war on the 'thick forest of hair' visible through the newly sheer fabric clothing covering women's lower limbs. The advent of package holidays, sunbathing and the beach body firmly entrenched the image of tanned, hair-free female pins. A survey of American women from 20 to 81 years old in 1991 found that 81 per cent shaved their legs and/or their armpits.[22]

The practice of hair removal travelled across the Atlantic in 1946, the consequence of the postwar arrival of the nylon stocking from the USA.[23] An inquiry conducted in 1972 found that 80 per cent of the French women questioned regularly removed hair from their legs and armpits, although 43 per cent of them

only did so when it was visible.[24] Hardly a ringing endorsement of the hairy French woman myth, then. And what of French women today? There again, believers in French furriness will be disappointed. According to a nationwide survey of 1,016 French people conducted by the marketing group Ipsos for the depilatory brand *Nair* in 2006,[25] 77 per cent of French people considered it important for a woman to be free of body hair to be seductive. Of the women questioned, 83 per cent removed leg hair, 73 per cent underarm hair, and 54 per cent hair on the bikini line. A sizable chunk of French men declared they would be most displeased if their partner stopped shaving (44 per cent), and even more of the men under 35 declared that this would be a serious relationship issue (57 per cent). Oddly enough, the French will tell you, if asked, that it is German women who don't remove body hair. But that is another story.

So French women are as busy plucking, waxing, threading, blitzing, depilating and electrolysing as everybody else. And they may even be venturing into more exotic pastures down under. For younger French women, the traditional bikini line wax or Brazilian triangle apparently are a bit *passé*, and the rage now is for a *ticket de Métro* (which is a… well, you can probably figure it out). There is even the increasingly popular total pelvic blitz, also known as the 'Hollywood' or the 'Sphinx' (the term 'Sphinx' allegedly derived not from the Egyptian monument but rather from the Sphynx, a naked breed of domestic cat originally created in Toronto in 1966).

But fans of hair as opposed to bare can take heart that women in the laid-back Scandinavian countries are still out there, defending the bush: in March 2012, a group of Swedish feminists demonstrated their 'hairy pits' in Malmö as a protest against beauty fascism, calling for women to return to the wild and 'reclaim the hair'. And believe it or not, there is also a free-spirited and hairy soul lurking in the depths of the plucked and perfected body of the archetypal French woman. If you don't believe me, take a look at what was until recently the second most famous painting in the Louvre Paris (now in the Louvre at Lens) – Delacroix's *La Liberté guidant le peuple* ('Liberty Leading the People'). The picture – an unofficial national emblem – portrays the bare-breasted figure of Liberty leading France to victory against the oppressor, the *Tricolore* held aloft in one hand, and a bayonetted musket in the other. Take a good look at the armpit of Liberty's right arm, the one brandishing the flag. No, look a bit closer. There! See what I mean?

Myth Evaluation: *False*.

3

Dangerous Liaisons

Myths about French Sex, Marriage and Children

The French are obsessed with sex

Behold, my love, behold all that I simultaneously do: scandal, seduction, bad example, incest, adultery, sodomy. Oh, Satan! One and unique God of my soul, inspire thou in me something yet more, present further perversions to my smoking heart, and then shalt thou see how I shall plunge myself into them all!

MARQUIS DE SADE, FRENCH WRITER AND LIBERTINE (1740–1814), *LA PHILOSOPHIE DANS LE BOUDOIR*, 1795

For many foreigners, the word 'French' conjures up one image, and one image only: sex. From the aggressive, *baise-moi* stare of the archetypal French male to the smouldering sensuality of the Gallic *femme fatale*; from the pervy libertinism of the Marquis de Sade to the heavy breathing of stubbly Serge Gainsbourg; from the febrile eroticism of films such as Jean-Jacques Beineix's *Betty Blue* to the explicit shagfest of Catherine Millet's best-selling memoir, *La Vie sexuelle de Catherine M* ('The Sexual Life of Catherine M') – in the fevered Anglo-Saxon imagination, copulation and the French are entwined in an inseparable embrace.

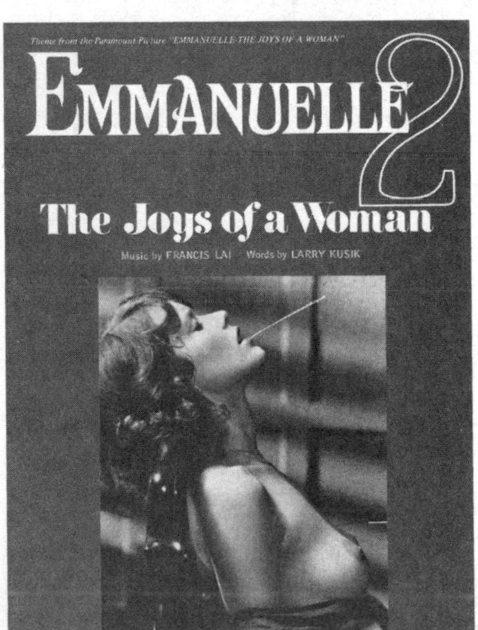

Like the origins of the 'adulterous French' myth (for which see pages 110 to 119), the sources of the myth of the sex-obsessed Gauls are hard to pinpoint in time. French literature has certainly much to do with it, Gallic writers having a well-known lack of inhibition when it comes to describing human sexual activity in all its forms. As far back as the sixteenth century, the French monk François Rabelais created one of the most priapic of literary personages in the form of the giant Gargantua, born sporting a yard-long erection. Seventeenth- and eighteenth-century French writing took up the literature of the libido with no less enthusiasm, delighting in the joy of smut from the explicit accounts of the sexual initiation of young girls in the writings of the Comte de Mirabeau to the darkly perverted violence of the Marquis de Sade. Even in the staid and moralistic nineteenth century, French poets and novelists kept the flame alight for the rude, the raunchy and the downright arousing: Alfred de Musset's 1833 erotic novel *Gamiani, ou deux nuits d'excès* ('Gamiani, or Two Nights of Excess'), with its graphic portrayal of the bedroom activities of a threesome, became a nineteenth-century erotic best-seller; while the poets Arthur Rimbaud and Paul Verlaine jointly composed what one imagines is the world's only 'Sonnet to an Asshole' ('*Sonnet du trou du cul*'). Throughout history, France has also been the haven for the 'dirty book', a shelter from censorship for Europe's literary refugees. James Joyce's novel *Ulysses* (1922) was published by a small private printing press in Paris, as was Henry Miller's banned, sexually candid *Tropic of Cancer* (1934), and the taboo-busting *Lolita* (1955) by Vladimir Nabokov.

Nor has French cinema shown any more coyness about the pleasures of the flesh than French literature. In fact, France practically gave birth to the soft-porn movie in the form of the 1974 erotic sensation, *Emmanuelle*. Based on the banned memoirs of a Thai-French actress, *Emmanuelle* spawned a whole series of hit movies and redefined a genre of the blue, as opposed to silver, screen: masturbation, the 'Mile High Club', skinny-dipping and rape were never to be off limits again, and the film even featured a scene in which a character lights a cigarette and puffs it with her vagina. Nor are erotic images confined in French films to the realms of erotica. Even (or perhaps especially) serious French art-house films have made an industry of exploring the pleasures of the flesh in graphic form: from Catherine Deneuve being ravished by a stranger in the woods in *Belle de jour* (1967), to Marlon Brando doing unmentionable things with butter in *Last Tango in*

It's true that the French have a certain obsession with sex, but it's a particularly adult obsession. France is the thriftiest of all nations; to a Frenchman sex provides the most economical way to have fun. The French are a logical race.

ANITA LOOS, AMERICAN AUTHOR AND PLAYWRIGHT, (1889–1981)

Paris (1972) and probably the most graphic scene of oral sex that has ever managed to escape the censor's cut in a mainstream movie, in the 1986 classic *Betty Blue*. 'Sex,' observed the Marquis de Sade (who knew a thing or two about the subject), 'is as important as eating or drinking, and we ought to allow the one appetite to be satisfied with as little restraint or false modesty as the other.' The French would seem to have taken him at his word.

Nowhere is the hard-wiring into the British psyche of the idea of France as a nation of erotomanes more evident than in the range of English slang expressions that associate the French with sexual or amorous activity. In fact, it is virtually a foregone conclusion that, if a slang word or phrase in English has the word 'French' in it, then it will usually be something to do with sex. Thus – to cite just a small handful of examples – a condom is a *French letter* (see page 105), an established branch of uniform fetishism is that of dressing as a *French maid*, and syphilis was notoriously known as the *French disease*. A particularly vigorous and sensual osculatory contact of tongues in kissing is known as *French kissing*. Do these terms have any basis in historical fact? As far as the term *French kissing* goes, this seems to have first appeared in English slang in the 1910s, although there is no reason to believe that the French were the inventors of the technique. There is some evidence, however, to suggest that certain sectors of the French population were especially proficient at it. The marsh-dwelling inhabitants of the Vendée in western France are famed for having long acknowledged a courtship rite of prolonged public kissing, traditionally under a blue umbrella, known as *maraîchinage* (see page 163). Before marriage or even engagement, young lads and lasses were granted the right to snog each other for hours under this sheltering umbrella, a practice to which the great politician Georges 'the Tiger' Clemenceau, French premier during the First World War, was said

THE ELUSIVE DR CONDOM

The allegedly Gallic origins of the 'French letter', or condom, are as murky as those of the 'French kiss'. 'French letter' appears to have been first used in relation to condoms in the nineteenth century, for no better reason than that condoms connote sex, and therefore must have something to do with the French. A nineteenth-century English guide to libertines entitled *The Man of Pleasure's Companion* refers to the fact that 'Gentlemen in London will be at no loss in easily obtaining these French letters.' (Interestingly, the French term for a French letter is *capote anglaise*, or 'English hood'.)

The more current English word for a 'French letter' or sheath – condom – is one of the great unsolved puzzles of etymology. Theories abound as to the origins of this very un-English sounding word. There are those who claim it derives from the Latin word *condere*, meaning 'to conceal or protect', or from the Persian word *kondü*, an earthenware receptacle for seeds or grains. Others assert that it came from the French village of Condom in the southwestern *département* of Gers, where the local butchers are said to have made condoms from animal intestines. It has been claimed that the word relates to a Dr Condom, personal physician to Charles II, who supposedly invented the device in the seventeenth century, but to date the existence of such a personage has not been established. The French would certainly have been baffled when, a certain Jean Condom playing for the French national rugby union team in the late 1980s and early 1990s, a banner appeared in the crowd during a Five Nations match versus England proclaiming: 'Play safe – pass it to Condom.'

to be especially partial. His biographer notes that he took full advantage of 'the custom of *maraîchinage*, or kiss on the mouth, prolonged to the very point of acute joy'.[1]

And what of the *French pox, French disease* or *mal français*, used to refer to venereal disease (in particular, syphilis)?* Did

* The above are just some of the most common slang terms for venereal

the French really have anything to do with the spread of this scourge of the libidinous? Here the French do have a lot to complain about, because – while the geographical origin of syphilis remains a mystery – if there is one place in which the disease almost certainly did *not* originate, it is France. The exact provenance of syphilis is to this day the subject of raging dispute, but the balance of the evidence seems to point to it being brought from what is now the Dominican Republic to Europe by the Spanish sailors on Columbus' ships returning from the Americas.[2] The first major epidemic of the great pox broke out in Naples in 1495,[3] when the French were besieging the city – hence the popular attribution of the disease to them. However, the outbreak also occurred only a few years after Columbus' return from the New World, after several of his sailors had been treated for a mysterious ailment on their return to Barcelona; moreover, many of those same sailors went on to serve as mercenaries in the French and Spanish armies fighting it out in Naples. Some of them then proceeded to fight for James IV of Scotland and his

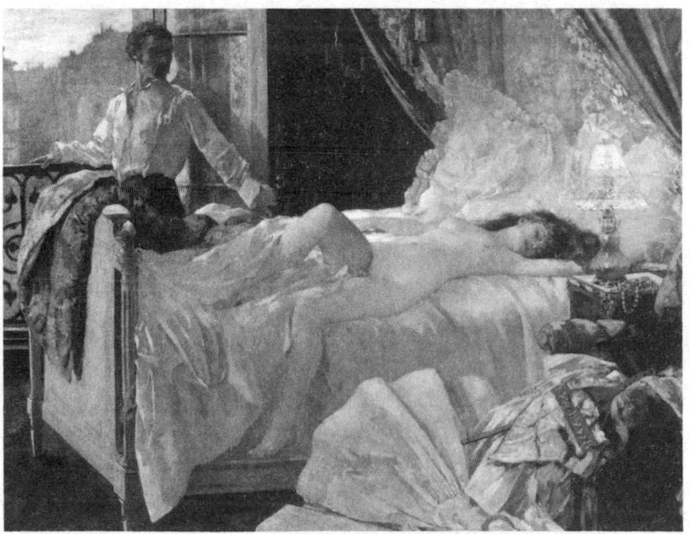

disease, especially syphilis, with the word 'French'. Others include: *The Frenchman, French measles, French crown, French marbles, French chilblains, French aches,* and *French cannibal.*

ally the English Yorkist pretender Perkin Warbeck, whereupon the mystery scourge hit Scotland, too. By the sixteenth century, syphilis had reached China and Japan, and by the 1700s even the remote islands of the South Pacific had succumbed. As the dreaded pox hopped from place to place, it was rechristened with the name of the country from which it last hailed: thus the *Christian, Polish, Spanish, Russian, Persian, Neapolitan, Portuguese, English,* and *Turkish pox* travelled all the way to Asia. But to the British it remained firmly a foul French disease that left Englishmen wasting away.* In fact, the image of the gaunt and palely syphilitic, opium-dosed English poet of the nineteenth century is matched only by that of the gaunt and palely syphilitic, absinthe-soaked French poet of the same period. As the French novelist André Gide once observed, 'It is unthinkable for a Frenchman to arrive at middle age without having syphilis and the *Croix de légion d'honneur*.'

More recently, 'French' has come to be associated in slang use with oral sex – viewed for many centuries as a 'French perversion'.† Thus a whole sub-genre of mainly gay terminology developed in the 1950s around the word 'French' to describe a wide range of oral sexual activity: *French artist, Frenching* or *French culture* (fellatio); *French active/passive* (the passive or active partner in fellatio); *French dip, French dressing* or *French-fried ice-cream* (semen or pre-coital fluid); and *French language expert* or *French by injection* (anybody well-versed in fellatio).[4] It is a telling point that in the leading modern reference work on slang, Jonathon Green's *Dictionary of Slang* (2010), more than 75 per cent of the slang phrases containing the word 'French' are connected with sex.

But are the French truly as sex-obsessed as their cultural output and our idioms and phrases for them might suggest? Certainly, they are less hung up about sex than the British. And, while their writings literally drip with the juices of often per-

---

* Interestingly, the French refer to syphilis as *la maladie anglaise*.

† The slang term *French art* in the late nineteenth century meant not the works of the Impressionists but the art of fellatio.

Of all the sexual aberrations, chastity is the strangest.
ANATOLE FRANCE, FRENCH POET AND NOVELIST (1844–1924), QUOTED IN *THE HERETIC'S HANDBOOK OF QUOTATIONS*

verse sexual fantasy, they are not nearly as obsessed as the British with sexual perversion in daily life. The French do not, for example, have tabloid newspapers that describe sex crimes such as rape in pruriently forensic detail, while simultaneously adopting a tone of shock and moral outrage (in fact they do not have tabloids, period). French crèches do not have fortifications, security cameras and alarm systems like their British counterparts. French nursery staff are not banned from dabbing sun cream on their charges for fear that such an act might generate accusations of sexual abuse. One is free to take pictures of one's children on a French beach, without fear of people suspecting you of being a paedophile. It is not that sexual perversion and/or paedophilia do not exist in France – it does, of course, as it exists everywhere. It's just that the French don't seem to be as paranoid about it, as ready to see perverts lurking on every playground, beach and street corner, as the British. The French would be far more shocked at the prospect of an ex-soft-porn model writing books for young girls, than at crèche workers smearing sun cream on kids in their care.

Nor would the French appear to be the permanently switched-on sex machines that the fervid Anglo-Saxon imagination would seem to suggest. A 2010 survey by the French polling group Ifop found that more than three-quarters of French couples have bad sex lives. More than one in three French women said they used excuses such as headaches, tiredness or the children to get out of having sex. And nearly one in six Gallic males did the same.[5] One of the world's leading sex surveys, the Durex 2005 Global Sex Survey,[6] found that only 38 per cent of French people were happy with their sex lives, compared with 51 per cent of Britons.

As for the legendary adventurousness of the Gallic lover, the Durex 2005 survey came up with some surprising results. According to the survey, only 14 per cent of the French liked experimenting with sex aids (as compared to 32 per cent of British), and only 33 per cent liked to try out new ideas in the bedroom (as compared to 42 per cent of Brits). Only 15 per cent of French (versus 17 per cent of British) had tried out three in a bed, and 3 per cent (versus 5 per cent) sadomasochism. Only 2 per cent of the French (versus 5 per cent of Brits) had experimented with tantric sex, and only 21 per cent (versus 37 per cent) had tried a spot of bondage. The Marquis de Sade must be turning in his grave. Most surprising of all, only 42 per cent of the French (versus 52 per cent of the British) had had a one-night stand. When it comes to the nitty-gritty, the favoured sexual position for French women is apparently 'doggie-style' (or rather more gracefully in French, the *levrette* or 'greyhound' position). This contrasts with the plain vanilla Americans who go for the missionary, and the buccaneering Brits who are alleged to prefer the 'cowgirl' (or 'woman on top', for the more prosaically inclined).[7]

In fact it seems that, in terms of innovation between the sheets, ordinary French folk are downright conservative compared to the kinky Brits. They seem to be into boring old unadorned, vanilla sex between a man and a woman, in bed, without the intrusion of any 'marital aids' made of plastic, leather or rubber, whips, chains, or wacky Oriental theories (although they do seem to be on the adventurous side in terms of sexual positions). 'Continental people have sex-life: the English have hot-water bottles,' the Hungarian writer and wit George Mikes once observed.[8] Perhaps that opinion needs to be revised to: 'Continental people have sex lives: the English have sex toys.'

Myth Evaluation: *False. The French are not sex-obsessed but they are less hung up about sex than the English. The English, on the other hand, are obsessed with the sex lives of everybody, including the French.*

The French are uniquely tolerant of adultery

Marriage: the cause of adultery and prelude to divorce.
LÉO CAMPION, BELGIAN ARTIST AND ANARCHIST (1905–92)

'Marriage is a prison whose doors are always open to adultery,' wrote the Swiss-French poet and dramatist Louis Dumur in 1892. His view of marriage is one widely believed to be representative of the French. French married couples, so the saying goes, are as ready to bed-hop as their Anglo-Saxon counterparts are to partake of a bedtime cup of tea and Digestive biscuit; and a *ménage à trois* is not just the norm, but virtually a requirement of the glamorous *haute-bourgeoisie. Liberté, Egalité, Infidélité*, in fact, could more or less be considered the unofficial motto of the French Republic.

Precisely where the Anglo-Saxon view of the French as a nation wedded to unfaithfulness comes from is hard to pinpoint. Possibly, it originated with the perceived sexual incontinence of the old French monarchy; or possibly, from the Anglo-Saxon Protestant suspicion of the moral laxity of Catholic Europe. On the other hand, it could simply be part of the age-old habit of attributing bad habits to one's neighbours and rivals. Certainly, during the *ancien régime*, infidelity was an institution for French monarchs. There was even a special post created for the official royal mistress at any one time, the *maîtresse-en-titre*. Louise de la Vallière, Madame de Maintenon, Madame de Pompadour, Madame du Barry… these sumptuous and shrewd women showed, by their often spectacular ascent to the dizzy heights of power, that the worlds of *le boudoir* and *le pouvoir* were not so very far apart in French politics. In this respect, the monarch sent to the guillotine during the French Revolution – Louis XVI – was something of an aberration, since he appears to have taken the unprecedented and somewhat bizarre decision to remain faithful to his spouse (although the same could not be said of his wife, Marie Antoinette). Clearly things were all up with the French monarchy if the king felt he could function without a mistress, and so after the unfortunate Louis was decapitated in 1793, the awards for the most high-profile royal mistresses of the nineteenth and twentieth centuries sadly passed from the French to the British.*

Nevertheless, the demise of the French monarchy did nothing to deter the new bourgeoisie from adopting the royal tradition of the kept mistress and the extramarital dalliance. It was quite common for a wealthy Frenchman of the nineteenth century openly to maintain a mistress in her own apartment, separate from the 'official' family – the poet and novelist Victor Hugo did exactly this, with his devoted mistress Juliette Drouet at his (other) side for almost fifty years, while the novelist Émile Zola also had a mistress to supplement his wife.† Casual affairs were elevated from necessity to an art: brothels, utilitarian places in the early 1800s designed simply to service the frustrations of men trapped in loveless marriages, became, by the century's end, extravagant palaces of luxury and hedonism, dedicated to serving every fantasy and populated by courtesans who famously rose up the social ladder on their backs. (The French referred to these ladies in colourful fashion as *les grandes horizontales*.)[9]

The obsession of the post-Revolutionary age with breaking marital taboos is reflected in Gallic literature of the period. An adulterous trail had already been blazed by Choderlos de Laclos in his classic 1782 epistolary novel of sexual duplicity during the *ancien régime*, *Les Liaisons dangereuses* ('Dangerous Liaisons'). The theme was further developed in Benjamin Constant's novel *Adolphe* (1816), the tale of a melancholy young man's infatuation for an older woman who happened to be another man's

---

* The French did in fact flirt with a few (brief) returns to a monarchical system after the Revolution of 1789, but none of these stood the test of the turbulent times.

† While this was also true of English public figures – such as Charles Dickens – the openness with which mistresses were accepted as a part of life in France differed from the British practice of covering up such matters. During his exile in England in 1898, Émile Zola was alerted to the contrasting attitudes between the countries by his friend Fernand Desmoulin, who advised him not to bring his mistress Jeanne over to see him 'in the country of cant'.

Women react differently: a French woman who sees herself betrayed by her husband will kill his mistress; an Italian will kill her husband; a Spaniard will kill both; and a German will kill herself.
BERNARD LE BOVIER DE FONTENELLE, FRENCH SCIENTIST, PLAYWRIGHT AND ESSAYIST (1657–1757)

mistress. The peak of the long-running affair of French literature with the theme of unfaithfulness was of course Gustave Flaubert's 1856 novel *Madame Bovary*, the tragic tale of the attempts by a provincial doctor's wife to escape the emptiness of small-town life with a string of liaisons. But *Madame Bovary*, towering as it does over the genre, was far from the end of the affair; Zola's *Thérèse Raquin* (1867) followed hot on its heels with a similarly doomed portrayal of a married woman's fall from grace. Even well into the twentieth century, it seemed that the French couldn't get enough of infidelity, at least in fiction: as late as 1923, the twenty-year-old Raymond Radiguet shocked a postwar readership with his at least partly autobiographical tale of a married woman's affair with a sixteen-year-old boy, *Le Diable au corps* ('Devil in the Flesh').

However, this obsession with infidelity in France in the nineteenth and early twentieth centuries – in life as in literature – concealed many deep-seated anxieties, and those who laughed at the farces of Feydeau, which famously dealt with the subject, did so through gritted teeth. As the old century gave way to the new, brothels became less outrageous and fantastical and more and more bourgeois: gentlemen would come to take tea with their mistresses in the afternoon to the background tinkling of a piano, the reception rooms of the whorehouse approximating more and more to the banality of the middle-class salon.[10] A whole window of the early evening – the infamous *cinq à sept*, or interval from 5 p.m. to 7 p.m. – became ritually devoted to extramarital dalliances, the space to play after a day's work before going home to family life. Tied down in arranged marriages, men paid to flirt with the idea of a meeting of minds and bodies, consorting with tarts who resembled, more and more, their bourgeois wives at home; while those very Emma Bovaries at home were beginning, slowly, to exhume a long-buried eroticism. The tart was becoming respectable, and respectable

Whatever it is that French women have, Madame Bovary has more of it!

MGM ADVERTISING SLOGAN FOR ITS 1949 FILM OF FLAUBERT'S *MADAME BOVARY*

women were discovering their inner tart. Just like the English late-Victorian and Edwardian obsession with double identity and concealing hidden lives behind a respectable façade,* the French fetish for the theme of adultery in the late nineteenth and early twentieth centuries was, in truth, a critique of existing social constrictions on personal relationships, an advance role-play for their dissolution in the century to come.

Now that those social constrictions have all but disappeared, in France as elsewhere in Western Europe, the evidence indicates that ordinary French people are no more unfaithful than anyone else. In fact, they are perhaps less so. Reliable figures on infidelity rates and attitudes to infidelity are rather patchy and hard to come by, not least because, when questioned, men have a tendency to exaggerate their past indiscretions, while women tend to minimize them. There is also often a big discrepancy between the almost universal condemnation of infidelity, and actual practice. A 2009 survey by the French magazine *Madame Figaro* found that 66 per cent of French people believed that fidelity was essential to a

* As exemplified by Robert Louis Stevenson's *Strange Case of Dr Jekyll and Mr Hyde* (1886) and Oscar Wilde's *The Importance of Being Earnest* (1895).

real commitment, while 19 per cent admitted to having actually cheated on their partner.[11] The United States, on the other hand, in a 1994 nationwide survey, was the most conservative country in condemning infidelity (94 per cent) but estimates indicate that between 20–25 per cent of married Americans will have sex with someone other than their partner.[12] And despite what many Froglit authors would have one believe, these days the old French window of dalliance – the *cinq à sept* – is little more than the equivalent of the British 'happy hour', a time to snatch a quick drink (as opposed to a quickie) with colleagues before heading home. If French couples feel the need to move on, like anybody else these days, they simply divorce.

None of this contradicts the fact that, for a very small group of the older generation of the French élite – notably French presidents – the old tradition of the mistress and/or 'kept family' has been maintained with panache. In terms of sheer *chutzpah* in this respect, first prize must surely go to the late François Mitterrand, president of the French Republic from 1981 to 1995. Because Mitterrand assiduously cultivated the image of a committed family man, it took twenty years for it to come to light that he had a whole second family – a mistress and secret daughter – who had been kept hidden from the world. At his funeral, all the three women in his life stood together by the grave. None of this shocked the French public unduly, until it was revealed that the 'second family' had been housed at the taxpayer's expense. Then there really was a scandal. But while Mitterrand must surely hold the supreme title for extramarital dalliances among the French *sexus politicus*, he is by no means the only French president to have allegedly had a complicated personal life. In October 1974, for example, the satirical French weekly *Le Canard enchaîné* caused a storm when it claimed that the then president, Valéry Giscard d'Estaing, had crashed into a milk float in the early hours of the morning, accompanied by a young actress in a Ferrari 250 that he had allegedly borrowed from the film-maker Roger Vadim. In the resulting furore a number of ironic remarks were made on the rumoured nocturnal perambulations of the president, including the observation by the former prime minister, Maurice Couve de Murville, that 'Giscard is the only Head of State in the world of whom one knows with certainty where he does not sleep.'[13] Jacques Chirac (president from 1995 to 2007) was likewise said to have been a vigorous pursuer of extramarital relationships. His many alleged conquests were documented in a 'drive-and-tell' book published in 2001 by his former chauffeur, Jean-Claude Laumond. According to Laumond, the steady stream of women walking into Mr Chirac's office was so constant that female staff would joke: 'Chirac? Three minutes. Shower included.'[14] Most recently, any sighs of relief heaved at the election of (the thankfully unmarried) President François Hollande in the 2012 *présidentielles* proved premature: the president's complicated love life has subsequently more than proved that love triangles are not the prerogative of married couples.*

So it seems that while ordinary French people are no more likely to bed hop than anyone else, they are less likely to judge those who do (especially their presidents). How does one explain the Gallic tolerance of infidelity in public office? The answer partly lies in the French bourgeois obsession with secrecy. The roots of this obsession are unclear: possibly, it dates from the days of the Revolution, when anybody with anything other than proletarian roots was wise to keep their head down, if they wanted to keep it. Or it could be derived from the strict separation of Church and State enforced by the Revolutionary government, the insistence that one's religion and morals are a private affair. In any event, privacy is a very public

Christ pardoned the adulterous woman. By God! It wasn't his wife.

GEORGES COURTELINE,
FRENCH ROMANTIC NOVELIST
AND PLAYWRIGHT (1858–1929)

* The alleged battle between the present companion of the French President, Valérie Trierweiler, and the mother of his children, Ségolène Royal, has been a subject of extensive speculation in the French press, not least when his children and former partner failed to appear at the presidential inauguration. When Hollande gave his former partner a peck on the cheek in public, Trierweiler swept in to give him a full frontal smacker on the lips. Matters reached a head with *Twittergate*, the infamous sending by Trierweiler of an indiscreet tweet in support of Royal's opponent in the 2012 legislative elections for the region of La Rochelle.

FUNEREAL FELLATIO

François Mitterrand wins the presidential prize for adulterous liaisons during his lifetime, but the nineteenth-century French president Félix Faure (1841–99) takes the laurels for the most spectacularly scandalous death. In fact, Faure has the dubious honour of being more famed for his death than his life: he suffered an apoplectic fit in the throes of an orgasm while in the arms of his mistress, Marguerite Steinheil.

Rumour had it that she was fellating him at the fatal moment, and since the French slang word for performing oral sex on a man is *pómper* (literally, 'to pump'), Steinheil was rechristened (rather unkindly) by the French press of the time as *la pompe funèbre* ('undertaker' or 'funereal pumper/blower', depending on how you choose to read it).

Faure's arch-enemy, the statesman and subsequent French prime minister Georges Clemenceau, played on this sense of the word when he delivered his salaciously punning epitaph on his late rival: *Il voulait être César, mais il ne fut que Pompée.* This translates as either 'He wanted to be Caesar, but ended up as Pompey', or – for those less charitably inclined – 'He wanted to be Caesar, but ended up being sucked off.'

obsession in France. Everybody, in the French view, is entitled to his or her *jardin secret.* This curious term – literally, 'secret garden' – is uniquely French, and used to describe a person's own world of private interests. It can include anything from cavorting naked in dog collars to stamp collecting. It's a hard phrase to translate into English, as 'secret garden' tends to suggest either nineteenth-century children's books or unmentionable parts of the female anatomy. 'Own private world' might be the best paraphrase. One facet of this obsession with privacy is the draconian French privacy law, which forbids the press from revealing details of a person's private life without their consent. Adultery in the French view is a private sin, not a public matter, and not of itself reason to exclude a person from public office (an exception is when heavy extramarital petting allegedly turns into something worse, as in the case of the disgraced former Socialist politician and IMF leader, Dominique Strauss-Kahn). Because they are seen as private sinners, adulterers in France are not subjected to public humiliation, and forever branded with the letter 'A' like the unfortunate American sinner Hester Prynne in *The Scarlet Letter*. This does not mean that adultery is tolerated by modern French people in the private sphere, any more than anywhere else: adultery is in fact the number one reason for divorce in France.[15] It simply means that playing the field is one's own affair. The relatively non-judgemental view of adultery adopted in France by the outsider to a relationship is echoed in French cinema's long-standing fling with unfaithfulness: French films typically tend to view marital infidelity with a blackly comic eye, or as angst-ridden self-exploration set to the music of Schubert.* This contrasts with a seminal Hollywood portrayal of infidelity as a pact with a she-devil that has disastrous family consequences, including bunny-boiling, acid thrown on the family car, and knife attacks in the shower.

Of course, in France as elsewhere a distinction has historically been made between the *adulterer* and the *adulteress*, the latter being guilty of a far worse misdemeanour than the former.† Under the *ancien régime*, men who had affairs were just being men; by contrast, a woman who took a lover was liable to have her head shaved and be immured in a nunnery. That the French have traditionally taken a more censorious view of the cheating woman is illustrated by the fact that, until as late as 1975, a French woman who committed adultery was technically liable to be sent to prison for three months to two years. On the other hand, a man who played away was simply liable for a fine (and

---

* As in Bertrand Blier's film *Trop belle pour toi* (1989).

† A difference in attitude towards male and female adultery is replicated in many cultures and probably links with the fact that female adultery can obscure or 'taint' the blood line. The very word 'adultery' has been argued to come from the Latin word *adulterium* or 'altered', meaning polluted or tainted blood. French children born of an adulterous relationship did not obtain equal rights with legitimate children until 1972, and were only entitled to half the inheritance of legitimate children until 2001.

OOH LA LA! ORIGINS OF THE FRENCH MAID FETISH

In addition to adulterous liaisons beyond the precincts of the family home, the nineteenth century was also the heyday of *le troussage de domestique*, or the ancient right of the master of the house to help himself to the personal services of the household maid in every sense of the phrase.

The *belle époque* had something of an obsession with maids: *le fétichisme du tablier* ('apron fetish') manifested itself by the innumerable appearances of maids in novels and plays of the time. There were, for example, titillating works such as the racy *Journal d'une femme de chambre* or 'Diary of a Chambermaid' of 1900 – full of keyhole observations of the bourgeoisie in compromising positions – and the sensationally popular farces of the playwright Georges Feydeau.

The relegation of maids to tiny bedrooms, or *chambres de bonne*, usually located on the sixth floor of Parisian houses, made them all the more accessible to a discreet knock on the door from the master of the house. These *chambres de bonne* exist in Paris to this day, and are generally rented out as studio apartments to students and poorer members of the Parisian population. Even as late as 2011, a member of the bourgeois establishment shocked the French public by referring to Dominique Strauss-Kahn's alleged rape of a hotel maid as *le troussage de domestique*.

By the twentieth century, the French fetish with the maid had migrated to Britain and America. A strongly modified style of their evening uniform of black dress and frilly apron – with necklines much lower and hemlines much higher than would have been tolerated at the time – had established itself as one of the most popular forms of fetish and fantasy wear, in countries as far afield as Japan. The symbolism of domination/submission inherent in the outfit presumably only added to its appeal.

this only if he committed the sinful act in the marital home).* French literature abounds in examples of adulterous women who suffer heinous consequences for their sins (generally suicide by ingestion of arsenic).[16] In contrast, French women who stand by their erring husbands in public are seen as paragons of wifely devotion. This was the case, for example, with the late Danielle Mitterrand, who when questioned by a reporter about her reaction to her husband's infidelity, made the extraordinary statement that it concerned his own private life and was therefore his affair. Yet actions speak louder than words; when Mme Mitterrand died in November 2011, she was buried in the cemetery at Cluny (Saône-et-Loire), and not beside her erring husband at Jarnac (Charente). Barred by social convention from voicing her real views in life, she stated them most eloquently in death.

Where does all this leave us in terms of the messy affair of the French and their views on unfaithfulness? Hopelessly muddled, unfortunately. One thing is for sure, and that is the fact that as long as men and women (of any race) commit to each other, some are bound to stray. And the ultimate difference between the French and their Anglo-Saxon counterparts is perhaps simply that they accept (but do not revel in) this reality. As the French writer Pascal Bruckner observed, 'One cannot imagine a way of loving more likely to generate discord. And that is why adultery is the eternal, universal road companion to marriage: they are unthinkable, one without the other.' Or, as W. Somerset Maugham more succinctly put it: 'You know that the Tasmanians, who never committed adultery, are now extinct.'

Myth Evaluation: *Partly true. The French are probably more tolerant of adultery than the puritanical British or Americans, at least in public office, but they actually practise it less.*

* France was one of the later European countries to decriminalize adultery for women, in 1975. The UK had done so as far back as 1857.

The French habitually have large families

La France a besoin d'enfants. ('France needs children')
SLOGAN ACCOMPANYING FRENCH STATE NATALITY CAMPAIGNS

This is not so much a myth as a fact. The French birth rate, at 2.01 children per woman on average, is (along with Ireland) the highest on the Old Continent of Europe.[17] And while most French families average two children (40 per cent), the French have one of the highest rates of families with three children or more (30 per cent).[18] In fact, France is one of the few countries in Europe which is not suffering from an ageing population, and which is likely to be able to reproduce itself in the foreseeable future. The French are the reproductive miracle of Europe, envied in particular by countries such as Germany, growing grey-haired even as its Gallic neighbours churn out bouncing babies.

The reasons for the fantastic fecundity of the French are deep-rooted, going back through centuries of state policy. Throughout history, successive French governments have tended to see

family matters as affairs of state, interpreting domestic policy as embracing what goes on in the conjugal bed. Even under the *ancien régime*, French monarchs considered their subjects' reproductive lives a royal prerogative. The French philosopher Montesquieu (1689–1755)[19] observed that a lord was only as great, rich, powerful and secure as the number of his vassals, and with this principle in mind, monarchs like Louis XIV set about ensuring that they would have as many subjects as possible. Under the influence of his finance minister Jean-Baptiste Colbert, Louis introduced in 1666 an edict exempting all men who married before the age of 20 years from paying tax until they reached 25 years; all men with ten or more living children were similarly exempt (priests and nuns excepted).[20] The Revolution of 1789 swept away as many old ideas as it did heads, but the concept of big is best as far as families were concerned remained intact. The Revolutionaries, in the name of *égalité*, introduced various provisions to equalize the position of those who had multiple children with those who did not. These included ascending tax breaks for men with more than three and six children, and – a foretaste of what was to come in later centuries – fiscal penalties on those who were not so fruitful. The French Revolutionaries also introduced one of the earliest examples of child benefit: every child under ten received a payment of 2 livres a month, until attaining that age.[21]

The treaty does not state that France will have many children, but it is the first thing that should have been written there. For if France does not have large families, it will be in vain that you put all the finest clauses in the treaty, that you take away all the German guns, France will be lost because there will be no more French.

GEORGES CLEMENCEAU, FRENCH STATESMAN, ON THE TREATY OF VERSAILLES, 1919

The nineteenth century saw – in Britain as much as in France and the rest of Europe – a shrinkage in family sizes, as writers such as Thomas Malthus preached pessimistically about the evils of spawning more ill-fated offspring than one could afford, flooding the crowded cities with an overflow of rank bodies and malnourished mouths to feed. But France's suppressed propensity for self-propagation was to resurface in

A country which has a high proportion of children and young people is a country which progresses, a country which adapts, a country which innovates, and a country which prepares for the future with confidence.
PRESIDENT JACQUES CHIRAC, SPEECH DURING PRESENTATION OF THE MEDAL OF THE FRENCH FAMILY, MAY 2003

the twentieth century, with added vigour, after the ravages of the two world wars. The French population had suffered significant losses on the battlefield, especially in the trenches of the Western Front in the First World War, and required replenishing. What was needed, in de Gaulle's celebrated words of March 1945, was *d'appeler à la vie les douze millions de beaux bébés qu'il faut à la France en dix ans* ('to bring into being the twelve million bouncing babies France needs in the space of ten years'). It was made quite clear, to French women in the postwar years, that the most patriotic thing they could do was to reproduce. Hence *le baby boom*. Posters sprang up featuring Madonna-like *materfamilias* surrounded by six or more children, with the slogan *La France a besoin d'enfants* ('France needs children').[22] A law of 1920 had already made abortion and contraception criminal offences; and in Vichy France in 1942, illegal termination of a pregnancy was declared a 'crime against the state' and made punishable by death. Of course, this just boosted trade for backstreet abortionists, who were given the grim soubriquet of *faiseuses d'ange* or 'angel-makers'. It was a risky profession – in 1943, Marie-Louise Giraud was guillotined for having performed 27 abortions in the area of Cherbourg.*

Because birth control was outlawed, condoms in the postwar period in France were strictly under-the-counter purchases – although pharmacy catalogues did refer discreetly to 'hygiene products for men'. This probably explains the widespread popu-

* Those under the impression that the guillotine was a grisly form of execution confined to the period of the Revolutionary Terror will be amazed to learn that the last case of its use in France was in 1977, just before the abolition of the death penalty in 1981. Although no longer in use, the guillotine is still an object of awe and dread for many French people; some commentators advance this as a reason why one virtually never sees sash windows, ubiquitous in English town houses, in France, where they go by the graphic name of *fenêtres à guillotine*.

larity of the bidet in France until well into the twentieth century,* as a source of flushing out not only germs, but seeds which were at risk of being sown into the wrong furrow. A special series of medals – *La Médaille d'honneur de la famille française* – was created in 1920, to honour mothers who had raised multiple children 'in a worthy fashion'. A bronze medal was awarded to the mother who had raised, in worthy fashion, four or five children; silver for six or seven; and gold for eight or more. The award is given in France annually to this day: it is usually a platform for the president to vaunt his latest political achievements in family policy. (France is not unique among pro-natalist countries in distinguishing champion breeders. The Nazi regime awarded the 'Cross of Honour of the German Mother' to fecund and suitably Aryan recipients, and the former Soviet Union had several awards for outstanding ovaries. Even today, the Russian Federation bestows the 'Order of Parental Glory' on worthy couples raising seven or more children as good Russian citizens.) *La France a besoin d'enfants* has in fact become something of a national motto: in the 1980s, a government publicity campaign was run under the slogan, with posters featuring assorted gurgling bundles of joy under such headlines as 'Life isn't just about sex'.

Is France in the twenty-first century as baby-crazy as ever? It would seem so. Luckily, one is no longer guillotined for performing an abortion (just as well, since 200,000 of them take place annually in France), and since 1967 it has been legal to take the Pill.[23] But, while two-thirds of French women today use some method of contraception, the French state doesn't rush to the aid of those seeking to stop nature's course: the public advertising of condoms was only finally permitted in 1987, in the heat of the AIDS crisis, and even now many contraceptive pills are not reimbursed by the French health service. Abortion costs are not at present fully repaid by the state (a subject of proposed reform), and abortion itself is only available up to 12 weeks of

* The role of the bidet in the French bathroom is examined in detail in the later chapter dedicated to this intriguing – and to the Anglo-Saxons mysterious – piece of sanitary ware (see page 148).

pregnancy for non-medical reasons (as opposed to 25 weeks in the UK). The overall message from the Republic, in fact, is still that it is one's civic duty to go forth, be fruitful and multiply.

But the French state's killer weapon in its baby-making arsenal is more subtle than a poster campaign, and sharper than a guillotine. From the postwar period onwards, successive French governments have adopted a stealthily effective policy to encourage the patter of tiny feet on apartment floors: that is, to put money in the hands that feed them. Spending upwards of 27.5 per cent of GDP per capita on each child, France in 2011 spent more on families than any other EU country.[24] Those happy families with more than three children – i.e. those who acquire the blessed status of *famille nombreuse* – immediately qualify for an avalanche of benefits, from reduced-rate public transport to tax breaks and preferential treatment in almost any administrative queue. In no other European country are there so many benefits and tax breaks for large families: child benefit in 2012 started at a generous €127.68 per month for two children (naturally, there is no benefit for having just one child), and €163.59 for each additional child, paid until the child reaches the age of twenty years.[25] Income tax is calculated on a scale that reduces according to the number of children: France's famous and unique 'family quotient'. From the age of three months, every child in principle is entitled to go to the local crèche, open all day, run to a high standard and means-tested (although in practice there is often a pitched battle for crèche places, particularly in areas of high demand. However, state-subsidized child-minders exist for those unable to obtain a crèche place). From the age of three, every child is entitled to a free place at the local nursery school (France has one of the youngest ages for starting school in Europe). Local *mairies* operate school pick-up and drop-off services, and evening care for children after school until as late as 7.30 p.m. During the school holidays, the *mairie* will also run a *maison de loisirs* or holiday activity centre, open from 7.30 a.m. to 7.30 p.m., inclusive of meals and with a range of activities, for a reasonable (and subsidized) charge. All in all, while France may not be at quite the level of the Nordic countries in terms of winning the Order of Glory for Child Propagation,[26] it certainly leads other European countries in the league and comes in for an Order of Merit. And unlike the Anglo-Saxon countries – which tend to see social benefits as the degrading resort of the poor – the biggest winners in the French system, particularly on the tax front, have traditionally been the fecund families of the comfortably-off bourgeoisie.

Will France be able to pay for another generation of bouncing babies in these increasingly straitened times? Only time will tell. But just remember one thing. Next time you feel like throwing yourself out of the window after reading yet another eulogy about the quasi miraculous ability of French women to have an enormous brood, hold down a glamorous job, get their hair done at lunchtime, and go out to dinner with their husbands, just remember that behind that supposedly miraculous achievement of Parental Glory lies a subsidized crèche, subsidized child-minder, usually excellent free local school, subsidized after-school activity centre, several hundred euros per month of child benefit, a reduced income-tax rate, and... a whopping tax bill for those beasts of burden, the black sheep of the happy French family: the Inglorious Order of the Childless.

Myth Evaluation: *True.*

French children don't throw food

'As well behaved as a picture'
(*Sage comme une image* = 'as good as gold').
FRENCH SAYING

This is a relative newcomer to the pantheon of French mythology. It is a myth that appeared overnight, with the publication of a best-selling book of this title in 2012 by Pamela Druckerman (although, unlike *French Women Don't Get Fat*, it does not appear to have been trademarked, at least not as yet).* According to this book and its imitators, it is not only French women who have an innate sense of 'balance' and restraint. French children are poised and self-controlled, too. They never say *non* to their dinner of *escargots de Bourgogne*. They do not throw public tantrums in the park, or charge off from the dinner table to cut the hair off their baby sisters' Barbie dolls, like their hooligan Anglo-Saxon peers. They politely join in with adults in debates about French philosophy, always say please and thank you and ask to be allowed to leave the table. Even as small babies, according to these new parenting bibles, French children show a mature consideration for others. They miraculously sleep through the night from the age of three months, unselfishly enabling their mothers to slip on a sexy number and sneak off with their husbands – thus proving that, for French women at least, reproduction does not put an end to *la séduction*. In fact, the myth of the preternaturally well-behaved French child appears to have established itself as a new theory of parenting. We've had Authoritarian Parenting, Permissive Parenting, Child-Driven Parenting, Fusion Parenting, and Chinese Parenting.[27] Now, it's French Parenting that's all the rage. Anglo-Saxon females should prepare themselves for another bashing. Not only are they fat, inelegant and

* The best-seller *French Children Don't Throw Food* (Doubleday, 2012) has predictably inspired a whole new breed of parenting books, eulogizing the allegedly saintly virtues of French children in all spheres from eating to discipline.

inept at cooking, but they are now apparently rubbish parents as well.

This paragon-like nature of French babies and children is supposedly due to superior Gallic methods of child-raising. Exactly what these methods are and how they are superior remains somewhat ill-defined, but many of the techniques described seem suspiciously reminiscent of what used to be called 'good old-fashioned parenting'. In truth, however, studies of French babies' and children's eating and sleeping habits suggest that they are not substantially different from others. Research into the sleep patterns of French babies found that 21–38 per cent of French children aged 1–2 years woke up at night,[28] and a further clinical study found that 72 per cent of French children aged between 16 and 24 months had sleep issues.[29] As for the much-vaunted omnivorousness of French children – their allegedly preternatural penchant for greens and all things gross to the non-French, imperfect child – a 2009 study found that many French toddlers were being given an unsuitable diet by their parents (including chips and *charcuterie*),[30] and an estimated 25–45 per cent of French babies and toddlers have food issues at some point or other (including fussy eating).[31] There has been much discussion in the French media recently about the so-called 'baby clash', a growing phenomenon of French couples separating in the first few months or years after the birth of a baby, owing to the pressures placed on their marriage by the arrival of a new bundle of stress into their lives. In fact, when one looks at the evidence, the French baby experience does not appear to be substantially different from that of any other harassed parents elsewhere in the world.

It has to be said that Pamela Druckerman's book is not exactly the work of a sociologist. The British weekly newspaper The Economist *is of the view that 'it sounds too good to be true.' It suspects her of confining herself to the wealthy families of Paris. And it advises her to go visit the 'French suburbs' to verify whether 'Bonjour, Madame' is really practised out there. One could also retort that even in the posh sandpits of Neuilly, the children are far from being angels…'*

REVIEW OF *FRENCH CHILDREN DON'T THROW FOOD* IN THE FRENCH NEWSPAPER *LE FIGARO*, 23 JANUARY 2012

So much for the feeding and sleeping habits of French babies and toddlers. As we know, babies when they become children do more than just sleep and feed, so there is also the question of behaviour to consider. Are French children more polite than their English or American counterparts, as the new French parenting bibles would have us believe? On the whole, at least in the presence of their parents in public spaces, it would seem that younger French children are. And for good reason. French parents, quite simply, are generally stricter than their English or American counterparts. France has not banned corporal punishment of children in the home, and *la fessée* – or smack on the bottom – is a venerable French institution, which 64 per cent of French parents in a recent survey were not ashamed to admit to using.[32] A comparative study by members of the University of Wittenberg in 2007 found that nearly half of French parents had resorted to severe corporal punishment (a resounding slap on the face, beating with an object or severe beating) of their children.[33] Some of the chastisements meted out in French schools, while never violent, do seem somewhat out of touch with the cutting edge of modern pedagogical practice. It is perfectly common in nursery school, for example, for naughty children to be sent to sit with their back to the class, in *la chaise qui fait réfléchir*.

The French and Anglo-American education systems, in fact, are as alike as chalk and cheese. For unlike the Anglo-American system – which is designed to produce free-thinking, freewheeling renegades – the French system is designed to produce obedient citizens of the *République française*. French schooling makes a fetish out of everything Anglo-American pedagogy condemns: rote learning, absorption of massive amounts of information, dictation, competition between pupils, and the ritual humiliation of those unable to keep up.[34] A favourite technique of French teaching from primary school onwards is the method known as *La Martinière*, where arithmetical problems are called out orally to pupils, who write the answer down on a slate. They are then told to hold up the slate, and those who have got the wrong answer are derided. As one British commentator noted, her children were trapped 'like rats in a cage'.[35]

With a strong tradition of individual achievement through effort and the idea of reliance on the state seen as a sign of failure, Anglo-American parents are expected to put huge personal effort into the rearing of their children. Getting one's hair smeared in finger paint, digging in sandboxes, introducing one's child to Sudoku at an early age, and killing oneself to pay enormous school fees, are considered entirely normal behaviour for British and American parents. How else will their precious offspring make their mark in a viciously competitive world, with no social safety net? French mothers would consider such behaviour preposterous, if not downright mad. The French state provides crèches, free schooling and after-school activities. Other people are paid to get their fingers covered in paint and mess with Play-Doh. The state has its own means of sorting the wheat from the chaff (see pages 189–96). Being a 'pushy parent' is not encouraged in France. There are no school parent–teacher meetings; in general, one only hears from a teacher if one's child has done something wrong. The French government has even gone so far as to ban homework from 2013, as this is said to place an undue burden on parents, and apparently privileges middle-class children whose parents can give them more help. Homework is to take place at school, after lessons are over for the day, supervised by teachers. All the more reason to relax with a glass of wine in the evening, *non*?

Does this weight of state-organized child intervention produce the models of exemplary behaviour intended, further down the line? It would appear not. A 2011 OECD survey of schoolchildren ranked France fifth from the bottom of 66 countries for discipline in class. When questioned, over a third of French pupils stated that there was noise and disorder in the classroom (the most disciplined classes were, perhaps unsurprisingly, the Japanese).[36] A UNICEF study of French primary schoolchildren in 2011 found that 25 per cent had been insulted often or very often at school, 21 per cent had been subject to regular taunting, 17 per cent had been frequently or very frequently hit by fellow pupils, and 7 per cent subject to frequent racism.[37] Almost a third of French children aged between 10 and 15 years old smoke, or have tried a cigarette. Of those who did smoke, 45 per cent said their parents knew about it, 27 per cent smoked in front of their parents, and 25 per cent said that their parents had thrown in the towel on them smoking.[38] On the basis that the toddler is father of the child, things don't look good. If those little French preschoolers are indeed so very preternaturally perfect, whatever happens to them in later years? A release of long-bottled-up resentment, perhaps?

> *In my practice as a clinical psychologist, I encounter more and more parents who are powerless before what I call their child's seizing of power at home: 'We don't know any more how to deal with him'... 'He does what he likes'... 'We can't cope any more.'*
>
> DIDIER PLEUX, DIRECTOR OF THE FRENCH INSTITUTE OF COGNITIVE THERAPY, *DE L'ENFANT ROI À L'ENFANT TYRAN*, 2002

There is, it must be admitted, much that is laudable about French methods of education, particularly at the primary level, where a certain amount of rote learning is essential. My children – all within the French state school system – can do maths, notably mental arithmetic, better than I could at their age (despite my expensive private school education in England). They write in deliciously French spidery handwriting, like the menu on the chalkboard in the bistro down the road. They can recite reams of the poetry of Verlaine. They are passionately French, in a way I never felt (nor was taught to feel) English – even though they don't have a French bone in their bodies. They are under no illusions about their ranking in the class. It does no harm for children to know that the world doesn't owe them a living, that learning involves application and hard work. That they would be better to aspire to being a nurse or teacher than the next David Beckham. But to crush every spark of creativity and enthusiasm from their little souls in the process, to make learning a drudgery from the word go, does seem to be rather a case of throwing the brat out with the bath water. And it is easy to forget that, behind every seeming French *wonderfemme* and her supposedly immaculate brood, there is the invisible arm of the French state controlling, funding and directing most of the moves. So next time you despair because your little Tom or Harry is chopping the fingers off his grandmother's gloves to make body bags for the corpses of his Playmobil pirates, just remember that it was the wayward Tom Sawyer, and not the sanctimonious Sid, who found the hidden box of gold at the end of the story; and that a horrid Henry – however horrid he may be – has got to be better than a not-so-perfect Pierre.*

Myth Evaluation: *False.*

---

* The motif of the renegade schoolboy who 'turns out good' is a familiar trope of Anglophone children's literature, from Richmal Crompton's *William* books and Mark Twain's Tom Sawyer to its latest reincarnation in the form of Horrid Henry. French children's literature, on the other hand, tends to feature whimsical and/or saintly characters like Antoine de Saint-Exupéry's *Le Petit Prince*.

4
MERDE ALORS!
MYTHS ABOUT FRENCH PLUMBING

French toilets are repellent

France is the only country where the money falls apart and you can't tear the toilet paper.

BILLY WILDER, AMERICAN SCREENWRITER AND JOURNALIST (1906–2002)

A scholarly tome on the design of public conveniences might seem an odd place to encounter a sweeping statement about French attitudes to relieving oneself *en plein air*. In *Inclusive Urban Design: Public Toilets* (Architectural Press, 2003), however, author Clara Greed notes that 'Overall, continental European attitudes to toileting seem to be more open.' She goes on to observe that 'Anecdotally, everyone informs me that if you ask a French policeman "where is the toilet?", he will look puzzled and shrug his shoulders and gesture to show that the whole of France can be used as a toilet.' Perhaps this is just as well, as public toilets in France are often hard to come by. 'Public toilets, signposted *toilettes* or *WC*, are surprisingly few and far between, which means you can be left feeling really rather desperate,' lament the writers of the Lonely Planet guide to *Provence and the Côte d'Azur*. And when you do finally track down a loo in France, you're often left wondering whether an open field might not be a preferable place to do your business. Although comparative statistics on the relative salubrity of toilets around the world are (unsurprisingly) rather thin on the ground, the candidacy of French toilets for the lavatorial laurel is attested by a number of surveys. This includes the only known global tourist toilet survey, in which public toilets in France rank as the third worst in the world, pipped at the post by China at no. 1 and India at no. 2.[1]

What ungrateful visitors to France do not realize, however, is that they are lucky to have access to any public toilets at all. For throughout history, even up to the 1980s, public toilets in France were in chronically short supply. At the court of Versailles up to the mid-eighteenth century, for example, there were no public conveniences at all, with the result that courtiers urinated and defecated on the staircases and corridors, or into whatever receptacles (including vases and fireplaces) were at hand.* In cities all over France until well into the nineteenth century, pots containing urine and faeces were routinely emptied out of the window onto whatever (or whomever) happened to be below. In a famous thirteenth-century incident, a chamber pot was emptied onto the head of King Louis IX by a student working in the early hours of the morning (he was subsequently given a stipend for being so studious).† Wiping one's *derrière* was the privilege of the wealthy few; while common folk made do with blades of grass, fingers or yesterday's newspaper, the rich enjoyed the smooth sensation of lace, hemp (Cardinal Richelieu's preference), merino wool (the favoured toilet wipe of Louis XIV's mistress and later morganatic wife Madame de Maintenon), or a valet to perform the ablution on one's commodious commode. The post of personal valet in charge of the king's privy affairs, including the maintenance of his nether regions, was one of particular privilege, known as the *Chevalier porte-coton* or, loosely translated, 'Knight of the Toilet Roll'.‡ Toilet business was a deadly serious matter: an impressive line of French kings (including both Louis XIII and XIV) held court on the privy, and the unfortunate Henri III was assassinated in 1589 while enthroned on one.

His apartment [i.e. Louis XIV's at Versailles] and that of the Queen have the latest inconveniences, with sight of private cubicles and everything behind them – the most obscure, shut away, and reeking.
MEMOIRS OF THE DUC DE SAINT-SIMON (1675–1755)

For many centuries the French public authorities battled to control this deluge of public urination and defecation. As early as 1374, Charles V issued an edict requiring every house to have

* There were no functioning toilets in Versailles until 1768. By the time of the French Revolution in 1789 there were only nine, and those belonged to the King and other members of the royal family.

† The English word 'loo' is popularly believed to derive from the shout *prenez garde à l'eau!*, the warning traditionally given to passers-by when chamber pots were emptied onto the street below.

‡ The English monarch's equivalent valet at this period was the Groom of the Stool, an office instituted by Henry VIII.

a cesspit (it was ignored). When the magistrates of the town of Troyes in the seventeenth century tried to stop the locals from using a village street as an outdoor toilet, they were faced with a mass protest by villagers in front of the *hôtel de ville*, chanting: 'Our fathers crapped there, we crap there now, and our children shall forever do so.'[2] Paris itself was a giant latrine, a stinking bog of excrement. In fact, it was not until the mid-nineteenth century that the first public toilets appeared in the capital. They were the innovation of one of the city's most enlightened and reforming public officials – Claude Philibert de Rambuteau, Prefect of the Seine from 1833 to 1848. Unusually for a public official of the time, Rambuteau was more interested in improving public services for the Parisians than in erecting grand monuments. (Rambuteau was a somewhat earlier counterpart to the Victorian engineer Sir Joseph Bazalgette, creator of London's sewerage system.) Cunningly concealed in tall columns plastered with advertising posters, the new cast-iron urinals he introduced quickly became part of the Parisian street scene, immortalized by artists of the *belle époque*. Initially, they were dubbed 'Pillars of Rambuteau' by a mocking public and press. Mortified by the unkind appellation, Rambuteau rechristened his brainchild 'Pillars of Vespasian', in honour of the Roman Emperor Vespasian, who had imposed the world's first tax on urine collected from public toilets in the first century AD. Of course, *Vespasiennes,* as they came to be called, catered only for the male population of the city. The women of Paris had to wait until the twentieth century for their toilet facilities, since it was assumed that they should be able to control their natural urges.

By 1930 there were 1,200 *Vespasiennes* or *pissoirs* in Paris. They were,

MISTRESSES OF THE ROLLS

There are few visitors to Paris who have not quailed at the sight of one of the city's formidable female toilet attendants, known to the French as *Mesdames Pipi*. Though they are principally associated with the French capital, the first professional qualification for female toilet attendants was offered in the eastern city of Strasbourg; the certificate including training in detecting viruses, microbes, moss and signs of damp, appropriate cleaning techniques, and how to deal with the amorous approaches of clients.

Some of the great fallen women of history ended up serving in this capacity, notably the actress Marguerite Weimer, Mademoiselle George, mistress of Napoléon III and the Tsar of Russia. The average *Madame Pipi* has an indomitable personality, necessary for the job, and it is not unknown for them to tip a bucket of water over clients who mistake their toilet for an impromptu place of fornication.

however, the focus of a continuing debate between the hedonists (such as the American novelist Henry Miller, who considered it charmingly French to be able to urinate while looking out at beautiful women passing by), and the moralists (who disapproved of places that were considered the haunts of the dissolute and narcotically dependent). This culture clash was perhaps most vividly illustrated by the 1934 satirical novel *Clochemerle* by Gabriel Chevallier, which centred on the brouhaha created in a small village in Beaujolais by the local mayor's proposal to install a *pissoir* in the village centre. The plan outrages local worthies such as the priest, lawyer and landed gentry, pitting social classes against each other and revealing the deep fault lines in French provincial society at the time.* As for real-life Paris, various alternatives to the *Vespasiennes* were tried, including an attempt to imitate London by installing underground lavatories

* The name of the fictitious village of the story, *Clochemerle*, has now entered the French language to designate any community riven by factional local feuding.

in the Paris Métro, supervised by a brigade of female attendants – known as *Mesdames Pipi* – who watched over their clientèle and their collecting saucers with an eagle eye. The figure of *Madame Pipi* has now become something of an urban legend for visitors to Paris (see page 137).

From the 1960s onwards the *Vespasiennes* were phased out, so that by the end of the 1970s, only thirty remained. They had been replaced by toilets in parks and on the Métro policed by the *Mesdames Pipi*, but with barely a few hundred of these available to satisfy the bulging bladders of visitors to one of the world's greatest tourist destinations, Paris was increasingly and embarrassingly being caught short. Then, in the 1980s, the city hit on the perfect solution for cleaning up its act: *Sanisettes*, the Parisian version of the Superloo. Bearing no resemblance to the elegant spires of the *Vespasiennes*, these new Tardis-like extrusions on the capital's pavements enabled the French public and visitors to relieve themselves in the tranquillity of a compact, self-cleaning box (as long as they did so in the twenty minutes allotted before the door automatically opened and the self-cleaning mechanism kicked in). Introduced by Jacques Chirac when he was Mayor of Paris in 1980, the *Sanisettes* have provided a belated imperial triumph for the French. J.C. Decaux, the French company that invented them (and which is most famous for its ubiquitous advertising hoardings), is now one of the world's leading suppliers of Superloos, supplying over 1,000 European cities. Thus the French can console themselves with the fact that, although only 72 million people worldwide speak French as their native tongue, several hundred million people use French-made toilets. Today, there are some 400 *Sanisettes* in Paris,[3] to which access has been free since 2006; a dwindling number of toilets manned by *Mesdames Pipi*, mainly in public parks; and a single, solitary working *Vespasienne*. This last is, somewhat bizarrely, situated on the Boulevard Arago in the 14th *arrondissement*, opposite one of the major Paris prisons – perhaps to discourage the newly released from celebrating their freedom by peeing against the prison wall.

All in all, the public toilet situation in the French capital has improved dramatically. But what of toilets in Parisian restaurants and cafés? There, in the words of a French commentator (note: this is a Frenchman speaking), there is a 'descent into hell'.[4] It is, regrettably, all too common for French café toilets to present scenes of medieval squalor. Nor is the so-called 'squat' toilet, or hole in the floor, unheard of, although to the gratitude of many, these are being phased out in central Paris. The curious thing about squat toilets is that, whereas Anglo-Saxons often refer to them as 'French toilets', the French themselves call them 'Turkish toilets' (*toilettes à la turque* or *WC turcs*). But in Turkey they are known as 'Greek toilets', while the Greeks insist they are 'Bulgarian'. In fact, it seems that no one wants to lay claim to this primitive form of public convenience. Even the Japanese call it the 'Chinese toilet'. The squat toilet has been variously defined as an Arabic, French, Chinese, Japanese, Korean, Iranian, Indian, Turkish, or Natural-Position toilet.*

A certain *laissez-faire* attitude to the state of public loos was noted by French and US surveys conducted in the 1990s. When asked whether they were careful to leave public toilets clean after use, 51 per cent of Americans considered this very important, compared to 31 per cent of the French (44 per cent of French people considered leaving toilets clean an optional extra, and 21 per cent considered it of no importance at all).[5] In a 2008 survey for the Swedish personal care product group SCA, France came top of a total of nine countries for the percentage of people who expressed concerns about using public toilets (80 per cent of French people were worried about the hygiene risks they posed).[6]

Other nationalities visiting France have likewise remarked on the malodorous state of the conveniences. In the words of one Japanese analyst: 'The Parisians don't stoop to such details, and it has to be recognized that they are not exacting on such

* The Turks have recently taken revenge on the French for naming the squat toilet after them – and incidentally for planning to make denial of the genocide of Armenians by Turkey in 1915–16 punishable in law – by giving a brand of toilet paper the now-outmoded appellation of *Sarkozy*.

matters'.[7] For the people of Nippon – where toilet etiquette is a national obsession – the state of the average French café toilet is enough to induce a nervous breakdown.* It is said that the only toilets most female Japanese tourists in France feel capable of using are those in luxury hotels. Which brings us to one of the most powerful arguments used by men in support of decent public lavatories for women: they stop them from going into shops and other expensive establishments on the pretext of spending a penny, only to come out having spent a fortune. But what of those poor unfortunates among us, who would appreciate a clean toilet in Paris, but can't afford the price of a cocktail at the Ritz? There are unfortunately but a couple of options – cross your legs and hold on, or check out a Japanese restaurant.

Myth Evaluation: *Mainly true.*

---

* The Japanese mania for toilets and cleanliness has been traced by some to the purity rites of the ancient Shinto religion. Japanese toilets will typically have a dazzling array of functions, including a blow dryer, heated seat, massage options, water-jet adjustments, automatic lid opening, automatic flushing, and air conditioning of the room. Some Japanese loos even serenade the user. Unfortunately for foreigners, control panels tend to be in Japanese only.

The French don't wash

The more the ram stinks, the more the ewe loves him.
FRENCH PEASANT SAYING

The myth of the Great Gallic Unwashed is one that sticks to the French like dogshit to a Parisian pavement. This is despite the fact that France is home to one of the largest perfume industries in the world, including the big beast of the global cosmetics and personal care product market, L'Oréal. But then, one of the charges traditionally levelled at the French perfume and toiletries industry is that it developed to its current height of sophistication precisely in order to conceal the nasty niff of what lurked beneath the scent of a French woman.

Certainly, at least until the end of the nineteenth century, there wasn't much difference in washing habits throughout Western Europe. Everybody was pretty stinky by current standards, the rich possibly slightly less so than the poor. As we have already seen, the Palace of Versailles in the reign of Louis XIV famously had no toilets, and courtiers relieved themselves wherever they happened to be. The Scottish writer Tobias Smollett, travelling in France and Italy in 1766, remarked of the palace that, 'In spite of all the ornaments that have been lavished on Versailles, it is a dismal habitation. The apartments are dark, ill-furnished, dirty, and unprincely.'[8] This was the heyday of so-called 'dry' ablutions, a period when bathing was avoided at all costs, as water was believed to be the carrier of germs and 'bad humours'. Thus courtiers seldom washed, and elaborate perfumes were devised to cover up the stink of sweat and other bodily emissions. Not that all French people despised bodily odours. Some positively revelled in them. 'Madam, I will be with you in eight days. Do not wash…' were the celebrated words allegedly uttered by King Henri IV to his mistress, and two centuries later Napoleon wrote to his mistress Joséphine in similar terms.[9] In a somewhat different context, the Duc de Villeroi is said to have congratulated his men on the 'strength of their goatish essences' before the Battle of Ramillies in 1706; and General de Gaulle is credited by numerous sources as having the most eye-watering halitosis. The equation of a certain pungent body odour with masculinity, and the view that overenthusiastic washing and self-daubing with perfumed concoctions was the sign of a pampered and emasculated dandy, persisted well into the twentieth century across many cultures. As late as 1975, for example, the British magazine *New Scientist*, while observing approvingly that Britain at that point led Europe in soap consumption, nevertheless warned:

'But our pride in standing top of the lather league should be tempered by heed to the warning of Mark Twain that soap and education are not as sudden as a massacre, but they are more deadly in the long run. As borne out by the decline of the Roman Empire when its people became so obsessed by lying around in hot baths that they could no longer face sleeping out on cold battlefields and thus succumbed to the unwashed barbarians.'[10]

Though Britain might have arrived at the head of the 'lather league' in 1975, it began the race to get there in the late nineteenth century. Regular washing with soap was a phenomenon that started in Britain in the 1880s, with the spread of piped domestic water supplies. British soap consumption per person per year stood at 3.1 lbs in 1791; in 1881, by which time soap use had reached a mass market, it stood at 14 lbs per capita. In that same year, French per capita soap consumption was only 6 lbs.[11] As early as the 1830s, English visitors to Paris such as the novelist Frances Trollope had noticed that the French public authorities seemed to prioritize city monuments over plumbing. Unimpressed with the splendours of the newly erected Church of the Madeleine, Trollope noted, 'I think it would have been more useful, for the town of Paris, to have saved the sums it cost to build for the construction and laying of pipes to distribute water to private houses.'[12] The Gallic aversion to washing was exacerbated by a profound Catholic mistrust of nakedness, and the perceived sinful possibilities of intimate contact with bodily parts that ablutions necessarily entailed. Many girls in convents were required to bathe in shirts or a shift, and a manual of

THE TRIALS AND TRIBULATIONS OF THE TUB

In 1819, an ingenious man by the name of Monsieur Villette came up with the clever idea of a home bathing service for Parisians, known as the *bain à domicile*. This consisted of a bath on wheels that was delivered to the door of apartments, complete with towels, hot water and other bathing requisites. The *bain à domicile* was the subject of numerous satires, songs and pranks, but somehow it never really took off. Paris continued to be highly suspicious of the bath tub, so the home bath remained a rare phenomenon, as attested by an incident when the painter Édouard Manet sank his coat in a tub of water in the hall of a friend, mistaking it for a smoothly reflective marble table top.

hygiene, published in 1844, stated that 'certain [unnamed] parts of the body' needed to be washed only once a day. Observing that some women washed these parts more than once, the manual admonished: 'We do not advise this. We wish to respect the mystery of cleanliness. We will content ourselves with observing that everything which goes beyond the boundaries of a healthy and necessary hygiene leads imperceptibly to unfortunate results.'[13]

In mitigation, it should be borne in mind that France remained a largely rural country for far longer than Britain, and mains water came to homes in France much later than was the case in the United Kingdom. In 1930, for example, 92 per cent of the homes in Bradford were equipped with piped water, had a mains water supply, and at least a WC, while 43 per cent also had a bathtub; as a result of which, in the words of one observer, 'the bathing habit has become more general'.[14] In France, on the other hand, only 10 per cent of homes in the 1950s had a bath or shower, and only 58 per cent running water. In that same decade, half of French people took a bath only once every two years, and three in ten washed their hair just once a year.[15] In 1951, the *Larousse médical* advised its readers 'to take care of appearances', and that 'a bath or shower can be taken weekly'. As late as the 1960s, when the English wife of the Vicomte de Baritault inspected his château, Roquetaillade, she found it contained sixty chamber pots, no toilets, and one bathroom.[16]

The late arrival of mains water in *la France profonde* is therefore almost certainly the source of the myth of the Great Gallic Unwashed. The sensitive nostrils of American GIs, returning from the battlefields of the Second World War (at a time when most French villagers still had to take a dip in the village fountain), were outraged. Two of the 112 *Gripes about the French* (a pamphlet produced immediately after the war by the US military, which was aimed at quelling rising anti-French sentiment among their forces) were that the French didn't bathe, and that they were not as clean as the Germans. The pamphlet explained that the French couldn't bathe during the war, because the Germans had nicked all the soap. And even four months after hostilities ceased, the soap ration for the French was 'two cakes of poor ersatz soap per month' – in other words, a mere 20 grams. Even if the Germans were cleaner, the pamphlet opined reproachfully, '*an untidy friend is better than an immaculate enemy*'.[17] The leaflet also reminded American troops that the French could not afford decent plumbing systems, that their standard of living was lower than that in the United States, and that even in the US, 9,400,000 homes still had no electricity, 80 per cent of farmhouses did not

have bathrooms and running water, and 3,607,724 homes did not have their own flushing toilets.[18]

Despite the efforts of the US military to defend French standards of hygiene, however, the mud simply seemed to stick. It is no accident that in 1945 – just as the GIs were returning home – a new Looney Tunes cartoon character appeared on American television screens: Pepé Le Pew. A skunk with a heavy French accent given to strolling around Paris in the springtime filled with thoughts of 'lurve', Pepé's numerous attempts to find a mate are stymied by his rank odour and obdurate refusal to take 'no' for an answer. And – like the Gallic male stereotype – he also spends a lot of time spraying on perfume to try and put his victims off the scent. (His surname, Le Pew, was probably an allusion to the words *pooh* or *phew*, a traditional exclamation in response to a disagreeable smell. Hard as it may be to believe, linguists have spent entire careers debating its etymological origins. Some believe it derives from the Latin *puteo*, meaning to stink; while others maintain it comes from the Indo-European word *pu*, meaning to rot or decay – as in 'putrid'. The most appealing theory – although, sadly, probably apocryphal – ascribes a Chinese origin to the exclamation, namely the ancient Confucian saying, 'He who fart in church sit in own pew'.) Most French people are blissfully unaware of the true nationality of Pepé Le Pew, since in the French version of the cartoon, he was dubbed with an Italian accent. Banished to obscurity for many years, rumour has it that Pepé is soon to be resurrected by Disney, with actor Mike Myers (*Austin Powers* /*Shrek*) voicing the character – though whether with a French or Italian (or indeed Scottish) accent, is as yet unclear.

In Paris, the devout do not wash their bottoms.
EDMOND AND JULES DE GONCOURT, *JOURNAL*, 1895

In spreading the stink about the French, the British – and their tabloid newspapers in particular – have been historically at least as much to blame as the Americans. During the 'lamb wars' of the 1980s, when French farmers responded to the threat of British meat undercutting the price of their home-reared product

by burning lorryloads of imported lamb, the editor of the *Sun* newspaper, Kelvin MacKenzie – who had read a report that the French used less soap than any other country in Europe – hit back with such headlines as 'The French are the filthiest people in Europe', and 'Many French people smell like kangaroos which have been kept in cages'. A Page Three girl was dispatched to the French embassy to deliver toiletries and clean underwear as British aid to the 'needy nation'.[19] In fact, as various surveys of the time confirmed, the French *did* use less soap than the Anglo-Saxons – but that was because they were already, along with other Europeans, leading the market in the consumption of liquid soaps and shower gels.[20]

But do the French of today really wash less than everybody else? In September 2011, the pollster BVA carried out a survey on behalf of the hygiene product company Tork, which found that 20 per cent of French people questioned skipped a shower every other day, 3.5 per cent had a shower only once a week, and 12.5 per cent omitted to wash their hands after going to the toilet.[21] On the other hand, a survey by US consulting firm United Minds for the Swedish personal hygiene product company Tena/SCA in 2010 found that 94 per cent of French women felt uncomfortable if they had left the house without showering, as opposed to only 74 per cent of British women. This poll also found that the French dedicated the most time of any nation questioned to the pursuit of cleanliness, with French men spending 35 minutes a day on personal hygiene, and French women 46 minutes.[22] A further, detailed comparative report on hygiene issues in nine countries by SCA in 2008 found that 73 per cent of French people showered at least once a day, compared to 71 per cent of Americans and just 61 per cent of British.[23] (Australians and Mexicans showered the most, and the Chinese the least.)

Admittedly, for older generations of French people, hygiene is a fraught issue, evoking images of cold showers during compulsory military service, or being whacked with a ruler at school for having dirty ears. Hygiene was incorporated in the French school curriculum by the great educational reformer Jules Ferry in 1882, and schoolchildren grew accustomed to dictations such as 'Conjugate: I know my duty. I wash my hands. I wipe and polish the brasswork.'[24] In the early twentieth century, the French government took on the task of spreading the word on cleanliness through its ranks of martial primary teachers, who were known as the *hussards noirs* ('black hussars') from their sombre militaristic uniform. Every class started with a 'cleanliness inspection' of the head, neck, ears and hands, and those found lacking were given a good hiding. In the 1950s, the role of the *hussards noirs* was taken over by the French company L'Oréal, with its pioneering shampoo DOP. DOP executives ran *journées des enfants propres*, or 'clean children days', when free soap and shampoo were handed out to schoolchildren, while the teacher expounded the rules of cleanliness at the blackboard. At the same time Eugène Schueller, the canny founder of L'Oréal, organized vast publicity campaigns to market DOP, including mass rallies of 30,000 people in Calais and 50,000 people in Brussels, all chanting the mesmerizing slogan, *DOP, DOP, DOP, c'est un shampooing qui rend les cheveux souples et vigoureux* ('DOP, DOP, DOP, the shampoo that softens your hair and beats the flop').

The French cleanliness cause, it must be said, has not been helped by certain of their intellectuals, who have taken a perverse delight in celebrating the bodily pungency of the French as a Gallic rebellion against Anglo-American germophobia and 'hygiene fascism'. As the social historian Alain Corbin has written, France is a 'somatic culture' that revels in the delights of everything sensory, from the enticing aromas of the kitchen to the pungent whiff of bodily effluvia.[25] This is in stark contrast to the puritanical Americans and British, for whom any hint of corporeal odour must instantly be obliterated and 'sanitized' by a deluge of soap and deodorant, as though the faintest whiff of animality were in danger of unleashing a destructive and rampaging animal instinct. 'The English think soap is civilization,' the German historian Heinrich von Treitschke once observed. The French reply to that assertion would likely be, 'But of what uncivilized force are they so afraid?'

Myth Evaluation: *False. Contemporary surveys show that the French now wash at least as much as most of the other countries of the developed world, although this was not the case in the past. Yet the French – unlike the British and Americans – are not obsessed with expunging all traces of bodily odour.*

Every French bathroom has a bidet

Will custom exempt from the imputation of gross indecency a French lady, who shifts her frousy smock in presence of a male visitant, and talks to him of her lavement, her medicine, and her bidet!
TOBIAS SMOLLETT, SCOTTISH NOVELIST (1721–71),
TRAVELS THROUGH FRANCE AND ITALY, 1766

We have already had cause to note that, while squat toilets still exist in France, they are definitely on the wane. There is, however, another Unidentified Foreign Object in the French bathroom that has acquired a mythic status for foreigners: the strangely squat, tub-like contraption sandwiched between the basin and the toilet, otherwise known as the *bidet* (pronounced 'bee-day'). To most British people, a bidet is as much a feature of the quintessential French privy as a pile of Sunday newspapers in the British loo. But do all French bathrooms really have one? And, most importantly, what on earth are they are for?

Those who do know what a bidet is for are in an élite minority of British people. They are also as likely as not to be middle-aged, as the heyday of the bidet in British bathrooms was the 1970s and 80s. In the age of water beds, jacuzzis and other such items of suburban luxury, Armitage Shanks sold hundreds of bidets for installation in the bathroom suites of newly cosmopolitan Britons, fresh from the first wave of foreign holidays in Europe, and eager to relax in luxurious bathrooms with continental fixtures. There was just one problem. Nobody knew – or at least, nobody dared say – for what purpose these arcane objects were intended (even Armitage Shanks gave no explanation in their catalogues). Many and creative were the uses to which the bidet was put in the British bathroom: watering pot plants, washing the dog, cooling beer. But few knew the dark and salacious reality of its true purpose.

Why, one might ask, such coyness over washing one's nether regions after going to the toilet? Nobody, after all, is reticent about the purposes of a toilet roll. The reason is because that's not what a bidet is *really* for (at least, not in France). No: a bidet in France has traditionally been used for female *hygiène intime* – in other words, intimate feminine ablutions. Bidets were probably invented in Italy,[26] and became popular in France in the eighteenth century: the earliest reference to one dates from 1739, on the business card of Rémy Pèverie, a master cabinet-maker of Paris.[27] In an age when showers were non-existent and having a bath involved droves of minions heating buckets of water on a stove and hauling them to a tub, the bidet (originally a free-standing item of furniture) developed as a convenient way for mistresses at Versailles to have a quick and convenient ablution after an assignation, without having to go to the inconvenience of a full bathe. No royal mistress would dream of going to bed without one: Louis XV's mistresses Madame de Pompadour and Madame du Barry, whom we encountered in the chapter dealing with adulterous affairs, both had splendid personalized bidets coordinating with the king's bathroom suite. One of Madame de Pompadour's many bidets, for example, was made of walnut, equipped with crystal flasks; its lid and back were covered in red leather with gold nails.[28] The word *bidet* itself comes from a French word, first used in the sixteenth century, meaning 'pony' (the reference is to the act of riding the contraption, an innately bawdy innuendo of which full use was made by less-than-highbrow French writers).[29]

The English adore horses, but know nothing of the bidet.
ALPHONSE ALLAIS, FRENCH WRITER AND HUMORIST (1854–1905)

After the French Revolution of 1789 and the fall of the *ancien régime*, the principal locus of bidet use shifted from the royal boudoir to the Parisian brothel. At *Le Chabanais*, for example – one of the most famous bordellos, established in 1878 by a certain Madame Kelly and the haunt of the playboy Bertie, Prince of Wales (the future Edward VII) – there was a magnificent bath and coordinated bidet in the shape of an enormous swan made of red copper, water streaming from its beak.* *Le One-Two-Two* down the road,† famous for its extravagant staging (hay barns with girls disguised as milkmaids; African huts; igloos; train carriages; the obligatory 'torture chamber', with handcuffs, whips, hunting crops and flails), had bidets on every 'set', cunningly concealed in the furnishings. The notorious Parisian restaurant *Lapérouse*, a place where the bourgeois rubbed shoulders with the *demi-monde*, was famous for its bidets concealed under its banquettes. The bidet was thus indissolubly linked to the *toilette intime* of the high-class courtesan. But the jasper and crystal bidets of the *grandes horizontales* had poor relations in their grimy tin counterparts to be found in the seedier red-light districts. The famous Hungarian photographer of the Parisian underclass, George Brassaï, recalled his Paris hotel in the 1930s as a place where 'each room had heavy, flowered curtains, a wardrobe with mirror, a large all-purpose bed… and that most important piece of furniture, a bidet. Down in the hall below, the patroness distributed towels and kept track of the tricks.'[30]

From high-end whores in kept apartments to the hookers who walked the boulevards around Place de Clichy, the bidet was the indispensable tool of the trade for the world's oldest profession – a receptacle for ablutions, a cleansing contraceptive, purger of venereal disease, and in some cases an aid to home abortion. Even the French dared hardly speak its name. French home inventories and bathroom catalogues of the nineteenth century discreetly skirt around the word *bidet*, tactfully referring to the 'unmentionable little piece of furniture', the 'device for watering the thighs', the 'indispensable little unit', or even that 'discreet item of furniture, with the equestrian name, impolite to mention'.[31] The term *eau de bidet*, or 'bidet water', came to refer to worthless people or things – any sort of scum.[32] At the

* The Japanese Room in this bordello was given an official prize at the 1900 World's Fair in Paris, as an example of French refinement and taste.

† *Le One-Two-Two* derived its name as an English translation of its address, 122 rue de Provence, in the 8th *arrondissement* of Paris. It was one of the most famous and luxurious of Parisian brothels in the early twentieth century.

SOME FRENCH SLANG EXPRESSIONS USING THE WORD 'BIDET'

chevalier de bidet (knight of the bidet) = pimp
l'eau de bidet (bidet water) = trash
rinçure de bidet (used bidet water) = abortion

same time, the French soft-porn industry had a field day with salacious prints and engravings of newly fallen young women from the provinces perched on bidets, assisted in their morning ablutions by the *Madame* of the house, playing on multiple forbidden connotations.*

In its early days the bidet was used by men as well as women, particularly cavalry soldiers, to soothe the aches and pains of a hard day on horseback (Napoleon – probably its last great male aficionado – bequeathed his splendid silver-gilt bidet to the King of Rome). By the mid-nineteenth century, however, the bidet in France had become the exclusive preserve of women, synonymous with the mysteries of female personal hygiene. But despite its dubious associations, the bidet somehow made the leap into the twentieth century as an indispensible component of the French *salle de bain*. The bathroom trio of toilet/basin/bidet endured (even as other relics of partial bathing, like the sitz bath and foot bath, were consigned to the dustbin of history). Somehow, the bidet survived the purge of other bathroom paraphernalia, even if its bland and sanitized new form was a far cry from the showy clothes in which it started life. Why this was the case has been the subject of much debate and speculation amongst French social historians. Could the key to the bidet's survival have been the alleged contraceptive powers of its cleansing water jet? The bidet had remained one of the few discreetly legitimate means of attempting to stay nature's course after a French law of 1920 decreed contraception a crime. Whatever the reason for its tenacity, the bidet was by the 1950s a

* As in, for example, the painting by Louis Leopold Boilly, *The Morning Wash: Woman on a Bidet*, c.1790.

standard fixture of most French bathrooms, including those in council housing.

Today, however, the bidet is no longer the ubiquitous presence in the French bathroom that it once was. The advent of the Pill, the pressures of space in modern French apartments, the ease with which water is now available on tap or in the shower, but most of all, its associations with the *demi-monde*, have all played their part in its gradual disappearance. In 1951, 62 per cent of French bathrooms had a bidet; by 1986, this had diminished to 47 per cent; and by 1993, it was only 42 per cent.[33] Successive changes to the criteria for hotel ratings also illustrate its demise: whereas all French three-star hotels and above were required to have a bidet in every bathroom in 1964, these days a bidet in a hotel room carries a few extra points, but is not obligatory on any rating level. (Just 25 per cent of French hotel bathrooms are now equipped with bidets.)

The irony of all this is that the start of the bidet's demise in France coincided almost exactly with its brief heyday in England. That the good-lifers of the 1980s, so eager to keep up with the Joneses, actually realized that they had in fact installed a piece of (outmoded) Parisian brothelware with their avocado bathroom suites is unlikely. Today, the proud title of Europe's most bidet-loving nation has passed from France to Italy, where, it would appear, there really is a bidet in every bathroom. But those who do possess a relic of a bidet in their 1980s bathroom suite need not despair. When filled with ice, they really do make fantastic wine coolers: the ultimate accessory for a truly relaxing, post-modern soak.

Myth Evaluation: *False. In fact, it is every Italian bathroom that has a bidet.*

5
BOF! JE M'EN FOUS!
MYTHS ABOUT FRENCH MANNERS

THE FRENCH ARE UNCOMMONLY RUDE

I like Frenchmen very much, because even when they insult you they do it so nicely.
JOSEPHINE BAKER, AMERICAN-FRENCH DANCER (1906–75)

If, in the celebrated dictum of William of Wykeham, manners maketh man, they maketh not the Frenchman. Or at least, so the popular belief goes. The French, and in particular Parisians, are famed for turning rudeness into an art form: from swearing taxi drivers and offhand shop assistants to the legendarily churlish Parisian waiter, they are world-renowned for their service without a smile. (The principle of 'The Customer is King' seems not to have reached Paris; or if it ever did, it was summarily dispatched the same way as the aristos of old.)

The French have traditionally topped virtually every rudeness poll going. For instance, for four years in a row an annual poll of some 4,000 world hoteliers conducted by the travel website Expedia has found that French tourists are the most reluctant at trying to speak English,* leave the lowest tips, yet are the first to complain about everything. According to a survey in 2012 conducted for the online ticket-seller Skyscanner, the French were voted the most impolite nation in the world towards visitors to their country (followed closely by the Russians). A TripAdvisor survey in 2010 found that tourists thought Paris had the least friendly locals, the rudest taxi drivers, and the most hostile and aggressive waiters. The proverbial rudeness of the French, in fact, is more than a national myth; it has become a part of global folklore. When a new cartoon character – Mr Rude – was added to the children's television series *Mr Men* in 2008, what other nationality could he possibly have

We decided that the French could never write user-friendly software because they're so rude.
DOUGLAS COUPLAND, CANADIAN WRITER (b.1961)

* Although the French tend to default to English at home to put foreigners down when they try to speak French.

been but French? (Mr Rude, who had a very British top hat in the original books, lost it in favour of a strong French accent in the TV series. He is also smelly, another archetype associated with the French.)*

The irony of the modern French reputation for rudeness is that it was certainly not ever thus. During the seventeenth and eighteenth centuries, French manners and etiquette were considered the peak of refinement (even if writers such as the seventeenth-century comic playwright Molière took great delight in lampooning the gauche attempts of the *bourgeois gentilhomme* to ape the refined habits and manners of the aristocracy). As one of the hundreds of nineteenth-century guides to French etiquette noted, 'Throughout all time, French courtesy has been cited as the model of grace, gallantry, and true *noblesse oblige*.'[1] Under the *ancien régime*, convoluted rituals were a means for the king to stop the nobles taking up arms against each other (or against him), by keeping them busy with the complicated codes of court etiquette. Of course, there was (as there always has been) a distinction between courtesy in the sense of an unselfish regard for others in daily life, and the more complex rules of etiquette or *savoir-vivre*, designed as unspoken codes to mark out the well-bred from the common rabble. French court etiquette was decidedly of the latter type.

After the Revolution of 1789, there was a general revolt against the rules of politeness that had been a means of dividing those who were *comme il faut* from those who were not. 'Rudeness is a form of resistance to oppression,' wrote the fanatical Jacobin Louis Antoine de Saint-Just: from now on, the new buzzword was *antipolitesse*. Attempts were made to ban the use of the polite form of address, *vous*, and replace it with the familiar *tu*, and the titles *Monsieur* and *Madame* were abolished in favour of the levelling *Citoyen*. While the common citizens were busy being rude to each other, however, the old rules of *savoir-vivre* were being codified by the new (and therefore deeply socially insecure) bourgeoisie into a system of rules that was positively

* A spokesman for the French ambassador in London at the time stated that the new Mr Rude was 'unlikely to improve Anglo-French relations'.

Byzantine in its complexity. At table, a 'man of good breeding' of the new ruling class was expected to know the difference between a snail- and an oyster-pick, the exact circumstances in which to use a three-tined rather than a four-tined fish fork, and to avoid the heinous *faux pas* of complimenting a hostess on a dish at dinner.

Bourgeois *savoir-vivre* as developed in nineteenth-century France extended from the mastery of manners to every aspect of genteel living – dress, food, arts of the table.* A woman *comme il faut* would never be seen outside without a hat, have more than one aperitif before dinner (such an act being a sure sign of an alcoholic or an Englishwoman), or wear precious stones if she were under thirty-five (this was of course reversed for those above that age, since no respectable woman in middle age could possibly be seen wearing a jewel that was not real, as that would be an admission of one's husband's failure in life). Her male counterpart, meanwhile, would not be seen without his *cravate* (the essential mark of the well-bred gentleman), or without his gloves, although of course not just any old gloves would do. As the writer, journalist and astute social commentator Alphonse Karr remarked, 'There now are only two classes of men in France… those who wear yellow gloves, and those who do not. When one says of a man that he wears yellow gloves, it is a concise way of saying that he is a man *comme il faut*.'[2] The intricate network of social mores was disseminated (and in many cases invented) by a formidable battery of books on etiquette, written by bourgeois housewives with often faux-aristocratic *noms de plume* like Baroness Staffe, Madame de Grandmaison, Countess Berthe and the Marquise of Pompeillan.

The French tendency to view politeness as an aspect of subservience to, or rebellion against, hierarchy and oppression, rather than a purely courteous consideration of others as in other cultures, was exacerbated in the twentieth century, particularly in relation to foreigners after the Second World War. In the immediate postwar period and under the strain of the Mar-

* The principles of *savoir-vivre* in so far as they impact on French bourgeois personal appearance and dress are discussed in detail on pages 75–80.

shall Plan, the hostility of the French to their former allies, now seen as cultural oppressors – in particular the Americans – was extremely strong, leading to a number of clashes with American visitors in Paris and a proliferation of 'rude French' stories.* The American writer Sylvia Plath recalls this simmering hostility in an incident that occurred on the Parisian Left Bank in the 1950s, when she attempted to buy a kilo of peaches from an 'oily' stall-holder in the rue de Buci market. Plath, who spoke French fluently, asked for a kilo of red peaches; the stallholder replied that everybody asked for red peaches, and proceeded to quickly fill her bag with green ones. She wrote:

'I looked in the bag whilst his back was turned to take the money; I found a solid rock-hard green peach; I put it back and took a red one. The man turned just as the hostile little old woman made a rattling noise of furious warning to him, like a snake about to strike. One is not allowed to choose, the man raged, grabbing the bag back and rudely dumping the hard green peaches on the counter. We fumed, sick at the outrage, meanness and utter illogic.'[3]

'Like it or not,' wrote the travel writer Temple Fielding, 'the American tourist of 1953 is despised by thousands of Frenchmen and Frenchwomen.'[4] The author John Steinbeck noted how sad it was that American visitors came to Paris all excited by their trip and keen to learn about the new culture, yet when they arrived, 'they find themselves scorned, and they suspect they are being cheated… They find themselves huddling together fearful of raised brows of headwaiters, the superior smiles of guides. Local people who have not in their lives been fifty kilometres from their village look down on tourists. They become lonesome and some of them grow angry.'[5]

The dual inheritance from the Revolution – levelling rudeness on the one hand and a highly codified set of manners to distinguish the genteel from the mob on the other – together with a residual hostility to Anglo-Saxon foreigners, has left an indelible mark on French social interactions with foreigners to

* For more on the Marshall Plan and anti-Americanism in France in the postwar period, see pages 206–7.

THE CHAMPIONS OF CHURLISHNESS

Rude as the French are generally considered to be, it is Parisians in particular who are widely regarded as the champions of churlishness. Even the French themselves take this view. In a 2010 poll by the French polling agency CSA (*Conseil, sondage, analyse*) for the French current affairs magazine *Marianne*, of 1,000 French people questioned, more than 70 per cent considered Parisians more snobbish than other French people; more than 65 per cent thought they were more aggressive and arrogant, 62 per cent more chauvinistic; 71 per cent found them unsmiling, 59 per cent unwelcoming; 58 per cent regarded them as navel-contemplating, and 61 per cent as lacking in wit. On the plus side for Paris, its inhabitants were generally seen as more chic, more switched on, and bigger party animals than their provincial counterparts.

In fact, Paris holds the dubious distinction of having a psychiatric condition named after it: Paris Syndrome, characterized by an acute delusional state, persecution complex, hallucinations and panic attacks. Paris Syndrome is a psychosis to which Japanese tourists in Paris are peculiarly susceptible, resulting in the hospitalization of several dozen a year. Theories as to why people from the Land of the Rising Sun are so adversely affected by the City of Light are legion, but the general consensus is that the root of the psychosis probably lies in the idealization of Paris by the Japanese media as a city of refined manners, glamour, romance and gorgeously slim women. This dreamy vision is rudely dispelled when the visitor from Tokyo or Kyoto encounters the reality of canine excreta on the streets, brusque waiters, dirty toilets, and the dawning realization that they themselves are slimmer and wear more Louis Vuitton than the average French woman. Japan's embassy in Paris has a 24-hour hotline for Japanese visitors in the throes of this reality crisis, and a whole department at the Parisian psychiatric Hospital of St Anne is devoted to caring for its victims. But the only known cure to date is to go back to Japan – and never return to Paris.

this day. On the one hand, there is the typically offhand manner of people in the French service industries (who are of course those with whom most tourists will come into contact), whose general attitude tends to be to equate civility to foreigners with servitude. On the other hand, there are the rarefied and aloof circles of the French bourgeoisie, who remain hidebound by the strict and obscure codes of French manners and etiquette. It is generally true that, even today, French social interactions are more formal and highly codified than in England or the USA. In France it is obligatory, for example, to say *Bonjour* to anybody in a shop, restaurant, bus or café before saying anything else. Not to do so is considered the height of discourtesy, and will guarantee a brusque response. And then there is the vexed question of when *Bonjour* becomes *Bonsoir* (generally, this nebulous transition occurs around 5 p.m. in the afternoon, but it can be later. It depends partly on the whim of the person greeting you. You will know you have got it wrong if you say *Bonjour* and receive an icy *Bonsoir* in reply, or vice versa). Not to mention the bewildering rituals of French greetings: the requisite order of introductions, form of handshake, and whether to give social kisses (and if so how many; see the next chapter for guidance), all of which are guaranteed to terrify the innocent visitor.

In fact, every type of social interaction in France has its established form. Even the wheedling of French beggars on the Paris Métro runs along set lines. It invariably begins with the address, 'Excuse me for disturbing you, Mesdames and Monsieurs', continues with a catalogue of the history of misfortunes the speaker has suffered, and concludes with a request for money or a restaurant ticket (again asking to be excused for disturbing everybody). The intricate web of formalities and set patterns of behaviour inevitably leave the foreigner in a state of confusion. Nor will a big smile help: smiling for the French (as with so much else) is usually a strictly private matter. Aware of the problems caused by the traditional French *froideur* in public spaces, the RATP* has done its best to jolly its compatriots up.

* The French transport authority that runs the Paris Métro.

'Two smiles exchanged with each other light up a journey,' reads one campaign poster. 'The person who exchanges a smile travels in happiness,' reads another.

In fact, it would appear that nowadays even the French are fed up with their own rudeness. An Ipsos poll in 2012 revealed bad manners and aggressive behaviour as the leading cause of stress for the French, greater even than unemployment or the debt crisis.[6] The government has reacted with a number of measures, including a return of 'morals classes', teaching basic manners, in French schools. The RATP has also for many years run 'politeness' campaigns on the Paris underground. In 2012, for example, it set up a project for the annual review of rudeness on the Métro, with a series of 'politeness forums' to instruct the citizens of the Republic in how to behave on the underground, and an associated poster campaign. But beware: smiles don't always have the intended effect on the Paris Métro. At 10 a.m. on a late August morning in 2012, travellers on Line 4 witnessed a fellow passenger behaving in a suspicious manner. The individual in question had given up his seat to an elderly person. Not only that, on entering the carriage, he had beamingly announced '*Bonjour, tout le monde*', before apologizing when he bumped into another passenger. Worse still, he proceeded to give his free newspaper to a fellow traveller. Tension mounted as he laughed when a girl trod on his toes: 'It's nothing, don't worry about it!' he said affably. The other passengers, alarmed by this bizarre display of bonhomie, phoned the security services. The man was arrested. Under examination, he admitted to having returned from his summer vacation in an ebullient and happy state. 'I just meant to be pleasant, not to arouse suspicion,' was his sad refrain. All of which goes to show that smiling on the Paris Métro can be a risky business. Better to scowl, hunch your shoulders and look vacantly ahead. You will be precisely *comme il faut*.

Myth Evaluation: *Partly true.*

French people always kiss when they greet you

The social kiss is an exchange of insincerity between two combatants on the field of social advancement. It places hygiene before affection and condescension before all else.
LONDON *SUNDAY CORRESPONDENT*

How do I kiss thee? Let me count the ways…

In his celebrated 1,040-page treatise on the art of snogging, *Opus Polyhistoricum de Osculis*, the seventeenth-century German philosopher Martin von Kempe identified no fewer than twenty kinds of kiss. They included the reconciliatory kiss, the kiss that marked social distinctions, the contagious kiss, the lusty or adulterous kiss, the hypocritical kiss, and the kiss bestowed on the Pope's foot.[7] But what about the art of the French social kiss? Alas, there the great polymath was silent. Which is a pity, as the mysteries of French social kissing – or *faire la bise*, as the French term it – remain in dire need of elucidation.

So, to kiss, or not to kiss? That is the question. And if the answer is the affirmative, how many kisses? Starting which side?

And what sort of kiss is expected – a light peck, an enthusiastic smack, a graze, caress, scrape, tickle, or flick of lips to cheek? Whose lips to whose cheek?

The good news for foreigners is that the answers to these questions are far from clear, even to native French people. Kissing as a form of greeting outside one's circle of close friends or immediate family was not widespread in France until the social revolution of May 1968. Just as *les événements* led to an increase in the use of the informal *tu* rather than the more formal *vous*, so they also resulted in an explosion in the exchanging of affectionate *bises* – and perhaps more intimate displays of friendship – between young people who had only just met for the first time. Since those halcyon days, it is fair to say that things have calmed down a bit. Contrary to popular foreign belief, it is never obligatory in France to kiss a person whom you haven't met before. Social kissing is still mainly reserved for relaxed occasions with family and friends of the same age, although it is gradually becoming more common between work colleagues who know each other well, as is the case in other European countries. Most disconcertingly for uptight heterosexual Anglo-Saxon males, it is perfectly acceptable – even commonplace – in France for straight men who are good friends or relatives to kiss each other. This causes acute consternation for some stiff-upper-lipped men of Northern Europe and America, who baulk at brushing beards with the same sex. As one Lieutenant Colonel D. M. C. Rose complained in a letter to the *Spectator* in 2003:

'Sir: I was horrified to see our Prime Minister kissing the President of Russia. Can you imagine Neville Chamberlain kissing Hitler, or Churchill kissing Stalin? Anglo-Saxon men have never gone in for this kissing performance. Sometimes they shake hands, but never the double two-handed shake or clasping of the arm. Only the Gallic race and the Arabs go in for hugging and kissing. No British general would even think of giving or accepting a kiss from another man, surely?'[8]

Aside from the question of whether to kiss at all, how many kisses to give – and which side to start with – is at least as prickly an issue. Every region of France has a different customary number of kisses and a different starting side, with the result that kissing collisions are an everyday occurrence, as even the French don't know half the time when to turn the other cheek. In most regions of France, especially the cities, one exchanges two kisses, starting on the right cheek; but in parts of eastern France one exchanges two kisses, starting on the left. In Finistère, at the furthest tip of Brittany, it is customary to give just one kiss; but in whole swathes of the South including the *départements* of Cantal, Aveyron and the Drôme, one exchanges three. And across the *départements* of northern France, the affectionate locals share as many as four *bisous* on average.

To guide the uninitiated through the labyrinthine landscape of French kissing, in 2007 a Frenchman named Gilles Debunne produced a wonderfully helpful kissing map of France, *combiendebises.free.fr*, an interactive site where over 69,000 French people have registered their kissing preferences by region. But even here, there is confusion within regions. In Pas-de-Calais, for example, roughly 50 per cent of respondents say they kiss twice as a greeting, while the other 50 per cent declare that they kiss four times. In the Charente, in southwestern France, the situation is even more obscure, with voters divided between two, three, and four or more kisses. In general, Parisians will limit themselves to two, starting on the right cheek; just one kiss gives a dangerous suggestion of secret intimacy, and more than two runs the risk of one being regarded as a provincial bumpkin (or, as they would disparagingly say, *un plouc*). Generally, the urban bourgeoisie limit themselves to fewer kisses than effusive provincials.*[9]

So much for the number of kisses; but what type of kiss are we talking about? The ancient Romans, after all, distinguished between the friendly peck on the cheek (*osculum*), the passionate meeting of mouths (*basia*), and the kiss involving the use of tongues (*suavia*). The French *bise* or 'social kiss' is none of these. In fact, it is barely a kiss at all. If done correctly, it involves merely

* If these French kissing conventions seem complicated, they are as nothing compared with Belgium, where one kiss is the norm for someone the same age as oneself, but three a mark of respect for someone at least ten years older. A social minefield, especially when it comes to women *d'un certain âge*.

THE SOCIAL KISS THAT IS NOW A SOCIAL DINOSAUR

Those who approach the rituals of the French social kiss with trepidation can be thankful that another form of French social kiss, the *baisemain*, is now all but obsolete.

The *baisemain* requires a man to bow slightly and, raising a woman's hand to his lips, lightly brush it with his chin. The practice was invented in the early twentieth century as an affectation of the *haute bourgeoisie*. Only a married woman is entitled to the *baisemain*, and that only in certain circumstances. It is, for example, generally limited to private receptions, and not usually permitted on the street – although some French etiquette guides have conceded that it could be practised in a street without too many passers-by, and where discretion can be assured.

The *baisemain* is anachronistically featured in a number of films that are set in a period prior to its invention – a prime example being Stephen Frears' film of *Les Liaisons dangereuses*.

the lightest brushing of cheek to cheek; but at the moment of brushing, one is expected to make a loud and explosive sound of the lips, as if to imitate a good 'mwah'. It is here that some Anglo-Saxons can get it wrong, with a slobby lip-to-cheek (or worse, lip-to-lip) contact that has the average Gaul cringing with disgust. To the extent that several Frenchmen abroad have remarked that they would prefer to shake hands, or even partake of a good, old-fashioned American-style hug, than wipe off saliva juices from a bearish foreigner.[10]

Which brings us to the time-honoured alternative to the *bise*, the handshake. Surely a safe retreat from the hazardous minefield of the social kiss? Not quite. It should not be forgotten that the French expression for 'shake a person's hand' is *serrer la main*, in other words, a *hand squeeze* and not a *handshake*. In France, it is not customary to grasp the hand and energetically pump it up and down, as Anglo-Saxon practice dictates. France – like Japan and China – is a country of limp handshakes. This is especially true if you are a woman, as it is considered the height of rudeness energetically to grasp or pump a woman's hand. So if your zealous piston meets a limp-wristed response, don't take it personally. Nor should you make the *faux pas* of proffering a hand to someone older or more senior than yourself. French bourgeois etiquette – always concerned with establishing boundaries and limits – dictates that the older or more senior person, or a woman, proffers their hand first.

Social minefield as it may be, those who would love to kiss goodbye to the French *bise* will be disappointed. Despite a brief period of panic during the bird flu epidemic of 2009, when the official advice was to avoid social kissing (some schools installed 'kissing boxes' in classrooms for pupils to post 'kiss-notes' to their friends rather than swapping possibly contagious pecks on the cheek), the *bise* has fought back with a vengeance. Social snogging is now pretty much *de rigueur* in France between friends – as it increasingly is among the chattering classes of Britain and the United States.

Die-hard enemies of the social kiss can, however, take comfort in the fact that in some parts of the world, including many parts of Asia and Africa, kissing is looked upon with repugnance. In China, for example, kissing was for many years considered a revolting allusion to cannibalism, and in southern Africa the native tribes people recoiled at the European habit of 'sucking each other's saliva and dirt'.[11] So if you really can't cope with friends and colleagues slobbering over you, there are places to escape to. But if you come to France, you have no real option other than to dive in and have a go at the kissing game; but if you botch it, be prepared to take it on the chin.

MYTH • EVALUATION •

Myth Evaluation: *True. The French kiss when they greet you most of the time, certainly between family and friends, but there is huge variation in the number of kisses and with which cheek to start. The safest bet is to give two kisses and start with the right-hand side.*

The French are a nation of inveterate smokers

There's nothing like tobacco; it is the passion of all decent men – a man who lives without tobacco does not deserve to live.
MOLIÈRE (JEAN-BAPTISTE POQUELIN), FRENCH COMIC DRAMATIST (1622–73)

The cigarette is as integral to our image of the archetypal Frenchman as the baguette, beret or bicycle. Be it a Jean-Paul Belmondo lookalike with a trilby hat, moodily puffing on a *Gauloise*, or a cluster of leather-jacketed intellectuals hotly debating philosophy in a Left Bank café, tobacco fumes are as essential a component of the French landscape as *crottes de chien* on the pavements. In terms of French literature and culture, smoking has traditionally held a quasi-spiritual significance. The poet Charles Baudelaire, for example, eulogized the pleasures of puffing in his poem '*La Pipe*', in which the pipe of a habitual smoker ('*un grand fumeur*') is described as gladdening his heart and reviving his spirits ('*...charme son coeur et guérit / De ses fatigues son esprit*'). Baudelaire had yet more praise for the subliminal qualities of the pipe in his *Paradis artificiels*, where he wrote:

'You are sitting and smoking; you believe that you are sitting in your pipe, and that *your pipe* is smoking *you*; you are exhaling *yourself* in bluish clouds. You feel just fine in this position, and only one thing gives you worry or concern: how will you ever be able to get out of your pipe?'

Admittedly, the substance being here consumed is less likely to be tobacco than a somewhat stronger narcotic. Even so, later French artists and writers have not been hesitant to proclaim the virtues of the humble weed. The goatish *chansonnier* Serge Gainsbourg, for example, once crooned that God is a smoker of Havana cigars. The sulphurous Sylvie Vartan, one-time wife of the veteran rocker Johnny Hallyday, famously sang in husky tones that *l'amour est comme une cigarette*, wishing she could turn into a sultry *Gitane* and go up in smoke between her lover's lips. The most famous poem by France's unofficial poet laureate, Jacques Prévert, concerns a fateful coffee and cigarette consumed on the morning after a night before, stubbing out a mysterious relationship. The poem, '*Déjeuner du matin*', is the most-recited verse in French schools, although the exact nature of the relationship concerned has been hotly disputed by French literary critics ever since it was first published in 1946. In fact, the only sure thing about the poem is that it introduces French

A RIGHT ROYAL HERB

The smoking of tobacco was first practised by American Indians more than 3,000 years ago and brought from the New World to Europe by Christopher Columbus in 1492. The use of tobacco in France, however, was popularized by a Frenchman, Jean Nicot (1530–1600). Believing that the 'sot-weed' had curative effects, Nicot sent some tobacco powder to Catherine de' Medici in 1560, after a visit to Portugal, to treat the terrible migraines of her son, the frail and sickly child-king François II. The treatment initially appeared to have been successful; tobacco was hailed as the 'queen's herb', and subsequently licensed for sale by apothecaries. The species of tobacco plant used to treat the French royal family was later christened *Nicotiana tabacum* in honour of Nicot, from whom we also derive the term 'nicotine'.

schoolchildren to desolation, existential angst, coffee and cigarettes at an early age.

Behind the *tabacomanie* of Anglo-Saxon myth, are the French really a nation of voracious smokers? The answer is yes, they are. With daily cigarette smokers making up 26 per cent of the population as a whole, the French do not smoke as much as the world's most ardent puffers, the Greeks (39 per cent), but they do smoke more than the British (22 per cent) or the tobaccophobic Americans (16 per cent).[12] 24 per cent of 15–19-year-old French teenagers smoke,[13] and the average age of first exposure to cigarettes for French smokers is a tender 11 years old. Moreover, for the first time in many years, smoking in France has recently been on the increase, particularly among women. Today, 38 per cent of French women aged between 20 and 25 smoke,[14] and a slightly worrying 24 per cent of pregnant women.[15] The cost of tobacco-related illnesses to the French state in 2005 was €47 billion or 3 per cent of GDP, the equivalent of an annual tax of €772 per citizen.[16]

The French government (which cheerfully flogged cigarettes to its populace for decades under the auspices of the state-owned cigarette monopoly SEITA until it was privatized in 1995)[17] has done everything in its power to extinguish the fire. Massive duties and price hikes have been slapped on cigarettes, smoking in public spaces was outlawed in 2007, and EU-imposed bans on cigarette advertising were observed. There are even proposals to follow the Australian example, requiring manufacturers to sell cigarettes in unbranded packets displaying shocking pictures of bodily parts afflicted with every type of smoking-related disease. The French reaction to all of this, perhaps predictably, is a great Gallic rolling of eyes, shrugging of shoulders, and a bored '*et alors...?*' In fact, the country's response to the new regulations – far from quitting – has simply been to go and puff in other, as yet unregulated, places: cars, for example (a great favourite), or the tent-like enclosures tacked onto café terraces which nowadays have become Dantesque infernos filled with swirling tobacco fog.

The French anti-smoking lobby lays the blame for the continuing high levels of French tobacco addiction partly on Gallic cinema, which has traditionally portrayed smoking as the epitome of cool – the preserve of virile men, sexy women, and rebellious teenagers.

I don't know. Everything. Living. Smoking.
JEAN-PAUL SARTRE, FRENCH PHILOSOPHER (1905–80), IN RESPONSE TO THE QUESTION 'WHAT IS THE MOST IMPORTANT THING IN YOUR LIFE?'

Given that having a Bond Street Classic at an elegant angle in your fingers seems to be as much a prerequisite for a French actress's credibility as a Gitane for the French male, most French actresses won't admit to not smoking. Catherine Deneuve, Eva Green, Sophie Marceau, Charlotte Rampling, Karin Viard, Delphine Chanéac, Béatrice Dalle, Anouk Aimée, Charlotte Gainsbourg, Françoise Arnoul, Audrey Tatou, Monica Bellucci, Nathalie Baye, Clémentine Poidatz, Jacqueline Bisset… all have been shot in moody poses with a cigarette held to their pouting lips. As early as the 1930s, smoking was glorified on French celluloid as a symbol of machismo for men and sexiness for women, with filmed competitions for the man who could smoke his cigar quickest, and, for women, the contest for the Most Graceful Smoker in France.

In 2012, the French League against Cancer commissioned a study by the market-research group Ipsos of the top 180 French films released in the five years from 2005 to 2010.[18] It found that 80 per cent of them contained at least one smoking scene, and 30 per cent more than ten. On average, smoking took up 2.4 minutes of movie time per film – the equivalent of five advertisements. One of the top films in the list was the 2009 film *Coco before Chanel*, which featured Audrey Tautou lounging in a white satin pyjama suit with a cigarette on one of its publicity posters. (The 2010 film *Gainsbourg: A Heroic Life*, which outstripped every other film in the survey by clocking up no fewer than 43 minutes of smoking time, was excluded from the analysis as 'atypical'.) The study also found that characters who smoked in French films had gradually become more and more 'respectable' over the years, and that the virtual world of the cinema portrayed situations which flagrantly flouted French law in real life, with characters on screen lighting up in cafés, schools and dozens of other places where smoking is banned.

Official disapproval of smoking has resulted in a certain amount of retrospective censorship, a revisionist approach that

If I had to choose between a last woman and a last cigarette, I would choose the cigarette: you can get rid of it more easily!
SERGE GAINSBOURG, FRENCH SINGER (1928–91)

outrages those who prefer to see their nicotine-stained past through smoke without mirrors. In 2005, for example, Jean-Paul Sartre was deprived of his second-best companion after Simone de Beauvoir by the French National Library, which airbrushed the cigarette he was pictured holding from the publicity posters of an exhibition dedicated to him. The French Post Office recently retouched a postage stamp featuring the celebrated French novelist and diplomat André Malraux, by removing his beloved *clope*. And the latest victim of the censor's stroke was none other than former president Jacques Chirac, whose memoirs were withheld from publication until the front cover – which had featured him in pensive pose with cigarette in hand – was changed. (Nobody to date, however, has ventured to suggest that images of Serge Gainsbourg be Photoshopped to remove the inevitable fag – presumably because to do so would be a form of cultural blasphemy.)

For their part, French film-makers see the restrictions on lighting up on screen as heralding a new, dark age of censorship and the fettering of artistic expression. For many in the French pro-smoking camp, puffing a cigarette is the ultimate gesture of *memento mori*, the post-modern equivalent of an Old Master *vanitas* painting of a skull beside a bowl of fruit (or other symbols of the transience of all Earthly things). It is the ultimate act of sheer hedonism, indulgence in the pleasure of a moment that carries with it the shadow of impending mortality. To defend such forbidden pleasure becomes an act of defiance against Anglo-American political correctness and health fascism, a Gallic stand for freedom: *eat, drink, smoke and be merry, for tomorrow we die.**

Myth Evaluation: *True.*

* Or, as the French might say, *Cueille le jour présent en fumant, sans te soucier du lendemain.*

The French are cruel to animals

Brutality to an animal is cruelty to mankind.
ALPHONSE DE LAMARTINE, FRENCH POET, DRAMATIST AND POLITICIAN (1790–1869)

Among the many things for which the French are known and celebrated, sentimentality towards animals is not one. The standard Anglo-Saxon view of the French, in fact, is that of a country of hunters prepared to shoot and kill anything that moves, in order to put its head on the wall and its body on a plate. This view is not a new one by any means. As early as the mid-eighteenth century, in his journal *Travels through France and Italy,* Tobias Smollett observed with distaste:

'You may pass through the whole South of France, as well as the county of Nice, where there is no want of groves, woods, and plantations, without hearing the song of blackbird, thrush, linnet, gold-finch, or any other bird whatsoever. All is silent and solitary. The poor birds are destroyed, or driven for refuge, into other countries, by the savage persecution of the people, who spare no pains to kill, and catch them for their own subsistence. Scarce a sparrow, red-breast, tomtit, or wren, can scape the guns and snares of those indefatigable fowlers. Even the noblesse make parties to go à la chasse, a-hunting; that is, to kill those little birds, which they eat as gibier, or game.'

The image of the ruthless Gallic hunter bent on sacrificing our helpless furry and feathered friends in the interests of the pleasures of the table persists in Anglo-Saxon popular culture to this day, most recently in the form of the insane female *flic* Chantel DuBois in the 2012 Dreamworks animation *Madagascar 3.* From the late twentieth century onwards, animal rights protesters have frequently pointed the finger at France for excessive cruelty to animals, citing such notorious *bêtes noires* of animal welfare as

When I play with my cat, who knows whether she is not amusing herself with me more than I with her?
MICHEL DE MONTAIGNE, FRENCH PHILOSOPHER (1533–92)

the production of that infamous national delicacy, *foie gras*, or the country's devotion to inhumanely reared crated veal.

There is no denying that a few traditional French foods* do involve a measure of cruelty in their methods of production. *Foie gras* – literally, 'fattened liver' – is notoriously produced by *gavage*, or the force-feeding of geese and ducks through a tube inserted into the oesophagus, to create an artificially distended liver. Despite the protestations of producers, there seems to be little doubt that the process is deeply uncomfortable and, probably, dangerous for the fowl concerned. *Foie gras* production by force-feeding has been banned in a number of European coun-

* Horsemeat, which also comes into this category, is dealt with in a separate chapter (see pages 26–34).

tries, including Britain, with many public institutions taking the offending delicacy off their menus (including the Houses of Lords and Commons, to name but two). The French response, typically, has been to convert a culinary anomaly into a cultural exception: the French rural code states: '*Foie gras* belongs to the protected cultural and gastronomical heritage of France.' Nor are the French less recalcitrant over the consumption of veal, condemned by animal rights activists as a meat all too frequently produced in appalling factory conditions. *Blanquette de veau* (veal in a viscous white sauce) has traditionally been and is likely to remain, for some considerable time, the French national dish.*

Do the French see animals differently? As far as animals destined for the dinner table are concerned, it seems, yes. Many visitors to France have referred to a 'Paris exception' on the din ing front, necessitating the suspension of certain ethical commitments towards animal welfare if one is to partake of the authentic French gastronomic experience.[19] And certainly, meat occupies a hallowed place in French cuisine. Out of the eight favourite dishes of France, seven are unequivocally of the fleshly kind, involving red meat or poultry.[20] Less than 2 per cent of French people are vegetarian, contrasted with 3.2 per cent of Americans and 6 per cent of the animal-loving British (although vegetarianism is reportedly on the rise in France, as elsewhere, not least as a result of the 'Horsegate' crisis).[†21] Recently, the French government provoked a storm of protest from vegetarians by issuing a set of protein requirements for school canteens, which in practice excluded vegetarian and vegan diets. Meat-eating, it would seem, is as quintessentially French as a plate of *steak-frites*.

---

* Though *blanquette de veau* has recently been challenged by *magret de canard* (see page 24). This is unlikely to be seen as a positive development by animal rights activists, since the latter is a duck dish produced from the meat of fowl that have been fattened by *gavage*, and whose livers are used for *foie gras*.

† The country with by far the largest vegetarian population is India, with 40 per cent of the population eschewing meat-eating for mainly religious reasons.

As for the proverbial French mania for hunting, it is true that the French are avid fans of the chase. Hunting, or *la chasse*, is the second biggest leisure pursuit in France.[22] And – unlike in the United Kingdom – hunting in France is not exclusive to the upper echelons of society. *La chasse à courre*, or hunting with horses and hounds, is and always has been the preserve of the privileged few; but the majority of hunters in France are not toffs on horseback in jodhpurs and red jackets, but farmers, manual labourers and ordinary working people, rambling the fields on foot with a rifle to shoot a pigeon, rabbit or hare for the family pot.[23] The continued popularity of hunting in France is a reflection of a society that still has – relative to the UK, at least – a significant rural population. Hunting, in fact, is an official way of maintaining the rural French ecosystem. The French Hunters' Federation has the primary duty of controlling the population of pests like rabbits, foxes, pigeons and wild boar, and every year pays out thousands of euros in compensation to irate farmers for the failure of local hunters to eradicate crop-trampling, munching and crunching four-footed and feathered interlopers. In 2011, for example, it handed over the tidy sum of €50 million. This is a cushy deal for French farmers (who are often in rural communities the hunters as well, not to mention the judge and/or injured party in the local court…).[24]

But the French lack of sentimentality towards the animals they eat does not mean that they are generally uncaring about animals not destined for the pot. With over 61 million pets, the French are the biggest pet owners in Europe: 36 million fish head the list, followed by over 10 million cats and more than 7 million dogs (the French Bulldog has been supplanted by the Labrador as the most frequently insured pet dog, while common-or-garden moggies predictably head the cat list, followed by Persian cats).[25] There are also literally hundreds of flourishing animal rights organizations in France – of which the flagship *Fondation Brigitte Bardot* is the most notorious – fighting for everything from banning the seal trade to saving tired horses from the knacker's yard. As with so many aspects of Gallic life, French society is divided by a Cartesian dualism on the animal welfare front: for all the rabbit-shooting, bull-baiting, *foie gras*-consuming inhabitants in rural areas, there are as many urbane, sushi-eating rescuers of enslaved circus animals in the cities.

A good illustration of this bitter internecine conflict was the recent debacle over *La Corrida*, or bullfighting, a 150-year old tradition originally brought from Spain to Bayonne, and which is still hugely popular in southern France. After spending months in 2012 hearing the opposing arguments over *La Corrida*, the French Constitutional Court ruled that it was to be preserved as a French cultural exception – despite the fact that most French people believe that bullfighting should be banned.

So the consensus on the French and their attitude to animals, predictably, is that there is no consensus. Perhaps the truth of the matter ultimately is that, with a few exceptions of undoubted cruelty which mainly relate to ancient and time-honoured French practices of significant importance to local economics, the French are not so much cruel to animals, as more willing to make a distinction between the *animal de compagnie* (animal companion) and those destined for human consumption. So, while the French are more likely to adopt a rational and unsentimental attitude to the cow on their plate, they are as likely as anybody else to anthropomorphize, idolize, drool over and buy diamond collars for their pampered pets. The former's welfare is more an issue of good animal husbandry than the suffering of a friend;* but as to the latter, no praise is high enough. For, in the words of the nineteenth-century French historian and philosopher Hippolyte Taine: 'I've met many thinkers and many cats, but the wisdom of cats is infinitely superior.'

Myth Evaluation: *False*.

* In other words, the French take farm animal welfare into consideration not primarily as an aspect of the animal's suffering but rather from the point of view that a happy, meadow-fed cow is likely to produce sweeter milk and more succulent, nutritious beef than its factory-farmed, hormone-fed, BSE-ridden counterpart.

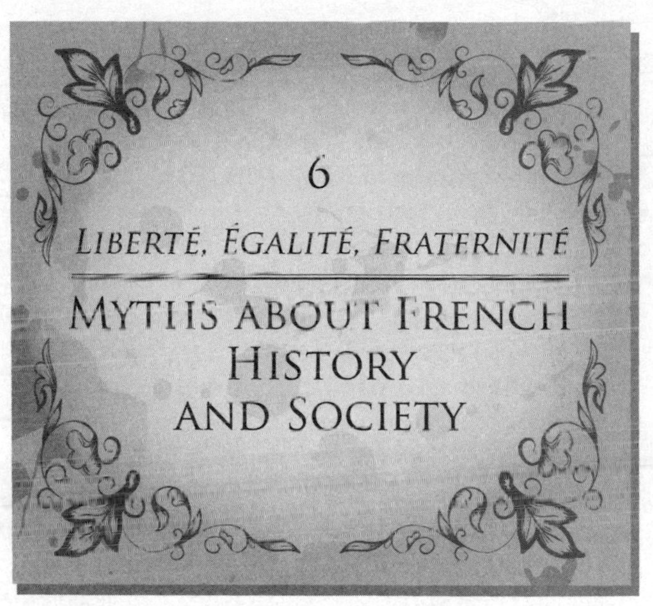

6

Liberté, Égalité, Fraternité

Myths about French History and Society

The French are a nation of Revolutionaries

Louis XVI: *So what is it, a riot?*
Duc de la Rochefoucauld-Liancourt: *No, sire, it is a revolution.*
EXCHANGE AT VERSAILLES DURING THE FRENCH REVOLUTION

There are few world events that have had as enormous an impact on cultural and political consciousness as the French Revolution of 1789. For those who lived through it – in France and abroad – the event defined the hopes and fears of the age. For some, the French Revolution was a beacon of light that gave a world crushed under the weight of aristocratic privilege and monarchical tyranny a hope of freedom; for others, it was the ultimate horror story of carnage unleashed by the abandoning of the established social order to the whims of the mob. Thus, while poets such as William Wordsworth waxed lyrical 'Bliss it was in that dawn to be alive / But to be young was very heaven!',[1] English politicians such as Edmund Burke saw a darker side to events unfolding across the Channel. Burke's treatise *Reflections on the Revolution in France* (1790) remains to this day one of the most cogent articulations of a 'conservative' position, viewing a gradual process of organic social change as preferable to the violent upheavals of revolution. He was confronted by a swift retort in the form of Thomas Paine's *Rights of Man* (1791), an equally cogent argument for a constitution based on reason, guaranteeing the natural rights of man.

The predominant contemporary view in England, however, was that Britain was a safe and prosperous haven compared to the horrors of what was going on in France; and thanks to the vivid picture of the Revolution portrayed in Charles Dickens' historical novel *A Tale of Two Cities* (1859), popularized by Hollywood movies such as the 1935 adaptation by Jack Conway, that is how it has largely remained in the English popular imagination. For a large sector of the British public, the French Revolution is synonymous with the atrocities committed during a very short period – the Terror of 1793–4, during which the climactic scenes of Dickens' novel are set. In the words of the historian Eric Hobsbawm:

'In Britain… this was the image of the Revolution that came closest to entering public consciousness, thanks to Carlyle and Dickens's (Carlyle-inspired) *A Tale of Two Cities*, followed by pop-literary epigones like Baroness Orczy's *The Scarlet Pimpernel*: the knock of the guillotine's blades, the sansculotte women knitting impassively as they watched the counter-revolutionary heads fall.'[2]

As recently as 2012, the Mayor of London, Boris Johnson, was able to play on these violent and negative associations in a speech comparing France's Socialist government with the revolutionary *sans-culottes* over their treatment of the steel magnate Lakshmi Mittal. Johnson's speech showed that even today, France is seen as a dangerous and mercurial harbourer of revolutionary sentiment, in contrast with the stable, business-friendly environment of shopkeeping Britain.

It is certainly true that the blood of rebellion against authority runs hot in French veins – so hot, indeed, that it must be considered a key element of the country's national DNA. Even now, well over two hundred years after the storming of the Bastille, Gallic citizens will be up in arms at the drop of a beret against some form of repression or other. In fact, the natural instinct of the French when faced with something of which they don't approve is to hit the streets. Thus, feminists in 2011 staged a demonstration against French media coverage of the Dominique Strauss-Kahn affair; in 2012, a group of random French people marched in protest at the French government's expulsion of gypsies; and in 2013, thousands of ordinary French people took to the streets to voice either their support for or objection to the government's proposals to allow gay people full rights to marry (the highly controversial project known as *mariage pour tous*). Even at a local level, the French are never slow to get together and noisily protest. For example, parents at a school in our area once demonstrated against a headmaster who was seen as excessively strict; and pupils at another local school recently saw fit

The right to strike is not a right, but a duty!
JEAN-MARIE GOURIO, FRENCH SCRIPTWRITER (b.1956), *BRÈVES DE COMPTOIR*, 1988

to protest against a Spanish teacher whom they claimed was incompetent. In the latter case, the pupils elected a fifteen-year-old representative to put forward a 'plan of action', to reform aspects of the school administration that they considered inadequate. In fact, not a day goes by in France without some group or other of *enfants de la patrie* taking up arms against repression: a confrontational approach to political issues from national to local level that raises the eyebrows of their more phlegmatic neighbours across the English Channel.

Taking to the barricades, in fact, holds a sacred place in French history and culture well beyond the 1789 Revolution. Worker revolt has traditionally been romanticized by French writers, the most classic example perhaps being Émile Zola's incendiary novel *Germinal* (1885), with its grim portrayal of the wretched lives of miners in the Nord-Pas-de-Calais, toiling blindly at the coalface while the wealthy, mine-owning bourgeoisie crack open champagne bottles and lobsters in their mansions above ground. *Germinal* (named after a spring month in the Revolutionary calendar), and based on the real-life strike of miners at Anzin in 1884, made no bones about sowing the seeds of a proletarian revolution. The last lines of the novel evoke the apocalyptic image of a final workers' uprising to end all uprisings, in a future mutinous Armegeddon that had the French bourgeoisie of the time seething with rage and alarm.* Zola was accused by the French press of being an 'artist without a conscience', who

* The 1993 film *Germinal* by Claude Berri, starring Gérard Depardieu, captures something of the gritty realism of the original novel.

had 'sown the seeds of revolt to the four corners of the earth'.[3] It was alleged that *Germinal* inspired a number of worker uprisings in the 1880s, including a savage strike of miners at Aveyron in 1886, which involved the defenestration of the mine's deputy director.

SOME CAMPAIGN SLOGANS OF MAY 1968

L'été sera chaud! ('Summer will be hot!')
La barricade ferme la rue mais ouvre la voie ('Barricades close the street but open the way')
Même si Dieu existait, il faudrait le supprimer ('Even if God existed, He would have to be abolished')
On achète ton bonheur. Vole-le. ('They are buying your happiness. Steal it')
Métro, boulot, dodo ('Subway, work, sleep'; slogan decrying the bourgeois humdrum)
L'imagination prend le pouvoir ('Imagination takes power')
Soyez réaliste, demandez l'impossible ('Be realistic. Demand the impossible')

The twentieth century, in its turn, saw another, albeit less bloody explosion of the French revolutionary spirit – the *événements* of May 1968. This epoch-making moment in French history began quite modestly, with protests by students at the University of Nanterre against the university administration. These protests spread like wildfire, leading to pitched battles between police and students in the Latin Quarter of Paris. Soon, strikes broke out all over France, culminating in a vast general strike. Fearing civil war or another revolution, the then president, Charles de Gaulle, fled to a military base in Germany before returning in June to dissolve the National Assembly and call for new legislative elections. This proved to be a political masterstroke. Naturally, it was much harder for the students to keep on protesting about government oppression when the president had agreed to submit to the popular vote, and so the protest movement petered out; not, however, without leaving behind some of the world's most poetic and memorable campaign slogans.

The Gallic population's natural propensity to take to the streets in revolt against oppression is both manifested in and contained by France's legendary tradition of striking. Striking in France – like street protests and demonstrations – is so much a part of daily life as to be almost banal, and the French are completely inured to their days being disrupted by an endless flow of industrial disputes. The newspaper *Le Parisien* includes strike forecasts in its daily schedule of likely traffic problems, consulted by Parisians in the same manner as folk in other countries might consult the weather forecast. Strike contingency plans are an essential part of any French commuter's armoury. Yet another strike? Time, then, to get on the bike, take the roller blades out of the car boot, or – a particularly favoured option – take a day off work.

However, striking in France is much more than organized protest against specific working conditions. Because of the country's Revolutionary history, every act of taking to the streets – even if it is just in protest at proposed job cuts – has traditionally been regarded as a microcosmic act of social rebellion: a sort of re-enactment of that great original revolt of 1789, the Revolution which created modern France. 'Every strike contains the germs of civil war,' wrote the Russian revolutionary Leon Trotsky in 1938,[4] and left-wing French political theorists echo the implicit link between striking and popular protest in a wider sense. 'A general strike, like all freedom wars, is the most powerful demonstration of individual strength in the uprising of the masses,' wrote the French theorist of revolutionary syndicalism, Georges Sorel (1847–1922).[5] Similarly, the French philosopher Émile-Auguste Chartier (known as 'Alain') observed that 'There is strength and a sort of war in the act of striking.'[6] The very French word for strike – *la grève* – carries with it dark, complex, and revolutionary connotations. *Grève* originally meant 'out of work', and derived from the fact that unemployed labourers seeking to be hired would traditionally go to the Place de Grève – a square in central Paris now occupied by the Hôtel de Ville – where potential employers would also congregate. It subsequently came to acquire the sense of 'put an employer out of work', namely by withdrawing one's labour, its first recorded use in the sense of 'strike' dating from 1844–8.[7] But the Place de Grève was also one of the places where executions took place in the years of the Terror. In Victor Hugo's novel *Notre-Dame de Paris* or *The Hunchback of Notre-Dame* (1831), for example, the location figures as a sinister reminder, with its pillory and gibbet, of the darker side of the French Revolution:

'The Grève had then that sinister aspect which it preserves today from the execrable ideas which it awakens, and from the sombre town hall of Dominique Bocador, which has replaced the Pillared House. It must be admitted that a permanent gibbet and a pillory, "a justice and a ladder", as they were called in that day, erected side by side in the centre of the pavement, contributed not a little to cause eyes to be turned away from that fatal place, where so many beings full of life and health have agonized...'

The fact that striking in France is inextricably linked to a struggle for rights in a much deeper sense than the right to an extra day's holiday or a protest against job cuts is illustrated by its use as a form of expression for those who otherwise would have no means to voice their views. In the twentieth century, working-class Frenchwomen played a major role in strikes long before they had access to the ballot box; while immigrant workers used strikes as a method – one of very few open to them – of voicing protest against their downtrodden position in society. French strikes in the earlier twentieth century were often festive affairs: the sit-in strike was traditionally accompanied by a ritual of dancing, seen as late as 1978 in the occupation of the Renault Flins factory. In 1973, women textile workers at Cerizay (Deux-Sèvres), protesting at the sacking of a colleague, set up an 'alternative' workshop, placing their sewing machines opposite each other rather than in rows and insisting on sewing whole garments rather than just endless collars or buttons, as a protest against being reduced to mere cogs in a production line. The clothes produced were exchanged rather than sold, local shops setting up collection boxes to help the strikers, in a strike of 'joy and song'.[8] The French left-wing activist Daniel Mothé eulogizes industrial action in no uncertain terms: 'The launch of a strike inspires in the activists, and sometimes the workers taking part, ecstasies comparable to those provoked by religious or sexual rites, or even by intellectual or artistic creation.'

But are French strikes today still the joyous expression of protest by an underclass that is battered but not beaten, echoes in microcosm of that great protest of the French people that led to the creation of the French Republic? Sadly not. A surprising fact, given the number of strikes in France, is that only a very small proportion of French people these days actually belong to a trade union. In fact, less than 10 per cent of French workers belong to one.[9] This compares with 27 per cent of UK employees who are trade union members, although union membership has been in decline throughout Europe in recent decades. Since the 1980s, a growing number of official strikes in France have been carried out by public-sector workers – in other words, those who in the main already enjoy the privilege of closed markets, extended retirement plans, paid additional work hours, and lengthy holidays. (Public-sector worker strikes increased from 443,725 strike days in the period 1982–5 to 830,924 in the period 1996–2000.)[10] For foreign observers in countries where workers are routinely obliged to work until their late sixties or later, it was hard to muster much sympathy for French public service workers on strike in 2010, in protest at President Sarkozy's relatively modest proposal to increase the minimum retirement age from 60 to 62. In fact, the French are extremely privileged compared to other countries, in that they can expect to be retired longer than almost any other nation in the world: 22 years for men and 27 years for women.[11] The truly exploited workers of France today – immigrants working on the black market and those on short-term contracts drafted to escape the generous social provisions – do not have recourse to a union to fight for them, or to organize a civilized street protest; periodically, they simply resort to torching cars instead, as was seen in the 2005 riots that hit Paris.

François Mitterrand once observed, with characteristic astuteness, that 'there are two ways to sabotage the right to strike: to regulate it, as does the Right, or to use it wrongly and perversely, as does the Left.' Many are the French services that are badly broken and in dire need of repair, yet paralyzed by vested interests that hit the streets at any hint of proposed reform. For example, the chronic shortage of taxis in Paris (there are a mere 17,000 licensed taxis in Paris, as against 25,000 licensed taxis and 44,000 minicabs in London),[12] is a direct result of the refusal of current taxi drivers to allow new licences to be issued. Every time any French government timidly suggests liberalizing the taxi market – as several have done – the taxi drivers protest *en masse*, blocking traffic in central Paris and airport routes with angry honking.

There is, however, an odd thing about traditional French street protests and strikes. That is, whenever the government of the day grows a backbone and toughs it out, the protesters tend to grumble for a while, then return to their old routines as if nothing had happened. So it was with the May '68 revolution, which actually saw the re-election of the Gaullist party the following year (just as Ronald Reagan's election as Governor of California in 1967 may well have been helped by his commitment to 'clean up' the anti-Vietnam War student protests raging in the state at that time). Similarly, the pensions furore of 2010 was essentially ignored by the Sarkozy government, and petered out into a grumpy acceptance of pension reform. Not that the French have much choice in such matters; as we shall see in the next chapter, they have invested so much power in their president that there is not much they could do to rein in his actions, other than protest. It is as though, in France, the traditional, time-honoured strike or mass demonstration is a massive social safety valve, a chance to let off steam, shout and have a tantrum, before returning to the real world. Which is perhaps just as well, because with five republics, two empires and a monarchy since 1789, perhaps the last thing the French need is another revolution.

Myth Evaluation: *Partly true. There is a historic tradition of street protest in France, of which striking is a manifestation. But although there is often a great deal of 'sound and fury', the result – equally often – is nothing.*

France is an egalitarian society

The French want equality, and when they do not find it through freedom, they seek it through bondage.
ALEXIS DE TOCQUEVILLE, FRENCH HISTORIAN (1805–59), EXTRACT FROM *L'ANCIEN RÉGIME ET LA RÉVOLUTION*, 1856

We are used to thinking of the French as the ultimate egalitarian nation. *Liberté, Égalité, Fraternité* was the motto of the French Revolution of 1789: principles that had already been articulated by French thinkers who led the world in championing the freedom of the individual as the basis for running a state. Most famously, the Francophone Swiss Jean-Jacques Rousseau wrote, in his 1762 treatise *The Social Contract*:

'If we ask in what precisely consists the greatest good of all, which should be the end of every system of legislation, we shall find it reduces itself to two main objects, liberty and equality — liberty, because all particular dependence means so much force taken from the body of the State and equality, because liberty cannot exist without it.'

Equality, for thinkers such as Rousseau and the leaders of the Revolution, was a counteracting force in the form of levelling laws imposed by the state to control the naturally selfish instincts of man; and ever since, the French have prided themselves on being (unlike the snobbish English) the nation of free-thinking, banner-waving, street-marching brothers-in-arms. Although, looking at the enormous upheavals of recent French history, one could be forgiven for thinking that the path to equality has been far from clear-cut. In fact, it's hard to see why people have problems understanding modern French history. Monarchy, Revolution, Republic, Empire, Monarchy, Revolution, Monarchy, Revolution, Republic, Empire, Republic. Dead easy, really. Few are the European countries that have had as many changes of regime, in as short a time, as the French. And yet, if you look behind the ostensibly breathtaking transformations in the French political landscape, one feature remains

I can think of hardly anybody except Jean-Jacques Rousseau who can be reproached with these ideas of equality and independence and all these fantasies that are simply ridiculous.

VOLTAIRE, FRENCH ENLIGHTENMENT WRITER (1694–1778), FROM A LETTER TO MARÉCHAL DUC DE RICHELIEU, 13 FEBRUARY 1771

constant as the northern star. And that is the centrality of the state.

L'état, c'est moi ('I am the state'), the *Roi Soleil* ('Sun King') Louis XIV once famously said. Napoleon could have said as much. And in recent times, little has changed. The president of France – thanks to the powers conferred on him by the Fifth Republic established by General de Gaulle in October 1958 – is the most powerful political leader in the Western world. Unlike the parliamentary democracies of countries such as the UK – where a system of checks and balances, in theory at least, places some restraint on the untrammelled exercise of power by any one individual – the French president reigns supreme. De Gaulle himself admitted as much, when he said to his minister of information, Alain Peyrefitte, that he had tried, in the constitution of the Fifth Republic, to create a 'synthesis between a monarchy and a republic'. 'What, a monarchic Republic?' Peyrefitte is said to have responded, astonished. 'No,' replied de Gaulle, 'let's say rather a Republican monarchy.' Once every five years, the president of the French Republic is required to go out on the street and answer to the rabble. For the next 1,825 days, he can virtually do what he likes.* A French president in office is immune from legal or criminal proceedings: no Watergate can unseat him, nor Chappaquiddick submerge him. That this should be the case in a country famed for its Republican revolution, and of which the motto is *Liberté, Égalité, Fraternité,* is profoundly ironic. It is as though the French people have never quite got over guillotining their royal family in 1793, and instead insist on appointing a walking and talking shadow to pay homage to the regal ghosts of the past.

Just as the Sun King surrounded himself with a tight circle of

* Although there is, occasionally, the inconvenience of *cohabitation* – that is, when the majority party in the French parliament is not the same party as the president's.

LIBERTY, EQUALITY, CONTROVERSY

The slogan *Liberté, Égalité, Fraternité* ('Liberty, Equality, Brotherhood') is one indissolubly linked to the ideals of the French Revolution. It is in fact France's official motto, found on the national logo inscribed on all official documents, along with the colours of the French *Tricolore* flag and France's national symbol, Marianne.

Credit for coining the slogan is traditionally given to Antoine-François Momoro (1756–94), a printer and politician during the 1789 Revolution. However, at that time it was simply one of several slogans in use – such as *Union, Force, Vertu* ('Union, Strength, Virtue') and *Force, Égalité, Justice* ('Strength, Equality, Justice').

Over the ensuing years *Liberté, Égalité, Fraternité* came to predominate over rival slogans, although the linking of the libertarian and individualistic ideals of liberty and equality with the levelling and collective ideal of brotherhood has always been a matter of controversy. At various periods – notably the Napoleonic era – the slogan was banned. During the Vichy régime in the Second World War, Marshal Pétain replaced it with *Travail, Famille, Patrie* ('Work, Family, Fatherland'), a motto that had a decidedly Nazi ring to it. After the war, however, the original slogan was reinstated, and incorporated into the French constitutions that followed.

The slogan has inspired countless imitations in many countries of the world, including the Universal Declaration of Human Rights and the constitution of the Liberal Democrat party in the UK, which refers in its preamble to 'the fundamental values of liberty, equality, and community'. However, the implicit tension between the conflicting values that the motto brings together has never been – and perhaps never will be – resolved.

lackeys, spies and sycophants to impose his laws on the land, so the French president has an army of executives – the *hautes fonctionnaires* or top civil servants in the administrative, financial and legislative departments of government – to administer his will. The tripartite structure of top civil servants, captains of industry, and – increasingly – bosses in the worlds of banking and commerce, form the technocracy that rules France. This *haute bourgeoisie*, or ruling class, remains aloof and hidden from the lives of ordinary French citizens. Most have been born into families that for years have occupied high functions in the civil service, industry or banking. As one French social scientist has observed, 'Birth remains in France one of the principal conditions of access to power.'[13] Hot on the heels of a silver spoon comes a sterling education. Many of the nation's elect bypass the French state schools, attending instead private, Catholic schools or top Parisian *lycées* known for taking the cream of the crop. And after school comes the most élitist institution of all: the *grande école*. Originally founded by Napoleon to train up a select cadre of officers to carry out his commands, the French *grandes écoles* are a league of super-graduate schools that exist over and above the normal French universities. Specializing in different disciplines, each has connections with the sector for which it trains up recruits. Thus HEC Paris (*Hautes Études Commerciales de Paris*), the leading business school, has close links with the world of banking and finance; ENA (*École Nationale d'Administration*), the élite school for civil servants, virtually guarantees its graduates the highest positions in the French administration; and the *École Polytechnique*, the top French maths and engineering school, trains hundreds of technocrats. (The *École Polytechnique*, known simply as *X*, is the *crème de la crème*, a quasi-military establishment under the control of the French Defence Ministry.) Entry to the *grandes écoles* is by a competitive entry examination or *concours*, for which entrants are hot-housed in top preparatory schools called *prépas* (the leading *prépas*, naturally, have close connections with the top *lycées* or secondary schools). Fees, except for the business schools, are virtually nil, and in fact in some *grandes écoles* (*École Polytechnique*, ENA and the *École Normale Supérieure*), students are actually paid a salary of €2,000 a month. The *grandes écoles* receive much higher government funding than the universities – they get 30 per cent of the national budget, with only 4 per cent of the students. A study in 2008 found that of the 27 French bosses of the CAC 40 companies (i.e. the top 40 companies in France), 20 had graduated from just three of the top *grandes écoles: ENA*, the *École Polytechnique*, and HEC Paris.[14]

Contemporaries at the *grandes écoles* hang out with each other, at work and play, for the rest of their lives. Though private social clubs were a British invention, the French have taken to them with an enthusiasm somewhat unbecoming a nation of Revolutionaries. The foremost private club – *Le Siècle* – was founded at the end of the Second World War, and counts among its members France's élite civil servants, businessmen, politicians, intellectuals, journalists and academics (some 40 per cent of the French government from the 1990s onwards, whether Socialist or conservative, have belonged to *Le Siècle*).[15] The club organizes an *apéritif* and dinner on the last Wednesday of the month at the Automobile Club of France in the Place de la Concorde, where the happy few can rub shoulders and discuss world affairs in confidence. Most of the mandarins of *Le Siècle* are male, middle-aged, the sons of industry bosses, civil servants or financiers, and many of them are *énarques* (that is, graduates of ENA; the powerful clique that runs France's civil service is known as the *énarchie*). More exclusive, but with less political clout, is the *Jockey Club de Paris*, with splendid rooms at rue Rabelais, a club for aristocrats presided over by the Duc de Brissac.

The French *haute bourgeoisie* – many of whom claim noble origins – are obsessed with distinguishing themselves from the newly and flashily rich. In fact, there is no greater social disgrace than being considered a *parvenu*. (Interestingly and perhaps not accidentally, the principal terms used in English to designate the newly and vulgarly rich are of French origin – *parvenu, arriviste* and *nouveau riche*.) It is as a result of this fanatical concern for demarcating old from new money, distinguishing the breadth of one's bank balance from the length of one's pedigree, that the bourgeois French obsession with the rules of *politesse* and *savoir-vivre* (see pages 157–8) arises; and it is in the *haute bourgeois* desire to set themselves apart from the vulgar *arriviste*

that the principles of discretion in dress, the choice of sober colours, the rejection of flashy designer labels and jewellery, take root. The big and vulgar noises in France – actors, celebrities and football stars – are listed in *Who's Who in France* (published since 1953), just as in the British version. The *haute bourgeoisie*, however, have their own directory – *Le Bottin mondain* – which lists precisely no French footballers, none of the best-paid French actors or singers, and only one top-selling French essayist. Instead, it features the handful of *grandes familles françaises* who form the inner circles of the Parisian élite.

To the average Frenchman, or indeed foreigner, nothing is more evocative of an aristocratic past than a name that includes the illustrious *particule* (i.e. the appellation *de* in a person's surname, as in Pierre-Augustin Caron *de* Beaumarchais); and nowhere is the allure of the *particule* so strong as in the land of ardent Revolutionaries. There are, in fact, so many *fausses particules* adopted by members of the French bourgeoisie in a bid to ennoble themselves that there is a counter-directory of fake nobility to name and shame them: the hefty tome *Le Simili-nobiliaire français*, by Pierre-Marie Dioudonnat, which lists all the *faux noble particules* and patronyms adopted by members of the bourgeoisie. The book caused a storm of protest on publication in 2002. Famous *faux noble* name-holders of bourgeois origin include: General Charles de Gaulle; the former French prime minister Dominique de Villepin; the one-time French president Valéry Giscard d'Estaing; and even the great nineteenth-century novelist Honoré (de) Balzac, whose humbly-born father added the *particule* to his name when he climbed the social ladder.[16]

The paradoxical devotion of the French to two conflicting principles – equality and privilege – inevitably generates a vast amount of cant and hypocrisy. It is also another reason for the excessive tact and discretion of that secretive, low-lying and hunted animal – the French *haute bourgeoisie*. After all, heads once rolled in France as a result of the overweening display of wealth and privilege. The impossible predicament of the prosperous in France was aptly expressed by the Franco Italian actor Fabrice Luchini, when he observed, shrugging his shoulders in despair:

'I don't have any gloating passion for money; at 58 years old, I am only beginning to learn how to profit from it. I am an insomniac, I don't derive pleasure from anything, but I don't have the right to complain because there are other people whose houses are being razed. So I shut my mouth. Either one keeps one's privileges and shuts up, or one gives it all to Emmaüs.'[17]

The latest round of bourgeois-bashing in France following the election of the Socialist François Hollande as president in 2012 triggered a flood of wealthy tax exiles from the country, most famously the noisy departure of former national treasure Gérard Depardieu, an exodus which has caused a certain amount of soul-searching.* The agony of self-doubt was exacerbated by a particularly mordant attack on the Gallic attitude to wealth by another national hero, the French pop singer Johnny Hallyday, in his best-selling 2013 autobiography.† Is it true, the French ask themselves, that they hate the well-off? If so, does such venom against the privileged sit well with a nation that prides itself on being the world's self-appointed arbiter of luxury

---

* For example, a documentary on French national television in February 2013 examined the question whether one has to leave France these days to succeed. (*L'argent : faut-il partir pour réussir?*, France 2, 7 February 2013.)

† Hallyday said: 'I have always asked myself why, in the USA, if you have a flashy car people smile and say "that's great", while in France they treat you like a thief. It's a sordid mentality.' (*Dans mes yeux*, co-written with Amanda Sthers, Éditions Plon, 2013.)

and refined taste, and which indeed lives in no small part off the trade in luxury goods? Right now, the French appear in grave danger of biting the very hand that feeds them.

Not that the French would ever openly admit that they were élitist, or money-grabbing, or insecure about wealth, or anything like that, of course. Discussing money is simply… well, too *vulgar*. Popular demagogues such as the left-wing Jean-Luc Mélenchon and even François Hollande have made a great show of denigrating the filthy rich and their 'dirty' money (although Hollande himself is an *énarque*, and Mélenchon owns both a Paris apartment and a country pad, so neither seem to have missed out entirely on the much-denigrated privileges in life). 'The French have a horror of "inequality", but they adore privilege. And often, 'inequality' is the name you give to the privileges of another,' the French comedienne and actress Anne Roumanoff has wisely said. But shhh, we are encroaching now on *private* matters. None of that is relevant. Let's return to the public mantra: *Liberté, Égalité, Fraternité…* and, above all, the greatest Gallic virtue of them all: *discretion.*

Myth Evaluation: *False. The French are at least as élitist as the British, if not worse, because they pretend that they are not.*

THE FRENCH DON'T WORK VERY HARD

Laziness is nothing more than the habit of resting before you get tired.

JULES RENARD, FRENCH WRITER (1864–1910)

Doucement le matin, pas trop vite l'après-midi goes an old French saying. In other words, 'slowly in the morning, not too fast in the afternoon'. And at first sight at least, for any visitor or foreign resident in France, the French would seem to be true to their word. Although shops in France are open on Saturdays, Sunday trading is generally for markets and small boutiques only. And then, naturally, all the shops that were open on Saturday close on Mondays to make up for the extra day of work (including, shockingly to most Anglo-Saxons, French banks). Turn up at any provincial shop other than a supermarket between 1 p.m. and 3 p.m. on a weekday at your peril: you will find the shutters drawn and the establishment steeped in a somnolent, postprandial haze, while the staff are lunching at the local bistro round the corner.

Do the French work less hard than other Europeans? The answer is, probably yes. With 30 days as the legal minimum for annual paid leave plus 10 days of public holidays a year (therefore 40 days of paid holiday in total), France is second only to Finland in the league table of holiday-happy states in the European Union.*[18] But the French official minimum holiday

* The stingy United Kingdom ties bottom of the EU holiday table with the Netherlands and Romania, requiring a minimum of only 28 days of annual leave and public holidays. This is nothing, however, compared with the United States, the ultimate no-vacation nation, which has precisely 0 days of legally obligatory paid leave.

requirement of 40 days doesn't include all the 'unofficial' days that are widely taken – such as the infamous *pont* or 'bridging day'. The classic case of this is where a public holiday falls on a Thursday: schools and most employers will shut up shop on the Friday as well, so that everybody gets a long weekend. And then there is France's celebrated 35-hour week, introduced by the Socialist government of Lionel Jospin in 2000. Although in practice many French people work more than this theoretical ceiling to the number of hours worked (above which employees must be paid supplementary hours), the average number of hours worked per year by the French (1,554) is below the average of OECD countries (1,749 hours).[19] The French also spend the greatest amount of time out of the OECD countries on 'leisure and personal care', including eating and sleeping – a whopping 68 per cent of their day, or 15.3 hours.[20]

However, try to confront a Frenchman with his relaxed approach to working, and he will likely call your attention smugly to one of the most celebrated of the so-called 'French paradoxes' – the 'French productivity paradox'. This is the apparently counter-intuitive claim that – despite working fewer hours than other countries – France has a preternaturally high productivity level. The country, in fact, comes fifth among the big economies of the OECD in terms of worker productivity per hour. Unfortunately, though, the French productivity paradox is more likely a myth. As a number of economists have pointed out, the real reason why French productivity levels are so high is because of the relatively high French unemployment rate, particularly among older and younger people. As workers in these age brackets are the ones most likely to be the least productive, their exclusion from the labour market artificially forces up the French productivity figure (never mind the 'informal' hours worked which are not counted in the official figures, particularly in the thriving employment black market). It has been estimated that if these unemployed, lowest-producing workers were factored into the French employment market to produce the same employment picture as in the United States, the French productivity rate would plummet by 10–15 per cent.

In fact, some commentators go so far as to claim that the high productivity rate in France is actually a sign of the inherent weakness of the French employment market, rather than its strength.[21]

The allegedly work-shy attitude of the French was the subject of a storm of controversy in February 2013, when the maverick chief executive of the American tyre company Titan – Maurice M. Taylor, nicknamed 'The Grizz' for his tough negotiating style – rejected a tentative inquiry by the French industry minister, Arnaud Montebourg, seeking to know whether Titan would be interested in taking over part of the struggling Goodyear tyre factory in Amiens. 'How stupid do you think we are?' Mr Taylor wrote, in a letter that was nothing short of extraordinary for its high-handed manner. 'I visited this factory several times. The French workers have high salaries but only work for three hours. They have an hour for breaks and lunch, chat for three hours, and work for three hours. I told the French unions that to their faces. They replied that this is how it is in France!'*[22] Insulting, unfair, and over the top as the letter undoubtedly was, even the French had to admit that it contained a grain of truth – which was no doubt why it was so widely discussed and reported, not without a touch of angst, in France.

What is going to count in the future is not work, but laziness. Everybody agrees that work is only a means to an end. People talk about a 'civilization of leisure'. When we get there we will have lost all sense of leisure. There are people who work for forty years in order to rest afterwards and when they finally get to rest, they don't know what to do and they die. I honestly believe that I would better serve the cause of humanity by lazing around than working. It's true, you need to have the courage not to work.

ÉRIC ROHMER, FRENCH FILM DIRECTOR (1920–2010) *ADRIEN, LA COLLECTIONNEUSE*, 1967

This is not to say, of course, that there are not people who work very hard in France. As in every country, there are the

* Maurice Taylor is no stranger to controversy. A staunch supporter of the 'Buy American' campaign, he once featured in a 2008 publicity campaign where he stated that putting Michelin tyres on an American tractor would be like 'putting a beret on a cowboy'. Given that he ran for the Republican presidential nomination in 1996, one can perhaps be thankful, for the sake of Franco-American diplomatic relations, that he did not win.

THE LAMENT OF THE WAGE-SLAVE

The classic French expression of existential *ennui* at the endless round of commuting, earning a living, and hitting the sack is the phrase *Métro, boulot, dodo* ('Subway–work–sleep'). This nicely rhyming coinage has revolutionary connotations, having been used as a slogan during the student revolt of May '68 to encourage workers to rise up against the perceived slavery of their daily drudgery. Its origins, though, lie somewhat earlier. It was first used by the Romanian-born, naturalized French writer Pierre Béarn (1902–2004) in his 1951 poem '*Couleurs d'usine*' ('Factory Colours'), the final stanza of which runs:

> 'Rush in boy, punch your number
> To earn your dosh
> For another dreary, routine day:
> Subway, work, bars, fags, sleep, nothing.'

In the event, the May '68 revolution petered out, General de Gaulle's party came back to power with renewed vigour afterwards, and the phrase turned from being a revolutionary call to arms to a resigned and cynical acceptance of one's lot. Cynics might point out, however, that given France's work record, an essential element has been omitted, namely, *Métro, boulot, dodo, vacances...*[23]

many self-employed people, who slog away with no paid leave or holidays; there are immigrants and workers on the thriving black market, who work like dogs for a pittance and no vacation at all; and there are the increasing number of people taking several jobs to try to eke out a living in the tough years of *la crise*. There are even employees who want to work more than their unions will let them – such as the staff of the DIY chain *Bricorama*, who in 2012 demonstrated against their union's refusal to let them work on Sundays. Generally speaking, though, France is a country where people work to live rather than live to work – an ethic that can be more than a little irritating for those who actually enjoy their job and consider it a major part of their life, rather than a tedious but necessary activity of which the primary purpose is to pay for one's next vacation. It also means that the holiday holds a sacred place in the national culture: the whole of the French year, in fact, turns around the school holidays, which set the pattern for French office workers as much as for the schools. The upshot of all this is that, when you come to France, like it or not, you just have to go with the flow. Don't expect a reply to a phone message without several chasers (and don't bother at all in August). Just turn on, tune in, and drop a beat. Remember: *doucement le matin, pas trop vite l'après-midi...*

Myth Evaluation: *True (relative to people in the UK and the United States, that is).*

The French are a nation of cheese-eating surrender monkeys

I would rather have a German division in front of me than a French one behind me.

GENERAL GEORGE S. PATTON, US SECOND WORLD WAR COMMANDER (1885–1945)

'Cheese-eating surrender monkeys' has become a modern stock phrase for allegedly lily-livered Frenchmen. France's propensity for cheese-eating has been the subject of a previous chapter (see pages 41–7); but the allegations of simian cowardliness merit closer inspection. Not that such allegations are anything new: the phrase 'Never trust a Froggy' was once common among British soldiers. Moreover, the slur has an exact French equivalent: *Perfide Albion*. In fact, the myth of the cowardly, treacherous and dastardly French in English history is matched only by the myth of the treacherous, dastardly and cowardly English in the annals of the French.

Whereas mutual mistrust between the Frogs and the *Rosbifs* goes back to the Norman Conquest, accusations of cowardice are relatively recent, dating in the main from the twentieth century. In fact, France's military history prior to the modern age is replete with as many tales of derring-do and heroism as that of any other country. Take, for example, the great French hero of the Dark Ages, the bold warrior Roland, who is the subject of the earliest literary work in French, the eleventh-century *La Chanson de Roland* ('The Song of Roland'). Battling the Saracens at Roncesvalles in the Pyrenees in AD 778 on behalf of the Emperor Charlemagne, Roland bravely refused to call for help by blowing on his horn (or *oliphant*), fighting a hopeless rearguard action until, finally, he was forced to blow for assistance but burst his temples in the effort, dying a martyr. Then there was the celebrated and dextrous Norman bard Taillefer who, according to the Anglo-Norman chronicler Wace, inspired the Norman knights advancing on the English troops at the Battle of Hastings in 1066 by singing the *Chanson de Roland* (all the while deftly juggling with his sword), before rushing the Saxons and being cut down.

Perhaps the most unlikely French military hero of all, however, is Joan of Arc, *La Pucelle d'Orléans* ('the Maid of Orleans'; 1412–31), a nineteen-year-old peasant girl who was inspired by divine guidance to lead the French to several important victories over the English in the Hundred Years War. Captured by the treacherous Burgundians,* she was put on trial by the pro-English Bishop of Beauvais and burned at the stake for heresy. And yet, having done away with her, the French – in a rather spectacular change of tack worthy of their reputation as turncoats – proceeded twenty-five years after her execution to turn her into a martyr: she was declared innocent by Pope Callixtus III in 1456, beatified in 1909, and canonized in 1920. Today, she is one of the patron saints of France† and has been the subject of countless songs, poems and plays, immortalized in works as varied as those of Shakespeare, Voltaire, Tchaikovsky, Leonard Cohen, and the 1980s New Wave group Orchestral Manoeuvres in the Dark.

France upheld its tradition of military prowess throughout the sixteenth, seventeenth and eighteenth centuries. The late medieval French knight Pierre Terrail, seigneur de Bayard (a.k.a. *le Chevalier de Bayard*) was noted for his chivalry and valour, and is famously known to posterity as *le chevalier sans peur et sans reproche.*‡ Bayard served three French kings (Charles VIII, Louis XII, and François I) before being killed in the Habsburg–Valois wars in Italy in 1524 (his

* i.e. supporters of John II, Duke of Burgundy.

† Along with St Denis, St Martin of Tours, St Louis IX, and St Theresa of Lisieux.

‡ From which phrase the French food critic Curnonsky (see page 43) derived his witticism, *La cuisine du Périgord est sans beurre et sans reproche.*

last words, reputedly, included the noble phrase: 'I die as man of honour ought, doing my duty…'). And then there were the commanders of the warmongering Sun King, Louis XIV – the likes of the Vicomte de Turenne and Louis de Bourbon, Prince of Condé, who helped consolidate French military supremacy over the Spanish during the Thirty Years War (1618–48). Nor was the eighteenth century short of Gallic war heroes: one of the most notable was the Marquis de Montcalm, commander of French forces at the Battle of Québec (1759), who died in that battle (as did his British opponent, General James Wolfe), and who remains a national hero in France to this day.

The wars of the Napoleonic era had their fair share of tales of tragic heroism, too. Take, for example, the case of Napoleon's commander Marshal Ney, nicknamed by his leader as *le brave des braves* ('the bravest of the brave'). Distinguished by his ser-

FALLING OUT WITH THE FRENCH

The most notorious national slur against the French for their alleged unwillingness to fight derives from Matt Groening's television cartoon series *The Simpsons*. In a 1995 episode called 'Round Springfield', the dour Scottish school janitor Groundskeeper Willie – who is unexpectedly saddled with the task of taking a French lesson at Springfield Elementary School – addresses the class with the greeting, 'Bonjour, you cheese-eating surrender monkeys.'

Since the day it was first uttered, the phrase has been endlessly repeated as a staple in the stock arsenal of insults against the French. It became especially popular in 2003, when it was used by the conservative US columnist Jonah Goldberg of the *National Review* to attack France's opposition to the invasion of Iraq.

Interestingly, if you mention the phrase to a French person, he or she will look at you blankly. This is because the voice-over was modified to 'cheese-eating monkeys' (*singes mangeurs de fromage*), when the series was broadcast in France.

vice, particularly during Napoleon's retreat from Moscow in 1812, Ney was arrested after the defeat and exile of Napoleon and sentenced to death by firing squad in 1815. He refused to wear a blindfold and was granted the (rare) right to order the squad to fire, reportedly saying:

'Soldiers, when I give the command to fire, fire straight at my heart. Wait for the order. It will be my last to you. I protest against my condemnation. I have fought a hundred battles for France, and not one against her… Soldiers, Fire!'[24]

Moving to the twentieth century, and the First World War, the magnitude of the French contribution to that conflict is reflected in their armies suffering more casualties and deaths than any combatant nation other than Germany or Russia. The number of Frenchmen sacrificed in the killing fields of the trenches far outstripped the (still enormous) number of British soldiers killed in action: French military deaths amounted to 1.3 million, as compared to 886,000 British.[25] Not even the most diehard Francophobe, then, could deny the enormous contribution made by the French to this most brutal and wasteful of wars.

How, then, did the nation of Bayard and Napoleon come to be tarred with the brush of cowardice? The suggestion that the French might be fight-shy largely arose from the part played (or rather, allegedly *not* played) by their forces in the *next* global conflict – the Second World War. 'There's always something fishy about the French,' sang Noel Coward in a number from *Conversation Piece*. This was amended by Ivor Novello in 1941 to: 'There's always something Vichy about the French.' The speed, and apparent willingness, with which France fell into the enemy embrace after the evacuation of Dunkirk by signing an armistice with Germany – allowing German forces to occupy the North and a puppet Nazi state to be created in the former spa town of Vichy in the South – astonished the British and Americans, and has provided Francophobes with a juicy opportunity to gloat over the carcass of French military glory ever since.

Certainly, there were many brave French Resistance figures: men such as Jean Moulin, who died at the hands of the Gestapo in Lyons. During the war, internal and external opposition to the

As far as I'm concerned, war always means failure.
JACQUES CHIRAC, FRENCH PRESIDENT (1995–2007)
As far as France is concerned, you're right.
REJOINDER BY US RIGHT-WING 'SHOCK-JOCK' RUSH LIMBAUGH

German occupation and the Vichy regime coalesced around the banner of the exiled Free French leader, General Charles de Gaulle, whose BBC radio announcements from London remained an inspiration to *la flamme de la Résistance française*. Even so, the accusation remains that, for most of this war, it was French collaboration that was rather more evident than French resistance. One of the most shameful episodes in modern French history is the deportation of some 75,000 Jews to German concentration camps, mainly via the temporary holding station at Drancy in the northeastern suburbs of Paris. These transports could not have taken place without the enthusiastic collaboration of the Vichy *Milice* and other French officials from 1940 to 1944. And although hundreds of Frenchmen joined the French Resistance – particularly towards the end of the war, when it became obvious that the Allies were going to win – thousands also volunteered to fight for the Nazis, by joining the 33rd Waffen Grenadier Division of SS Charlemagne (1st French).

Even after the war ended, Anglo-Saxon accusations of French cowardice and ingratitude continued. The postwar US Marshall Plan – one of the largest aid packages in history – poured 13 billion dollars into the reconstruction of Europe. Were the French grateful for these sacrifices in blood and cash from their erstwhile allies across the Atlantic? It seemed they were not – or at least, not as much as they should be in American eyes. The Marshall Plan, according to widespread French opinion, was simply an extension of American self-interest, a means of setting Europe back on its feet to begin spending money again on American consumer goods. As such, it was just a figleaf for the 'Coca-Colonization' of French society. The general view of the United States was that it was the country of 'mass-produced goods, mass-produced culture, and mass-produced feelings'.[26] Horror stories circulated of American tourists who, after trying some rare Vosne-Romanée, ordered Coca-Cola to wash it down. In the year immediately after the war, tensions mounted between GIs waiting to be sent back home and their French hosts, with outbreaks of violence. The result was that the average GI returned from France with his anti-French prejudices mightily reinforced.

But the moral balance of virtuous versus reprehensible behaviour in time of war is, of course, infinitely more subtle than popular folklore would suggest. No single event embodies the contrasting versions of history favoured by different sides in the conflict as much as the evacuation of Dunkirk in late May 1940, the fateful action that confirmed the triumph of the German armies in the West and was followed by the fall of France a matter of weeks later. Between 27 May and 4 June 1940, in Operation Dynamo, as it was called, nearly 340,000 British and French troops were rescued by sea from the French port, in a mass evacuation that Winston Churchill described on 4 June as a 'miracle of deliverance' (he had characterized the plight of the Franco-British forces as a 'colossal military disaster' only the previous week). The legend of Dunkirk, as created by Churchill and the British press, was a tale of the heroic rescue of French and British soldiers, trapped by the German advance, achieved with the help of fishermen and other ordinary folk, who braved the high seas in their 'little ships'. Majority French opinion, however, classified it as a craven act of desertion, which left them fighting a hopeless rearguard action against the Germans alone, and which ultimately led to their surrender and the signing of a shameful armistice with the enemy.[27]

While the French, British and Americans officially came out of the war as victorious allies, the French never again had real faith in perfidious Albion or gung-ho Uncle Sam (nor, indeed, did the latter two ever totally trust the dodgy Froggies). De Gaulle manifested his hostility by repeated refusals to allow Britain's application for membership of the Common Market, on the basis that Britain was a free-wheeling loose cannon and too much in the US camp, and therefore not truly compatible with the other countries of Europe.* With the benefit of hindsight, De Gaulle's hunch

* The British, for their part, have always considered de Gaulle's repeated *non* to Britain's EU membership to be a manifestation of his shameful ingrati-

may well have been right. Since joining the Common Market in 1973, Britain's relationship with the EU has been punctuated by spats over budgetary contributions and opt-outs, and bursts of Europhobic invective on the part of right-wing Conservative MPs and the tabloid press on matters great and small – from the single currency to French farming subsidies, and from increasing European political integration to the imposition of a uniform shape for bananas.†

Despite falling out over such issues as the 1956 Suez Crisis (America v. Britain and France), British lamb imports in the 1980s (France v. Britain), the French refusal to allow US aircraft to fly over their airspace for the bombing of Libya in 1986 (France v. America), and the BSE crisis of the 1990s (Britain v. France), the uneasy truce between the wavering allies continued for several decades after the Second World War. In fact, it was not until 2003 that the reluctant bedfellows had their biggest row since the war, when France refused to join Britain and America in their headlong rush to invade Saddam Hussein's Iraq, in order to neutralize the dictator's non-existent stockpile of weapons of mass destruction. Contrary to Anglo-American rhetoric, President Chirac had the temerity to say that he would not support military intervention in Iraq unless Saddam Hussain ceased cooperating with the UN weapons inspectorate. In this he was supported by Germany, Russia, China, the Pope, the Secretary General of the United Nations, the ex-US president Jimmy Carter, and 70–80 per cent of European (including British) pubic opinion.[28] In response, he was denounced by *The Sun*, which ran a French edition with the headline *Chirac est un ver* ('Chirac is a worm'); in the United States, French fries were rechristened 'Freedom fries'; and the old *Simpsons* quip 'cheese-eating surrender monkeys' came back into circulation.

Now that the desert dust has settled on the diplomatic crisis over the Second Iraq War, Anglo-American relations with

---

tude for their sheltering him after he fled France in June 1940.

† i.e. by the European Commission in EU Commission Regulation (EC) No. 2257/94.

Going to war without France is like going deer-hunting without your accordion.
GENERAL NORMAN SCHWARZKOPF, US COMMANDER OF COALITION FORCES DURING THE GULF WAR, 1990–1

France seem to have returned to an *entente cordiale*. Matters were helped during the presidency of the more NATO-friendly Nicolas Sarkozy, dubbed by barbed French opinion as *Sarko l'Américain*.* Sarkozy's keenness to dive into Libya would have been worthy of George W. Bush himself. More recently, the French have played a role of no small significance on the world stage, even winning the praise of US Vice President Joe Biden in February 2013 for their proactive stance against Islamist militants in Mali.

Will the treacherous Froggies and perfidious Albion ever get over their mutual mistrust of each other? Never, perhaps. But one thing is certain, and that is that their future in war and peace is forever intertwined. Just as, in many a corner of a foreign field, there lies a richer dust concealed – more, in fact, of that British dust in northern France than in any other country in the world.

Myth Evaluation: *False. There are heroes and villains on all sides in war.*

* Many French were horrified when Sarkozy brought France back into the NATO integrated military command structure, which it had left in the 1960s. This was seen as the ultimate betrayal of Gaullist values and proved that 'Sarko' was a traitor.

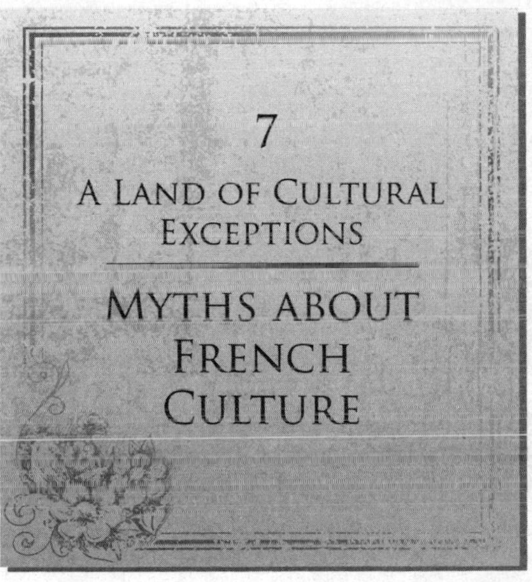

7
A Land of Cultural Exceptions

Myths about French Culture

The French are paranoid about their language

In Paris they simply stared when I spoke to them in French; I never did succeed in making those idiots understand their language.

MARK TWAIN, AMERICAN NOVELIST AND HUMOURIST (1835–1910)

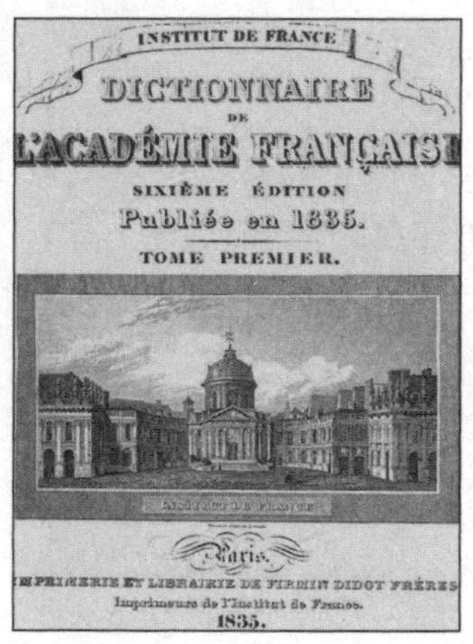

INSTITUT DE FRANCE

DICTIONNAIRE

DE

L'ACADÉMIE FRANÇAISE

SIXIÈME ÉDITION

Publiée en 1835.

TOME PREMIER.

Paris.

IMPRIMERIE ET LIBRAIRIE DE FIRMIN DIDOT FRÈRES

Imprimeurs de l'Institut de France.

1835.

For generations of visitors to France from the English side of the Channel, the scenario is an all too depressingly familiar one. It runs something like this. Using his or her rusty – but possibly still serviceable – school French, the British tourist makes a game effort to order a *café au lait* or *verre de vin rouge* in the language of the locals. In response to these halting efforts, the typical Gallic waiter's reaction is a sneer, followed by a quick switch of the conversation to (inevitably very bad, heavily accented) English. For foreign visitors to France, such supercilious rejection of their tentative forays into the language of Molière is deeply disheartening. So much so that many British people living in France give up trying to communicate with the locals, and simply hang out with other expats instead. And then, of course, the French have the temerity to complain that the British and Americans 'don't bother to speak their language'.

The mixture of pride, *hauteur* and lurking insecurity that is felt by the French towards their language and its status in the world, particularly relative to the dreaded *langue de Shakespeare*, has deep and complex roots. In this context, one should not forget (the French never do) that the language of Molière really *was*, once, the primary language of government, the ruling classes, and culture in the Western world. From the days of the cunning and ruthless Cardinal de Richelieu (1586–1642) – credited by some as the world's first diplomat* – to the mid-twentieth century, French was the language of international diplomacy. The multitude of diplomatic terms of French origin still in use today bears this out: *accord, attaché, aide mémoire, communiqué, entente, détente, chargé d'affaires*... the list goes on. The French language has also traditionally dominated many areas of culture and the arts, synonymous with the most exalted and refined tastes. The terminology of the loftiest branches of the culinary world, for example, even the word *cuisine* itself, derives from French; as does the language of classical *ballet*, itself also a French word.†

Even in England, the language of the ruling classes was for many centuries not English but the Gallic tongue. After the Norman Conquest of 1066, William the Conqueror established French as the official language of England. Consequently, though English remained the language of the common people, the northern French dialect called the *langue d'oïl* became the language of the English court, parliament and aristocracy. (Even so, some Norman kings are reputed to have uttered obscenities in English, since profanities apparently sounded more forceful in the Anglo-Saxon vernacular.) Several English monarchs of the medieval period barely spoke English at all. Richard *Coeur de Lion* or 'the Lionheart' (r. 1189–99), for instance, was famously uninterested in England: he grew up speaking French in Poitiers, hardly spoke a word of English, and kept away from England as much as possible, spending most of his short reign fighting the

---

* The great American diplomat, Henry Kissinger, credits Richelieu as the first diplomat worthy of the appellation in his book *Diplomacy* (1994). Richelieu notably developed the concept of *la raison d'état*, or the idea that there are in certain circumstances reasons for pursuing a line of foreign policy that override other legal or moral considerations.

† Although ballet technically originated in Renaissance Italy, it was in France under Louis XIV that classical ballet truly developed. An avid dancer himself, Louis founded the first ballet academy, the *Académie royale de danse*, in 1661. To this day, French remains the international language of the ballet world, and countless ballet terms are French-derived: *alonge, arabesque, attitude, barre* and *battement*, to name but a few.

Third Crusade. In fact, it was not until Henry V (r. 1413–22) that the English language began to come to the fore; Henry was the first monarch to promote the use of English in court and government, as well as the first English king since the Norman Conquest to use English in his personal correspondence. And even when English was finally established as the official language of court and government, English monarchs were generally perfectly conversant in French as a second language until the seventeenth century, when Dutch took over briefly (with the arrival of William III), followed by a settled tradition of German (with the advent of the Hanoverians).

Perhaps with an eye to preserving its lofty associations with power and the ruling classes, the French have throughout history shown a particular zeal in protecting the purity of their language. As early as 1635, Cardinal Richelieu founded an extraordinary institution to police and safeguard the French tongue – the *Académie française*, which survives to this day. Presided over by forty sage dignitaries known as the *Immortels* ('Immortals'), the principal role of the *Académie française* is to pronounce on the correct usage of the French language (although technically, its opinions are advisory and do not have the force of law). To this end the *Académie* periodically publishes new editions of a vast dictionary of the French language called *Dictionnaire de l'Académie française*, the ninth edition of which has kept the *Immortels* busy for the past twenty years (the first volume: *A–Enzyme* – appeared in 1992; the second: *Eocène–Mappemonde* – in 2000). Since the *Académie's* foundation, over 700 distinguished persons have graced the ranks of the Immortals. They are chosen from the highest ranks of government, literature, philosophy and the arts; of these, a grand total of six have been women.* Needless

Mathematicians are like Frenchmen: whatever you say to them they translate into their own language, and forthwith it is something entirely different.

JOHANN WOLFGANG VON GOETHE, GERMAN WRITER (1749–1832), *MAXIMS AND REFLECTIONS*, 1832

* An *Immortel* is designated as such for life, and very few of these dignitaries have been divested of their title. Those who were included some collabo-

to say, the *Académie* is not an institution associated with radicalism or innovation: it was, for example, one of the principal objectors to French regional languages being given protected status under the French constitution in 2008. It has been subject to much ridicule by the more radical elements of the French literary establishment – including the French playwright Edmond Rostand, himself an Academician, who in his 1897 play *Cyrano de Bergerac* included a recitation of the names of the first generation of *Immortels* (all of whom had been long forgotten).

Despite the best efforts of institutions like the *Académie*, one of the principal historical obstacles to a codified French language came from within France itself: namely, the absence of a single language spoken throughout the country. Until relatively recently, in fact, it could be argued that France was hardly a 'country' at all, but more a hotch-potch of regional tribes with different languages, dialects and customs. The Northern French dialect – the *langue d'oïl* – had a natural advantage, in that it was the language spoken in Paris and the surrounding region. This was the dialect that was to develop into modern French. After the fall of the monarchy in 1789, the heirs of the French Revolution decided that the only way to unify the country was

rators in the Vichy regime of the Second World War, most famously Marshal Philippe Pétain, head of state of Vichy France.

Into the face of the young man who sat on the terrace of the Hotel Magnifique at Cannes there had crept a look of furtive shame, the shifty hangdog look which announces that an Englishman is about to speak French.

P. G. WODEHOUSE, ENGLISH COMIC NOVELIST (1881–1975), *THE LUCK OF THE BODKINS*, 1935

to stamp out all other languages apart from French. Shortly after the Revolution, a government report – appropriately entitled 'On the need and ways to annihilate dialects and universalize the use of French' – noted that only 3 million of the total population of 25 million in France at that date actually spoke French.[1] How was the civilizing language of Voltaire to be brought to this unruly Babel of different tongues? The answer was – by outlawing all dialects and regional languages, and imposing a uniform standard of French. As a 1794 report on regional languages by the revolutionary zealot Bertrand Barère de Vieuzac made clear:

'Federalism and superstition speak Breton; emigration and hatred for the Republic speak German; counter-revolution speaks Italian, and fanaticism speaks Basque. Let us destroy these instruments of damage and error.'[2]

Revolutionary legislation ensured the propagation of French as the unified national language in a number of ways: the conversion of private schools into state schools, where the language of instruction was French; a decree banning the use of German in Alsace; a decree to ensure that the population would not be 'abused' by the use of regional languages; and a decree enforcing the use of French for official purposes.[3]

The policy of linguistic centralization was sustained in France throughout the nineteenth century, reaching its peak in the reforms of the revered statesman Jules Ferry, who as French minister of public instruction in the 1880s laid the basis of the modern, secular French education system. Even to this day – when regional languages have been all but eradicated in France – the fear of them and their perceived potential for creating discord has not completely abated. France has not, for example, ratified the European Charter of Regional or Minority Languages, which would give regional languages official status (as the UK has done with Welsh and Irish, among others). The

French government did, however, concede regional languages a 'protected' if not 'official' status, by a revision to the French constitution in 2008, recognizing regional languages as part of the 'patrimony of France'.* In other words, regional languages have about the same status as French regional cheeses: quaint relics of the past, adding a splash of local colour and piquancy to a summer vacation spiced with a few Breton songs accompanied by bagpipes. And with about as much political clout as a lump of Camembert.

Having eradicated regional languages, the French government was faced with a new threat to linguistic purity in the latter half of the twentieth century: foreign invasion in the form of English terms entering the French language. The first blast of the trumpet against the monstrous regiment of new words was sounded in 1964, with a book that caused a furore in France – *Parlez-vous franglais?*, by René Étiemble. 'Franglais' is the incorporation of English words into French, and *Parlez-vous franglais?* was a tirade against the colonization of the French language by such words: 'le weekend', 'le businessman', 'le boss', 'le playboy', 'le shopping', etc. According to Étiemble, the French language would soon lose its status as a 'pure' language of culture, turning France into a trashy country of 'free enterprise' and 'hamburgers, cheeseburgers and eggburgers – filthy things that I didn't eat even when I was poor in Chicago'.[4] Concern over the new linguistic threat grew over succeeding decades, leading to the enactment of a new law to try to stem the onslaught – the so-called 'Toubon Law' of 1994. Under the provisions of Toubon, the use of French was obligatory in official government publications; French as the predominant language

The French don't care what they do actually, as long as they pronounce it properly.

PROFESSOR HENRY HIGGINS PRONOUNCES ON THE FRENCH, IN THE FILM *MY FAIR LADY*, 1964

* France has stated that it is constitutionally blocked from ratifying the Charter, since to do so would jeopardize the status of French as the single official language of the state. As noted above, the constitutional concession of 2008 was objected to by the *Académie française*. President François Hollande, however, has declared that he intends to ratify the Charter.

was a requirement for schools to receive state funding; advertisements had to be in French, or if in English, with a French translation; and legal or other key documents in the workplace – such as computer manuals – had to be in French.

In addition to the Toubon Law, the *Académie française* was also drafted in to stem the onrushing tide of English words, by inventing French equivalents and attempting to impose them on the public. Thus the *Académie* caused a stir in 2003, when it rejected the words then in use by French people for 'email' (*e-mail*, *mail* and *mél*) as too close to English. Instead, the *Académie* declared that the word used by French Canadians, *courriel*, was the correct native word (somewhat ironically, as Canadian French would usually be looked down upon by purists as not 'true' French). A few days after the *Académie*'s decree, the French culture ministry banned the use of the word 'email' in any official or government documents. It has been of little use – most French people still use the words *mail* or *mél*, and not *courriel*. And many advertisers flout the Toubon Law, which requires a French translation of non-French words, by brazen use of *Franglais*. '*Pokez, taggez, likez!*' proclaims an Orange France advertisement to young users. '*Have fun, c'est Noel!*' says another, for Etam lingerie. The Toubon Law, in fact, has become something of a national joke.

There is, in fact, an argument that it is precisely the French obsession with the 'purity' and 'correctness' of their language that has contributed to its downfall. In other words, French linguistic chauvinism goes a long way to explaining why French is not the universal language of world business today (as it was once the international language of diplomacy). 'English,' George Bernard Shaw once quipped, 'is the easiest language to speak badly.' The English language is massacred every day in boardrooms, hotels and restaurants around the world, but nobody cares because as long as what is being said is understood, it doesn't matter if you cannot distinguish correctly between the simple present and present continuous tenses, or do not make the proper elisions between words, or generally speak English with an execrable accent. The French, on the other hand, will always correct you if you don't speak with the precision of a school textbook, and take great delight in doing so. They have a habit of telling you how much more difficult, how much 'richer' their language is than English (even though English has a vocabulary approximately five times larger than French).* In spite of all attempts by the French to stem the English linguistic incursion, however, the invaders keep on coming. The latest threat to French linguistic purity comes, of course, from the Internet, and the French have responded characteristically by setting up a watchdog to guard the chastity of their technical jargon. Among the snappy French equivalents proposed for English computer and Internet terms are *informaticien bricoleur* for 'geek' and *élément d'une image numérique* for 'pixel'. As yet, though, there is no official committee to police the influx of new (English) social networking terms, so, for the time being, you can write *un blogue*, *poker* someone on Facebook, and *tweeter* fellow *twittos*. A particular problem is posed by the subversive younger generation of French, who plunder US television series, bagging colourful words that they then use in ways unauthorized by the *Académie* – such as the *très cool* term *swag*. (*Avoir le swag* means to be 'classy' or 'hip'.) Not to mention the evocative, rebellious and impenetrably rich *argot* or slang coming out of the immigrant housing estates, in the *banlieues*.

Yet the latest word on the street is that the French may finally be loosening up a little on the linguistic front. Ministers in the Socialist government of François Hollande, elected in May 2012, have actually been heard hazarding a few sentences in English – and even German – on occasion. Some courses at the major French élite educational institutions, or *grandes écoles*, such as Sciences Po (*L'Institut d'études politiques de Paris* or Paris Institute of Political Studies) are now in English as well as French. And there is even a proposal to teach English in primary school

* The French are convinced that their language is more difficult than English, and therefore superior. The fact is that the two languages present completely different challenges. French has greater grammatical complexity and more rules than English, but when those rules are mastered, there is great consistency in their application. English is a language of few rules, but a thousand exceptions and idiosyncrasies that must be individually mastered.

at *Cours Préparatoire* level (Year 2).* In a marked difference of opinion from the stance traditionally adopted by their government, 90 per cent of French people in a 2012 survey regarded the arrival of new words in the French language as a good thing.[5] Every year, some 20,000 new words jostle for recognition in the French language; a privileged few will make it into the dictionaries. Indeed, Gallic publishers are even mooting the shockingly revolutionary idea that a dictionary might record the French language as actually used by people in daily life, as opposed to the officially authorized usage. There is even an annual festival of the *mot-valise*, the French translation of a 'portmanteau word', or – as Lewis Carroll's Humpty Dumpty put it – two meanings packed up into one word. The former presidential candidate Ségolène Royal herself unwittingly coined one a few years back, when she referred to *bravitude* (*brave* + *attitude*): surely an endorsement of lexical innovation from the highest authority. In fact, while linguistic traditionalists are fruminous about it, the radicals are chortling in glee; for finally, it seems, the smog of tradition may have lifted from the French languagescape.

Myth Evaluation: *Historically true, although this appears to be finally changing.*

---

* The recent government efforts to improve the quality of English teaching in French schools was in response to the general recognition that French ability in English was abysmal and actually handicapping young French people in the international workplace. The TOEFL results of 2008 placed France 69th out of 109 countries for proficiency in the English language.

French pop music is irredeemably naff

Life is always love and desolation – life is always the same songs.
GEORGES BRASSENS, FRENCH *CHANSONNIER* (1921–81)

It is an established fact: the French are as bad at pop music as they are brilliant at *haute cuisine*. Or at least, so we like to think. For while we are quite happy to accept the outstanding contributions the Gallic race has made to classical music – with names such as Berlioz, Bizet, Debussy or Fauré regularly topping British concert bills – we are less ready to accept their musical output of a more populist kind. It is part of a wider myth that the French can do 'high' culture, but are rubbish at 'pop' culture – the preserve, naturally, of the British and Americans. France's historic pop-musical isolationism is underlined by the fact that, although Anglo-American songs have often made it big in France, French-language songs in the UK charts are rarer than snow in June.* 'French rock music,' John Lennon once said, 'is like English wine.' The chilling put-down has haunted French pop music ever since.

In the mind of the average Briton, the words 'French pop music' conjure up traumatic images of televised Eurovision Song Contests featuring Gallic crooners with permed mullets and backing singers in satin hotpants. Among further offences to be taken into consideration: the writers of the 1980s song 'Agadoo' by Black Lace (recently voted the fourth most annoying pop song of all time)† [6] were French; the country's most famous rock star is a superannuated Elvis wannabe with the unlikely moniker 'Johnny Hallyday' (real name Jean-Philippe Smet); and the second-best-selling pop song of all time in France is '*Danse*

* There are, of course, the rare exceptions that prove the rule: such as the Belgian Plastic Bertrand, whose vaguely punkish *Ça plane pour moi* made number 8 in the UK singles chart in 1978.

† 'Agadoo' was originally recorded in French in 1971 by Michel Delancray and Mya Symille, and was the Club Med theme song from 1974. It was re-released by Black Lace in 1984.

des canards', the French version of 'The Birdie Song' (the number one most annoying song of all time in the aforementioned poll)[7]. Need one say more? Well, perhaps just a little…

The first and most important thing to know about French pop music is that it is intimately and inextricably linked to an age-old French genre of song called the *chanson*. It is hard to explain to a non-French person what the *chanson* is: like an elephant, one knows it when one sees it (or rather hears it), but it is difficult to define. It is, basically, a ballad. The modern *chanson* grew out of the popular music played in the French cabarets and dance halls of the late nineteenth century, producing such acknowledged masters of the genre as Edith Piaf and subsequently Jacques Brel, Mireille Mathieu, Charles Trenet, Georges Brassens and Léo Ferré, to name but a few (ironically, the great Jacques Brel, the ultimate exponent of the French *chanson*, was in fact Belgian). The *chanson* was a genre of music intimately linked to the lives of ordinary people, recording the joys and sorrows of the everyday and mundane, with often thoughtful, even poetic lyrics and the simple accompaniment of piano, guitar or accordion. Above all, the *chanson* is and has always been quintessentially *French* – as much a part of the French cultural landscape as Gauloises and *vin ordinaire*.

> *For most of the past 50 years, French music has not been cool, with a reputation stuck between 'Allo 'Allo-style theme tunes and a desperate desire to ape Anglo-Saxon sounds, the latter with cringe-worthy results often delivered in breathless Franglais.*
>
> TOM DE CASTELLA, *BBC NEWS MAGAZINE*, NOVEMBER 2010

In the 1950s and 1960s, however, a giant wave from the outside world burst onto the French popular music scene, threatening to sweep everything (including the *chanson*) aside: the tide of rock 'n' roll, led by Elvis and a host of rockabillies, swiftly followed by The Beatles and The Rolling Stones. Everybody the world over wanted to groove to the new beat, but the French public (not unreasonably) wanted to groove to it in their own language. Enter the *grand fromage* of French rock, Johnny Hallyday. Johnny *who*? You will have to trust me on this one, but Johnny Hallyday is the biggest French pop star ever. He is probably the biggest pop star of whom you have never heard. Indeed, 'Johnny' (as he is affectionately known in his native land) is a star of such gigantic proportions there that a 2006 French film had as its central conceit a nightmarish parallel world in which Johnny Hallyday doesn't exist (unthinkable for most French people, reality for everybody else).[8]

The 'Johnny phenomenon' presents an enduring puzzle to foreigners. Why all this un-ironic fuss and bother about a guy with a quiff and a bad line in Mad Max outfits, who seems to spend most of his time belting out cover versions of British and American rock classics like 'Let's Twist Again' ('*Viens danser le twist*')? Because, quite simply, 'Johnny' more or less single-handedly brought *le rock 'n' roll* to France, while remaining canny enough to alternate the new beat with French *chansons* to keep the traditionalists happy. It was down to him that the French could persuade themselves that they were participating in the rock 'n' roll revolution as equals, rather than as victims of Anglo-American musical colonization. The French have idolized him ever since; to everybody else, he remains the biggest French cultural exception.*

Johnny's groundbreaking exploits gave rise to a whole new slew of French pop singers in the 1960s, collectively known as the 'yé yé generation'. Some acts were purely imitative, but many were the real deal. And the biggest deal of all was Serge Gainsbourg. A chain-smoker and alcoholic who introduced designer stubble as a style statement, Gainsbourg made high art of bad taste, with songs as diverse in their subject matter as farting, oral sex, incest, cabbages, urination, and Nazi death camps.† Undoubtedly his most (in)famous song, the duet '*Je t'aime...*

---

* For a full explanation of this term, see the chapter on French cinema (page 229). The phrase 'French cultural exception' was first used in the context of the negotiated French exception to the provisions of the GATT relating to cinema. It has subsequently been extended to include all areas in which the French are perceived to be unique in cultural terms.

† Making an art of bad taste is not, in fact, a new concept in French cultural output. As early as 1857, Charles Baudelaire shocked the public with a poem in his collection *Les Fleurs du Mal* called '*Une Charogne*' ('A Carcass'), in which he daringly compared a woman he was courting to the rotting corpse of a dead animal.

moi non plus' (performed with his lover, the English actress Jane Birkin, in 1969) refers to him as a wave entering and receding from the loins of his lover.* The soundtrack included such orgasmic pants and groans that it was long believed it had been recorded by placing a tape recorder under the couple's bed. On its release, the song was instantly banned in most countries and

was denounced by the Vatican (which also excommunicated the record executive who had released it in Italy). Gainsbourg reacted by stating that the Pope was 'our best PR man'.

Gainsbourg continued to shock and titillate the French bourgeoisie throughout the 1970s and 1980s, notably by recording in 1979 a reggae version of the French national anthem, *La Marseillaise*; by burning a 500-franc note on live television in 1984; and by recording a song called 'Lemon Incest' with his then twelve-year-old daughter Charlotte, featuring a cover with them sprawled semi-naked on a bed. On his death at the relatively early age of 62 (his obituary in the newspaper *Libération*

* '*Je t'aime... moi non plus*' was originally recorded in 1967 by Serge Gainsbourg with Brigitte Bardot, but after one scandalous broadcast on the radio station Europe I, Bardot's then husband, the German businessman Gunter Sachs, threatened legal action. The couple split up shortly after the broadcast. At Bardot's request, the Bardot/Gainsbourg recording of the song was not played on the radio again and has never been officially released.

claimed he had died because '*il a bu trop de cigarettes*' – 'he drank too many cigarettes'),[9] he received something close to a state funeral, while President Mitterrand eulogized him as 'our Baudelaire, our Apollinaire'. Gainsbourg had managed to take elements from the 'new' music coming from abroad and combine it with the French *chanson* to create something that was quintessentially French: as heady and lethal as a pack of *Gauloises*.

Everything ends with a song.

PIERRE-AUGUSTIN CARON DE BEAUMARCHAIS, FRENCH PLAYWRIGHT AND REVOLUTIONARY (1732–99)

As for the present, recent French polls indicate that the *chanson* is still a big hitter, drawing 51 per cent of the total music-listening French public (although the share of *chanson* is gradually giving way to mainstream rock and pop music, including international pop).[10] The classic *chansons*, with their focus on universal and everyday issues, do not really date. Unlike Anglo-American pop songs, which tend to deal in angst-ridden teenage problems, the subject matter of the French *chanson* reflects life in all its stages. For example, it is hard to imagine the average English chart topper dealing with such uncool subjects as a child-custody battle, the love of an elderly married couple, attachment to one's home town, or the destruction of a small terraced Paris garden to make room for a parking lot.* But this is one of the charms of the French *chanson*. It doesn't have to be about chains and whips, not wanting to go into rehab, or everything being cool because you're getting thinner or smacking up your bitch. (This said, some *chansons* are best left shrouded in obscurity. Do, for example, try to avoid Eddy Mitchell – he of the bouffant hair and skimpy leather jackets – and Gilbert Bécaud. Generally, any French singer with an English name – Johnny Hallyday, Eddy Mitchell, Dick Rivers – should be approached with extreme caution.) Whereas the Anglo-American tradition tends to identify a song very strongly with its originator, the French take the view

* The songs referred to are, respectively: '*Mon Fils, ma Bataille*' (Daniel Balavoine); '*Les Vieux Mariés*' (Michel Sardou); '*Toulouse*' (Claude Nougaro); and '*Le Petit Jardin*' (Jacques Dutronc).

that a good song floats free of the original singer and becomes part of the national canon, open to reinterpretation across the generations. For instance, a classic like '*Ne me quitte pas*' (literally 'Don't leave me', but popularized in English as the ballad 'If You Go Away'), originally composed and sung by Jacques Brel in 1959, has subsequently been reinterpreted over fifty times, by such diverse artistes as Edith Piaf, Barbara, Johnny Hallyday, Jane Birkin, Juliette Gréco, Nana Mouskouri, Nina Simone and Sting. In France, cover versions, far from being naff, are seen as a way of keeping good songs alive, fresh and relevant. This applies not only to French songs, but foreign songs too: I for one rediscovered English songs like Kate Bush's 'Wuthering Heights' and 4 Non Blondes' 'What's Up' through French cover versions. Classic songs in France thus tend to reinforce the link between generations – the children of each decade have their quintessential expression of '*Ne me quitte pas*'. In Britain, by contrast, each generation tends to identify very strongly with a particular era of pop music, so reinforcing generational divides.

Outside of and overlapping with the *chanson*, the French pop music scene today is hugely rich and complex. French rap and hip hop make up the second-largest market in the world, with Parisian rap groups such as Sexion d'Assaut regularly topping the charts. French electronic dance music is also an international chart leader, with bands such as Air and Daft Punk hitting the decks of DJs around the world (dance music has the undoubted advantage of few if any words, and so is more easily exportable than the traditional *chanson*). Multilingual singer Manu Chao mixes languages with Spanish-French tracks like '*Me Gustas Tu*'. Even the infamous *frog rock* so despised by John Lennon has undergone winds of change with the advent of French rock bands such as the Bordeaux group Noir Désir ('Black Desire').*

* Noir Désir have frequently been compared to their gurus The Doors, and certainly the lead singer Bertrand Cantat seems to have followed in Jim Morrison's footsteps in terms of the melodramas of his life: he was imprisoned for the killing of his girlfriend Marie Trintignant (daughter of veteran actor Jean-Louis Trintignant) in 2003, and his wife subsequently committed suicide in 2010. The band dissolved shortly after the Trintignant killing, but they had already towered over the French rock scene for twenty years with

DOING IT CLOCLO'S WAY

It is a little-known fact that the classic ballad 'My Way,' made world-famous by the Italian-American crooner Frank Sinatra, was originally a French song. It was first made a hit in 1967 by the French pop star Claude François (1939–78), under the title '*Comme d'habitude*' ('As Usual'), the lyrics telling the story of a couple going through the motions of life together as their relationship breaks down. It is thought that the original lyrics referred to the breakdown of Claude François' then relationship with the petite blonde star of the 'yé-yé generation', France Gall. The American lyricist Paul Anka heard Claude François singing '*Comme d'habitude*' during a holiday in the south of France and reset the melody to English lyrics as 'My Way', completely changing the theme to one of a man looking back on his life. In the hands of Ol' Blue Eyes it became a global smash hit, the most-recognized pop song in the world today and frequently chosen by people to be played at their, or their relatives', funerals.

Affectionately known to his adoring French public by the nickname 'Cloclo', Claude François died at the untimely age of 39 when he was accidentally electrocuted in the shower in his Paris apartment. With his blonde flick and glitter suits, he was for many years derided by the French intelligentsia as a naff homegrown version of Liberace, a purveyor of songs heavy in schmaltz and light in content. But more recently he has been re-evaluated by a generation nostalgic for the upbeat melodies of a happier age. His annoyingly catchy song '*Alexandrie Alexandra*' is still a French disco standard, and '*Comme d'habitude*' remains one of the best-selling French pop songs of all time.

their poetically tortured songs. Listen, for example, to the haunting ballad '*Le Vent nous portera*'. Morrison himself, of course, was famously interred in Père-Lachaise cemetery in Paris after dying of a heroin overdose in the French capital in 1971. His graffiti-covered sepulchre has become a place of pilgrimage for angst-ridden teenagers of all nationalities.

In fact, it all seems a long way from the satin hotpants of the Eurovision Song Contest. And now, perhaps, it is the smug world of English-language popular music that needs to watch out. The French are striking back, with revenge attacks on the excesses of bad taste of a different kind peddled by Anglo-American pop music. Early in 2012, for example, French comedian/singer Max Boublil released 'Put your sex in the air', a song that takes a sharply satirical swipe at the Rihannas and Lady Gagas of this world, who pepper their song lyrics with words and phrases that are, some might say, not wholly appropriate to their early teenage audience. Boublil's song runs: '*Dans mes chansons j'aime faire des danses obscènes / Pour que mes petits fans de douze ans refassent le même*' ('In my songs I like to do obscene dances, so that my twelve-year-old fans can do the same…'). In all probability, the title of Boublil's song alludes to Rihanna's 'S&M', which contains the lines 'Sex in the air, I don't care, I love the smell of it…'

So next time you hear a French pop song and snigger, think again. They might just be sniggering at you, too.

Myth Evaluation: *False.*

French films are uniformly pretentious

French films follow a basic formula: Husband sleeps with Jeanne because Bernadette cuckolded him sleeping with Christophe, and in the end they all go off to a restaurant.
SOPHIE MARCEAU, FRENCH ACTRESS (*OBSERVER* INTERVIEW, 26 MARCH 1995)

The air is filled with the sound of seagulls screaming. Jerkily, the camera pans past some sections of concrete pipe towards an enormous rubbish tip that towers on the horizon. At the edge of the rubbish tip, a woman with blonde, flowing locks sits on a chair, gazing moodily into space. She holds a large cabbage on her lap. A man in a loosely-tied cravat and dark glasses, with a cigarette hanging out of his mouth, sidles up to her. There is a long silence, punctuated only by the incessant cries of the gulls. '*Bonjour*,' he says, finally. '*Bonjour*,' she replies, after a pause. 'I see that you have a cabbage.' 'Yes,' she replies. They remain staring for a while in moody silence…

Georges Franju: Movies should have a beginning, a middle and an end.
Jean-Luc Godard: Certainly, but not necessarily in that order.
INTERVIEW IN *TIME* MAGAZINE, 14 SEPTEMBER 1981

The opening sequence of a late Godard movie? One might be forgiven for thinking so. In fact, this is the opening scene of a Monty Python sketch ('French Subtitled Film') from the legendary BBC comedy series of the 1970s.[11] Parody though it is, the skit is easily matched – and even surpassed – by many French films of the *Nouvelle Vague* or New Wave era* for moody silences, clunking symbolism, stilted dialogue and pregnant pauses.

And yet – aside from the excesses of the late New Wave, which have been largely to blame for its not totally unjust reputation for extended exercises in navel-gazing – French cinema has a great

* That is, European and especially French art cinema of the 1950s and 1960s.

TO ANGLO-AMERICANS, THE FLICKS: TO THE FRENCH, THE SEVENTH ART

The curious term 'the seventh art' is frequently used by the French to describe the cinema, and reveals the deep veneration with which film-making has traditionally been viewed in France, as an art of the highest order. The term derives from the definition by the German philosopher Georg Wilhelm Friedrich Hegel (1770–1831) in his *Lectures on Aesthetics* of the first six arts. The Italian film critic Ricciotta Canudo then invented the term 'seventh art' in a manifesto published in 1911 to describe cinema, which he contended was a synthesis of the spatial arts (architecture, sculpture and painting) with the temporal arts (music and dance). The other six arts are:

First art:	*Architecture*
Second art:	*Sculpture*
Third art:	*Painting*
Fourth art:	*Dance*
Fifth art:	*Music*
Sixth art:	*Poetry*

deal of which to be extremely proud. It was, after all, two French brothers – Auguste and Louis Lumière – who invented the concept of cinema in the first place, giving the world's first commercial public movie screening with ten grainy, hand-cranked projector shorts at the *Salon Indien du Grand Café de Paris* in 1895. Unfortunately, setting what was to become a general precedent for French movie-making – that is, giving birth to *avant-garde* ideas and then leaving others to make a fortune out of popularizing them – the Lumière brothers were loftily convinced that the cinema was 'an invention without any future', deserting film for new photographic projects. Other French film-makers took up the baton to help shape what was to become the dominant new creative medium of the twentieth century: early special effects in the multiple exposures and dissolves of the first 'Cinemagician' Georges Méliès; pioneering work in the first sound movies

by giants of French cinema such as Marcel Carné and Jean Renoir. Son of the illustrious Impressionist painter Pierre-Auguste, Renoir carried the subtle social commentary of his father from canvas to the silver screen for a new age.

'Cinema is an industry but it is also – unfortunately – an art,' the French dramatist Jean Anouilh once observed. One of the strengths (and perhaps weaknesses) of French cinema lies in precisely this statement. For to the French, serious cinema has traditionally been primarily an art form, over and above mass entertainment – *le septième art*, or 'seventh art', as it is routinely referred to in the French media (see page 230).Thus, while ordinary French people have traditionally lived on a diet of comedies, the grand set-pieces of 'serious' French art cinema have in the past been the preserve of the chattering classes: the French bourgeoisie and international film critics. The lofty aspirations of French cinema reached their apogee in the hugely influential film magazine *Cahiers du cinéma*, which from the 1950s onwards defined the quintessentially French concept of the film director as *auteur*. That is, that film is essentially a vehicle for the creative vision and voice of the director or *author*, a 'voice' that somehow manages to penetrate through the myriad other voices and elements of the production process. It was faith in the messianic message of the *auteur* that produced the quirky, fabulous, idiosyncratic and sometimes downright freakish films of the French *Nouvelle Vague*.*

* French film-makers were making *avant-garde* and quirky movies even before the *Nouvelle Vague*. As in, for example, the weird Surrealist movie *Un Chien andalou* by Luis Buñuel and Salvador Dali (1929), or Jean Vigo's daring *Zéro de conduite / Zero for Conduct* (1933), an unsettling portrayal of schoolchildren rebelling against institutional violence that inspired Lindsay Anderson's 1968 film *If*.

The films of the 1950s and early 1960s *Nouvelle Vague* included some of the greatest ever made – Godard's *À Bout de souffle* ('Breathless') or Truffaut's *Jules et Jim*, for example – but in later years the movement became a parody of itself, producing exercises in French existential emptiness that were beyond the ken of virtually everyone. Take, for example, Jean-Luc Godard's 1967 movie *Weekend*.[12] A bourgeois couple with secret lovers (incidentally planning to kill each other), take what seems to be an interminable ramble across the French countryside. The film includes a single tracking shot of over eight minutes, following a car crawling through a traffic jam. Subtitles appear at various intervals, providing the viewer with such pearls of wisdom as that he or she is watching a film 'adrift in the cosmos', or a movie which was 'found on a scrapheap' (possibly revealing the inspiration for the Monty Python sketch). The film ends with a scene set in a camp populated by hippie cannibals, during which the viewer is treated to cameo appearances by Emily Brontë and Sir Walter Scott, and a long lecture on the virtues of communism (not forgetting the on-screen killing of a chicken along the way). A film about boredom and pretentiousness, apparently. Or maybe, just a pretentious and boring film?* 'The cinema is truth 24 times per second,' the character Bruno Forestier says in Godard's 1963 movie, *Le Petit Soldat* ('The Little Soldier'). In *Weekend*, we have to endure every one of the 151,200 nanoseconds of 'truth' that make up the film.

As to the French cultural exception, contrary to what has been said by a PDG [company chairman] who subsequently lost his job, it is not dead: it consists in making exceptionally boring movies, exceptionally rubbish books, and in general works of art that are exceptionally pretentious and self-satisfied. It goes without saying that I include my own work in this sad statement.

FRÉDÉRIC BEIGBEDER, FRENCH WRITER AND LITERARY CRITIC, *WINDOWS ON THE WORLD*, 2003

Cosseted by a system of subsidies and by the protection conferred by the French 'cultural exception' – and possibly also

* Another New Wave director in whose splendidly aesthetic films very little happens is Eric Rohmer. A character in the 1975 US film *Night Moves* describes watching Rohmer's films as 'kind of like watching paint dry'.

wishing to put clear blue water between their high-minded *oeuvre cinématographique* and the popular American blockbuster – French art-house cinema makers in the 1990s took to producing extensive, tedious exercises in navel contemplation.* Take the *Three Colours* trilogy of films by the Polish-French film director Krzysztof Kieślowski, for example. In *Three Colours Blue* (1993)[13] – possibly the most animated of the three movies – there is hardly any dialogue whatsoever, but instead a lot of pregnant pauses during which Juliette Binoche stares at a cup of coffee in a café or lasciviously licks a blue lolly. It is a combination of soft porn and pseudo-intellectualism that characterizes much of this period of French art-house cinema, possibly designed to appeal to the *louche* Serge Gainsbourg types who once hung out in cafés on the Left Bank. There is, in fact, a brief period in early adulthood when these kinds of film do appeal, especially to male university students, largely because they combine soft porn with a cred-salvaging leavening of intellectual angst.

Unsurprisingly, the general French public does not flock in droves to see these art-house films, which seem to be mainly designed as a French cultural export in the same way that the Merchant-Ivory genre of films were for Britain in the 1980s. (Existential angst in unfitted Parisian kitchens did for French cinema what lavish Edwardian period sets featuring top British actors – playing genteel heroes struggling with repressed emotions – did for British cinema in the same period.) 'The French cinema lives off its comedies and gives awards to its dramas,' the French comedian Michel Colucci (called 'Coluche') once observed. And true enough, the films that have traditionally been big hits in France are not art-house movies but Holly-

* The French 'cultural exception' is a phrase the French are very fond of using, in a wide sense, almost in any context, to signify their cultural difference from – for which read superiority to – everybody else. In the narrow sense, the French 'cultural exception' was an exception negotiated by the French government to the GATT provisions regulating international trade in the 1990s, with respect to 'cultural' products such as cinema, enabling the French to maintain subsidies for the native French cinema industry and limiting foreign (especially American) film imports.

wood blockbusters, Disney animations and French-made situation comedies (although the art-house movies are generally the ones that carry off the awards at the Cannes Film Festival). In fact, the top-grossing film ever in France is the very American *Titanic*, and the top ten box-office hits include *Snow White and the Seven Dwarfs*, *Gone with the Wind*, *Avatar* and *The Jungle Book*. Of the top ten grossing domestic films, virtually all are comedies.[14]

French situation comedies present something of a puzzle for foreigners. Mainly because – to anybody who is not French – they simply aren't that funny. The buffoonery, in fact, is much like that of Shakespeare or Molière – sharp wit to appeal to the bourgeois members of the audience and slapstick for the groundlings, with little in between. Take, for example, the French hit film *Camping* (2006).[15] This is a comedy set on a beachside campsite, on which a stuck-up Parisian and his daughter land by accident. Horrified at first to find themselves in such unrefined company, they end up being spiritually renewed, their bourgeois hang-ups exorcised by the jolly camaraderie of the working-class campers. A key running gag in the film is an extended wordplay on the expression *rouler une pelle* (literally 'to roll a spade'), meaning 'to kiss with tongues' (i.e. to French kiss). A woman in the throes of a midlife crisis reproaches her husband that he doesn't kiss her with a 'spade' any more. The point is hammered home with repeated visual references to 'spades' both in the literal and metaphorical sense. Of course, at the end of the movie, sundry mishaps and marital affairs later, they do enjoy a raunchy 'spade' kiss. French audiences find all this hilarious.

There is little doubt that there has been a general *mésentente cordiale* between the French and the Anglo-Saxons as to what is funny in a film. This is illustrated by the fact that many French comedies, huge hits in France, bomb when released abroad. For example, the tastefully named 1982 French comedy film *Le Père Noël est une ordure* ('Father Christmas is a shit') was a spectacular flop in the US. And yet the French can be considered world leaders in certain types of humour – satire, for example (as can be seen in the distinguished tradition of French cartoons and

THE TOP TEN HIGHEST-GROSSING FILMS IN FRANCE

1. *Titanic* (1998)
2. *Bienvenue chez les Ch'tis* (2008)*
3. *The Intouchables* (2011)
4. *Snow White and the Seven Dwarfs* (1938)
5. *La Grande Vadrouille* (1966)*
6. *Gone with the Wind* (1950)
7. *Once upon a time in the West* (1969)
8. *Avatar* (2009)
9. *The Jungle Book* (1968)
10. *One Hundred and One Dalmatians* (1961)

(* = French comedies)

Figures: J.P.'s Box Office, March 2013

THE TOP TEN HIGHEST-GROSSING FRENCH FILMS IN THE WORLD

1. *The Intouchables* (2011)
2. *Taken 2* (2012)
3. *The Fifth Element* (1997)
4. *Bienvenue chez les Ch'tis* (2008)
5. *Taken* (2008)
6. *Amélie* (2001)
7. *Perfume* (2006)
8. *The Artist* (2011)
9. *Asterix at the Olympic Games* (2008)
10. *March of the Penguins* (2005)

Figures: J.P.'s Box Office, February 2013

the daily TV satire of the French equivalent of *Spitting Image*, *Les Guignols de l'info*). And then there are classic French comedies of a nostalgically gentle kind, like Jacques Tati's *M. Hulot's Holiday* (1953). The French are also masters of black humour –

the very term *humour noir* was coined by the French Surrealist André Breton. 'Humour is like coffee – best taken black,' the French wit Bertrand Cèbe once remarked, and perhaps thanks to their heritage of the Revolution combined with existential angst and a blanket rejection of political correctness, the French love nothing so much as a wickedly morbid jest. Take a *soupçon* of the truly *tragique*, mix in a hint of the *absurde*, stir it up with a *tabou* or two, and a touch even of *sadisme*, and you have the classic French joke: as dark as a *café noir* and sharp as a guillotine. So why does this biting humour not come through in the traditional French comedy? Why was *film noir* an American invention rather than a French one?

There is nevertheless a wind of change blowing through French cinema. Since the early 2000s, a whole new crop of French films has been coming out: films that have a complex humour much subtler than wordplay or farce; films that are wickedly whimsical, reflecting out to the world rather than inwards to the director's umbilicus. A renegade breed of French film directors has begun to break down the traditional French divide between 'art-house' and 'commercial', producing darkly funny, quirky or moving films that have been huge world box-office successes (*Amélie, L'Auberge espagnole, The Artist, The Intouchables*). Many of these directors have spent time studying abroad, outside the restrictions of the French cinema schools. They include, for example, Cédric Klapisch, the director of *L'Auberge espagnole* ('The Spanish Apartment', 2002), who was rejected by the major French film schools because of his apparent lack of reverence for the classics of French cinema, and so studied in the United States instead. *The Intouchables / Intouchables* (2011)[16] is a so-called 'buddy movie' charting the relationship between an aristocratic quadriplegic and his carer, a young black man from a bleak local housing estate who has just been released from jail. The possibilities for crassness and mawkish sentimentality in such a set-up are legion. Yet the film manages to steer a course through all of these potential pitfalls, being moving and – most surprisingly of all – *funny*, in a daring French way. Only the French, after all, could make a joke as *politiquement incorrecte* as someone playfully pouring boiling water over a paralyzed (and hence unfeeling) person's legs.

The Intouchables became, within months of being released, the second-highest-grossing domestic French film ever. As at March 2013 it was the third-highest-grossing film in France of all time. It has also recently become the highest-grossing French film in the world market, surpassing films like *Amélie* and *The Artist*. But the humour in *The Intouchables* could not be more different from that of the traditional French comedies, and its impact a world away from the navel-contemplation of the worst of the New Wave. In fact, it seems that the French are, at last, moving away from the concept of cinema as the lofty seventh art, and coming round to the idea of cinema as a commercial art. Finally, it seems, there is an alternative to the tedium of waiting for Godard.

Myth Evaluation: *Was once true, is now increasingly false.*

8

City of Light

Myths about Paris

The Left Bank is a haven of writers and intellectuals

Whoever has not experienced the Left Bank of the Seine, between rue Saint-Jacques and rue des Saints-Pères, knows nothing about human life!
HONORÉ DE BALZAC, FRENCH NOVELIST (1799–1850), *LE PÈRE GORIOT*, 1835

The Left Bank (*Rive Gauche*) of Paris is a *quartier* of legend. Its warm hotchpotch of bars, cafés and underground cellars is where the intellectual fabric of the early twentieth century was woven. Cubism, Surrealism, Existentialism, Impressionism – the cafés of the Left Bank (and to a lesser degree, of Montmartre in the north of the city) were the birthplace of most of the -isms of Modernism (if not Modernism itself). But what is meant by the term 'Left Bank'? Geographically, it denotes anywhere on the left bank of the Seine (i.e. on the left-hand side while travelling downstream, or the river's southern bank). However, 'Left Bank' as a cultural term essentially refers to the areas of St Germain-des-Prés and Montparnasse, and the small network of streets in between. The Left Bank is also the student quarter of Paris, being the home of the university of Paris (the Sorbonne) and its various successor institutions. In this context, it is sometimes referred to as the 'Latin Quarter' (named after the Latin spoken at the university in the Middle Ages). What made this miniature piece of Paris the centre of the earth's cultural map, and is it still the hub of the creative world?

The tradition of the Parisian café as a hotbed of artistic, intellectual and political life goes back a long way. Even under the *ancien régime,* King Louis XIV became so anxious about the incendiary political debates going on in the Paris coffee-houses that he sent his police prefect to spy on them.[1] A Revolution and several regime changes later, many things had been turned on (or lost) their heads, but the tradition of the café debate continued. In 1867, the visiting American journalist Edward King observed that 'the huge Paris world centres twice, thrice daily; it is at the café; it gossips at the café, it intrigues at the café; it plots, it dreams, it suffers, it hopes, at the café.'[2] From the mid-nineteenth century onwards, radical artistic groups – notably the Realists and the Impressionists – congregated in cafés on the Left Bank and later in Montmartre. These meeting places became centres of rebellion against the stuffy directives of the French art academy.

As an artist, a man has no home in Europe save in Paris.
FRIEDRICH NIETZSCHE, GERMAN PHILOSOPHER (1844–1900)

The cafés were also temples devoted to the cult of a beverage that became both the nectar and poison of the French intellectual and working classes: absinthe. A lurid green and potently alcoholic cocktail of wormwood, anise and fennel with reputedly hallucinatory effects, absinthe – or the 'green fairy' (*la fée verte*) – was both the muse and the scourge of French poets and writers. Charles Baudelaire, Arthur Rimbaud and Paul Verlaine all struggled against its effects. Baudelaire noted in his diary: 'Now I suffer continually from vertigo, and today, 23 of January 1862, I have received a singular warning. I have felt the wind of the wing of madness pass over me.'[3] The 'green fairy' left her indelible footprint on the café art coming out of France in the late nineteenth century. To her potent spell have been attributed the psychedelic greens and yellows of Van Gogh's paintings, as well as his incipient madness. And many a café portrait of the period reveals the paradox of the absinthe addict, surrounded by jovial company yet trapped in his or her private phantasmagoria of shadows – as in the gloomy Degas café portrait *L'Absinthe* (1876), featuring a working-class woman slumped dejectedly over a glass of green liquor in the cold light of an approaching day, or the lonely figures collapsed in a drunken stupor beneath the sulphurous yellow glare of overhead lights in Van Gogh's *The Night Café*.

While Realists such as Gustave Courbet (he of *The Origin of the World* infamy)* hung out in brasseries on the Left Bank, the Impressionists tended to favour the Right Bank and Montmartre – the area around Batignolles, and subsequently the café *La Nouvelle Athènes* in Pigalle. The real heyday of the Left Bank came in the early twentieth century, in the period between the wars, when the cafés and bars of Montparnasse, and subsequently closer to the river at St Germain-des-Prés, became havens for the 'Lost Generation' that emerged from the devastation of the First World War. The celebrated café *Les Deux Magots* was an important hangout for the Surrealists in the 1930s, whereas the *Brasserie Lipp* was favoured by the political set. Drawn by the intellectual hubbub, *laissez-faire* morals, and a plethora of small printing presses springing up, hundreds of foreign literary and artistic members of the Lost Generation flocked to the area like moths to a candle-flame. James Joyce, Henry Miller, Ezra Pound, F. Scott Fitzgerald, Ernest Hemingway, Pablo Picasso, Djuna Barnes, Ford Madox Ford, Gertrude Stein… all contributed to the rich ferment of ideas brewing in the Left Bank cafés. Gertrude Stein and her partner, Alice B. Toklas, were famed for their Saturday night salon, invitation to which was a passport to recognition for any aspiring artist or writer.

During the Occupation, many went to the cafés simply to avoid freezing. 'Towards the end of the Occupation, in the winter of 1943–44, everyone came there to keep warm,' remarked one writer of the *Café de Flore*. 'One had the impression that the first-floor room was a classroom. Sartre was installed at a little table, writing *Paths of Freedom*, Simone de Beauvoir, at another table, was writing *All Men Are Mortal*… close by, Arthur Adamov was writing too, doubtless one of his plays…'[4]

Jean-Paul Sartre was undisputedly king of the Left Bank. American students came to the *Café de Flore* just to sit in his usual chair, and the café scene made him a bigger star on the world student circuit than such distinguished French predecessors as Montesquieu, Voltaire or Diderot. Simone de Beauvoir

* For more on Courbet and his controversial painting, see the chapter on French women and shaving, on page 96.

America is my country and Paris is my hometown.
GERTRUDE STEIN, AMERICAN AVANT-GARDE ART COLLECTOR AND WRITER (1874–1946)

was also a huge hit with nascent feminists at American universities: like Sylvia Plath two decades later, her combination of severe beauty and tortured women's lib, ferociously feminist yet hopelessly in thrall to a dominating male, were the stuff of sophomore fantasy. Sartre himself wrote of the *Café de Flore*: 'We installed ourselves completely: from 9 to 12 a.m., we worked, then we had lunch, and at 2 p.m. we came back and spoke with friends we had met, until 8 p.m. After having dinner, we received people with whom we had fixed an appointment. This could seem strange to you, but at this Café, we were at home.' He later asserted that, 'during 4 years, the road to the Café was for me the Road to Freedom.' The actress Simone Signoret has even said, 'I was born in March 1941 at night, on a bench of the *Café de Flore*.' Not that everybody was amused. 'Sartre?' the owner of the *Café de Flore* later commented, 'he was my worst client. Hours of scribbling on a piece of paper, sitting in front of a single drink, which he didn't renew from morning to night.'[5]

Despite the furore around Sartre and de Beauvoir, however, after the Second World War the Left Bank was somehow never the same again. There continued to be a flow of writers and artists to the area – notably Samuel Beckett and the new Beat Generation of US writers, including Allen Ginsberg and William Burroughs, who established themselves in a seedy no-star hotel just off the Seine – but the golden age of the Left Bank was drawing to a close. Already by the summer of 1948, the *New Yorker* columnist Janet Flanner (a seasoned resident) was commenting disparagingly about the hordes of American postwar college students flooding St Germain-des-Prés:

'The Café de Flore serves as a drugstore for pretty upstate girls in unbecoming blue denim pants and their Middle Western dates, most of whom are growing Beaux-Arts beards. Members of the tourist intelligentsia patronize the Rue de Bac's Pont-Royal bar, which used to be full of French existentialists and is now full only of themselves, often arguing about existentialism.'[6]

The right-wing backlash after the *événements* of May 1968* made Paris seem dull and conservative, just as other cities around the world were beginning to let their hair down. The United States, for example, which had emerged from the repressive McCarthy era, was suddenly becoming an improbable haven for free speech, with important victories over literary censorship in the court cases concerning Henry Miller's *Tropic of Cancer*, Allen Ginsberg's *Howl*, and William Burroughs' *The Naked Lunch*. In San Francisco, Lawrence Ferlinghetti opened

* For a closer look at the events of May 1968, see the chapter on the French as Revolutionaries, on pages 180–8.

the pioneering *City Lights Bookstore*, after many on the Parisian Left Bank had closed down – including the famous *Shakespeare and Company*, founded in 1919 by the American Sylvia Beach, a long-time refuge for writers and the original publishers of James Joyce's *Ulysses*.* Suddenly, Paris didn't seem to be where it was happening any more. As the bookstores and artists moved out, the luxury boutiques and bankers moved in. Alain Souchon, a celebrated French crooner, captured the inexorable decline in his bleak *chanson* dedicated to the Left Bank, 'Rive Gauche':

> Farewell, Rive Gauche of Paris, farewell my home
> Of music and poetry; misguided salesmen
> Who have taken everything
> Come to sell clothes in the bookshops, the bookshops.
> Tender as the night may be, it has passed;
> Oh my Zelda, it's finished, Montparnasse...[7]

These days, the Left Bank is a poor echo of its glorious heyday. True, a handful of bookshops remain, nestled among the fashion boutiques – including a new Shakespeare and Company, named after the original Sylvia Beach enterprise. The cafés of the Lost Generation are still there. One can still check out *Les Deux Magots* or the *Café de Flore*, if forking out a mini-fortune for a continental breakfast is not an issue. But don't expect to find a philosopher sitting next to you, if you do. Most likely, you will be nudging elbows with another tourist like yourself, trying to catch a glimmer of the elusive past through a glass darkly. The sixth *arrondissement*, home to St Germain-des-Prés, is the most expensive in the whole of Paris: at €9,790 per square metre,[8] it fits the budget of bankers and film stars more than the ideas-rich and cash-poor intellectual of the avant-garde. There are a few corners left that retain a trace of authenticity: the *Café Fleurus*, a place where film deals are still made; the tranquil and birdsong-filled tearooms of the *Grande Mosquée* or Great

* The original Shakespeare and Company closed down during the German Occupation of Paris in 1940, never to reopen. Another bookstore was later rechristened with the same name, in honour of Sylvia Beach.

If you are lucky enough to have lived in Paris as a young man, then wherever you go for the rest of your life it stays with you, for Paris is a moveable feast.
ERNEST HEMINGWAY,
AMERICAN WRITER (1899–1961)

Mosque of Paris, a favourite haunt of the actress Catherine Deneuve;[9] or the lively rue Mouffetard near the Sorbonne in the Latin Quarter, bustling with small restaurants and shops and a thriving street market. The student area around the Sorbonne, in fact, is the part of the Left Bank that has best retained its authenticity, alive with the vitality that comes from the presence of the young.

But where are the Paris *avant-garde* now? Many are in London, Dubrovnik or Istanbul. Although some of the artists and writers who stayed on in Paris do rent tiny *chambres de bonne* on the Left Bank – all that is now available to them at an affordable price – many others have found new haunts in which to cogitate, deliberate and procrastinate: mainly on the now trendy Right Bank of the Seine. Initially, there was the Jewish quarter of the Marais, and then – when the bankers and clothes boutiques followed them there – they fled further to the north of the city, to the picturesque and rustic banks, bridges and ateliers of the Canal St Martin. Take a stroll on a sunny evening along the bridges of the Canal, past the row of sugar-cube-coloured, pink-, yellow- and green-painted ateliers running along the cobbled bankside, and you might – if you are really lucky – eavesdrop on a conversation about Existentialism. And it might – you never know – even be in French.

Myth Evaluation: *False. The Left Bank is a haven of bankers, lawyers and established film stars.*

The Paris Métro stinks

Métro c'est trop / The Métro's too much

TITLE OF A SINGLE BY FRENCH PUNK BAND TÉLÉPHONE, 1977

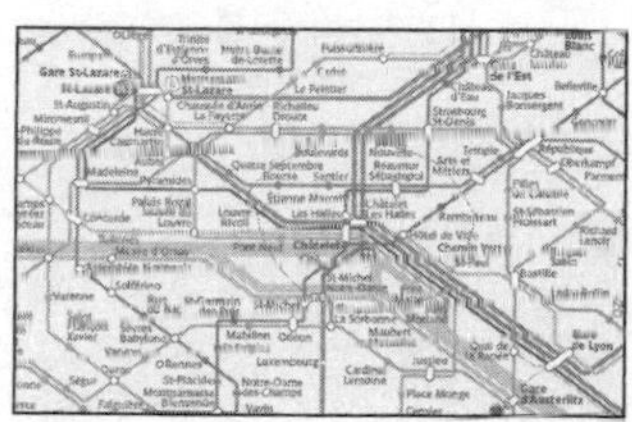

Anybody who has visited Paris and taken the underground will have been at least once assailed, on descending the escalator into the bowels of the station, by the unique and pungent odour of the Paris Métro. A distinctive exhalation even today, it appears – if historical accounts are anything to go by – to have been overpowering in the past. US Occupation Forces handbook attempting to dispel American GIs' prejudices against the French, *112 Gripes about the French*, refers to the common American complaint that 'you ride on the subway and the smell almost knocks you out, Garlic, sweat – and perfume!' The author of the leaflet goes on to explain that the odour of garlic arises from the fact that the French, 'who are superb cooks, use more of it than we do'; that the stench of sweat is due to the French having to use 'a very poor ersatz soap'; and that the perfume comes from the fact that 'French women would rather smell of perfume than unwashedness which they dislike as much as you do.'* Fifty years later, although certain constituents of the old odour had changed, a peculiar smell nevertheless still lingered in the subterranean passages of the Métro. The British journalist John Lichfield observed in 1998:

'The smell of the Métro – something between burnt air and rotting bananas – is a characteristic Parisian experience: as much a part of the city for visitors as the Eiffel Tower or the Champs Elysées. The magic formula is, or used to be, a delicate blend of scorched rubber, sweat and sewers. It also used to include the heavy scent of Gauloises and Gitanes, until cigarettes were banned from the Paris underground a decade ago.'[10]

* The origins and causes of the myth of the unwashed French are examined separately in the chapter dealing with this subject, on pages 141–8.

The Métro is an eminently Sartrean place where, in claustrophobic confrontation, each passenger becomes the prey of all the others.

FRANÇOIS MAURIAC, FRENCH AUTHOR AND NOBEL PRIZE WINNER (1885–1970)

Nor have complaints about the emanations in the Métro been limited to foreigners. 'I hate people. They stink in the Métro, and they stink on the pavements,' wrote the modern French philosopher and writer Pierre Boudot; and the American-French author Julien Green noted in his journal in 1949 that his friend, the writer André Gide, 'descends into hell in the Métro'.

These days, the Parisian Métro no longer reeks of garlic (as we have already seen, consumption of this pungent herb has declined sharply in France), nor of Gitanes (cigarettes were banned, as Lichfield notes, in the 1980s). Yet it is certainly true to say that the Métro still retains a distinctive *parfum* of its own. Every station offers a different olfactory cocktail. It might be top notes of sulphur, rotten eggs, dirty socks and urine, counterpointed by base notes of cleaning products containing fake lavender (Châtelet-Les Halles); or mouse droppings combined with scorched train brakes, permeated with a hint of cheap aftershave (Pigalle); or the damp odour of tourist sweat, tinged with fake Chanel 5 and Rive Gauche at the Champs Elysées, the underground car parks adjacent to the station being regularly sprayed with cheap scent to give a refined impression to those visitors too naïve to smell a rat.* And not only does the Métro's unique bouquet vary from station to station, but it also differs according to the season and time of day: sour body odour in the summer; clammy raincoats and damp fog in the autumn; wheezy exhalations and coughs in the winter.

But there is more to the undoubtedly peculiar scent of the Métro than mere bodily exhalations. Analysis by experts has found that the different underground aromas are in fact due to a

* *À propos* of which: if you think you smell a rat on the Paris Métro, you probably can. There are estimated to be 6–8 million sewer rats in the city, and in 2011 there were 1,716 complaints related to the presence of rodents.

complex mixture of chemical reactions, unique to each station. Take, for example, the distinctively pungent odour to be experienced in the central Parisian station of Madeleine – unfortunately nothing like the appetizing aroma associated with the eponymous cake of Proustian fame. Especially powerful at the notorious platform where Métro Line 14 stops at Madeleine station, this subterranean exhalation is caused by the slow release of hydrogen sulphide (the gas that famously smells of bad eggs, an essential component of the stink bomb) into the station tunnels. Its presence here – fortunately in quantities well below asphyxiation level – is said to be due to fluid from the water table above the station seeping down through organic matter, and infiltrating the station through walls and ceilings.*

The often unsavoury smell of the Paris Métro has long been a source of concern to the city's transport authority. The RATP (or *Régie autonome des transports parisiens*, the French government agency that runs the Métro) devotes some €65 million a year to trying to combat the infamous underground odours, including enlisting the assistance of an army of trained perfume experts to try to find a cure for the Métro's malaise. These consultants are members of an élite group of French master perfumers known as *Les Nez* (literally 'Noses'), whose more traditional vocation is to concoct commercial fragrances for the massive French perfume and pharmaceuticals industry. In 1998, the authorities even tried to introduce a new, specially designed perfume in the Métro cleaning products: named '*Madeleine*' after the notoriously malodorous station of the same name, it was said to be composed of 'lemon, orange and lavender, with an extra hint of floral bouquet and underlying woody notes, accompanied by vanilla and musk'. (This same scent was also introduced into the London Underground on an experimental basis in 2001, but was withdrawn after just one day when passengers complained of feeling sick.) The authorities have tried everything, all in vain: perfume pulverizers on the trains, scented cleaning products, sprays, even 'micro-balls' of perfume on the ground, invisible to

* This seepage not only releases a nasty niff, but also produces a wonderful array of rusty-brown ferrous stalactites on the Métro ceiling.

the human eye, which are said to explode under passengers' feet and prolong the diffusion of the scent.

On the other hand, while it may be repugnant to foreigners in Paris, there is evidence that many Parisians take a tolerant, and even affectionate, view of the familiar and comforting scent of the Métro. In the process of researching the olfactory preferences of Métro users in the late 1990s and 2000s, the RATP made the surprising discovery that, while customers equated certain specific smells – particularly human body odour and excrement – with danger, they also had a distinct concept of a defined and unique 'Métro' scent, to which they were extremely attached. They felt very strongly that the Métro did and should continue to have an odour of its own, that it should 'smell of itself', retaining its unique imprint or *griffe*.[11] Thus, despite the fact that Parisian commuters expressed revulsion for the Métro's ranker odours, they apparently harboured feelings of nostalgia for the steamy, womb-like security of the carriages, their tang of disinfectant and bleach, and for the warm stench of scorched tyres and burnt-out train brakes at the end of the day.

There's no better place than the Métro for hating the human race.

PHILIPPE JAENADA, FRENCH WRITER (b.1964)

For the ingénue just arriving in the Métropolis from the provinces (a motif that has been endlessly rehearsed in French cinema and literature), the subterranean emanations of the underground represent part of the essence of life in Paris, along with the smell of tobacco in the streets in winter and the scent of bleach in the cafés in the early mornings. Thus the child heroine of Raymond Queneau's cult 1959 novel *Zazie dans le Métro* ('Zazie in the Métro'), newly arrived in Paris for a weekend with her uncle, has only one desire: to plumb its depths (she never does, because the Métro is characteristically on strike for the whole of her visit). With their down-and-outs, graffiti-scrawled trains and troubling palette of aromas, Métro stations – like the *Vespasienne* public urinals of old (see pages 136–7) – remain louche places of both fascination and danger, where the humdrum life of the city teeters on the brink of something darker.

And so to this day, despite the best efforts of the RATP to fumigate the Métro, it defiantly clings to its age-old smell. The nostrils of the traveller who gets off Line 14 at Madeleine are, as they have been for decades, still assailed by the stench of rotten eggs. Visitors to Paris who cannot abide the perfume that most characterizes the subterranean passages of the city would perhaps be well advised to take a taxi; alternatively, one can just adopt the Parisian point of view, and revel in the poetry of the city's olfactory psychogeography. As Queneau said of his heroine Zazie, in an unpublished note to the original novel, in which he finally allowed his heroine to achieve her desire to enter the legendary labyrinth:

'The mouth of the Métro smelled powerful… an odour of dust, of an iron-rich and dry dust, an odour which Zazie thought of as new and raw, and which she inhaled with enthusiasm.'[12]

Myth Evaluation: *True. The Parisian Métro still smells most peculiar, although garlic and Gitanes have now been replaced by unusual chemical odours. However, for complex socio-cultural reasons comprehensible only to Left Bank intellectuals and Deconstructionist philosophers, the unique and irrepressible odour of the Paris Métro is not noxious, but apparently – in anthropological terms – a nexus of urban experiences encompassing alienation, excitement, repulsion and danger.*

Paris is the European capital of canine excreta

Q: How can you tell an American in Paris?
A: He's the one picking the poop up after his dog.
POPULAR JOKE AMONG AMERICAN EXPATS IN PARIS

This is one of the longest-running foreign beliefs about the streets of Paris. From Carrie Bradshaw's hazardous and ill-fated excursion to the city of smoke, strange language and dog poop in the series *Sex and the City* (involving the inevitable skidding of her stilettoed heel in a pile of viscous dung) to the *Merde* series by Stephen Clarke, the evacuations of man's best friend have become as much a part of the Parisian scene as the bistros or the cast-iron street lights. It seems, moreover, that even the French agree that the City of Light has a somewhat murkier aspect to its pavements. The French journalists Laure Watrin and Layla Demay, for example, make the following unflattering observations relating to the development of their children's vocabulary in Paris as compared to New York:

'Paris has not falsely assumed its status as the City of dog poop. If in New York, the first word of our children was "taxi", in Paris it was "dog mess". And when our Big Boy was seized with an urgent need without a toilet in sight, he said: "It's no big deal, I'll do it on the pavement." Faced with our horror and categorical refusal, Big Boy replied: "But it's not fair, the dogs have the right to do it, why not me?" That really is a dog's life. Here, Rover has more rights than Junior.'[13]

Oh God, murmured Durtal forlornly, What whirlwinds of ordure I see on the horizon!
JORIS-KARL HUYSMANS, FRENCH SYMBOLIST WRITER (1848–1907): A PRESCIENT VISION OF PARIS FROM THE NOVEL *LÀ-BAS* ('DOWN THERE'), 1891

Unfortunately, a survey of the available evidence – including many years of walking (or rather, slipping on) the streets of France's capital city – would tend to validate the myth. Paris' canine population of some 300,000 dogs dump about 20 tonnes of dog dirt on the pavements every year, which amounts to a kilo of *merde* hitting the capital's sidewalks every five seconds (enough, in total, to fill three Olympic swimming pools).[14] In fact, it is rumoured that the Olympic dimensions of Paris' dog-fouling problem is what lost it the chance to host the 2012 Olympiad. The Japanese, a people famed for their cleanliness, are said to have been particularly concerned about the health hazards raised by the prospect of athletes pounding slippery pavements. Possibly with good reason: every year, 650 Parisians are hospitalized from slipping on pavement dog deposits.[15] And the problem is not limited to Paris, but extends to most of the major cities of France (and even to the Francophone enclave of Brussels in Belgium).

The municipal authorities have done their utmost to try to reduce the amount of *merde* on the pavements of France's major cities. When Jacques Chirac was Mayor of Paris, he introduced a fleet of bizarre and much-ridiculed motorbike poop-hoovers known officially as *caninettes* and in the *vox pop* as *motocrottes*: a strange breed of green *tuk tuk* equipped with an aspirator to zap up offending deposits, the cabin at the back serving as a repository not of passengers, but collected ordure. However, the *motocrottes* cost a fortune and only dealt with a tiny percentage of the problem, so they were abandoned in 2002 and are now just an eccentric footnote in Parisian municipal history. Since then, the authorities have sensibly focused not so much on cleaning up after the canine culprits as educating them – or rather, their recalcitrant owners – to clean up after themselves. Allowing one's dog to foul the pavements in Paris, as in many other European capitals, is now punishable by a fine. A recent poster produced by the *mairie* of Paris, featuring a paradisal beach besmirched by canine defecation, seems to have prompted a certain amount of soul-searching and consequent poop-scooping by Parisian pet-owners. Yellow-jacketed 'canine counsellors' wander the city streets at the times and places known to be favoured by dog-owners for dumping excursions, ready to deliver a lecture on canine hygiene practices and armed with free collection bags. There is even a programme of street lectures and talks on pavement etiquette, including how to get one's

dog to defecate in the gutter (a virtually impossible feat, as any dog-owner will testify). It is an uphill task. Accustomed to delegating most things (including waste disposal in all its forms) to the state, French dog owners are proving characteristically recalcitrant on the canine excreta issue. As one French writer has observed: 'A French dog-owner won't accept someone telling them to make their dog use the gutter. Endowed with civic spirit, Americans take care to clear up their dogs' mess. The French would never stoop to do such a thing. They don't have the same sense of civic duty.'[16]

But although canine deposits are the French capital's most infamous excretory output, they are not the only things causing a stink on the city's streets. Paris' formidable population of pigeons – unaffectionately dubbed *rats volants* ('flying rats') by the natives – come in for a good deal of invective, especially from those city-dwellers who have been foolish or drunk enough to park under a tree. Pigeons are a curse of many of the world's great city spaces, from Trafalgar Square to the Piazza San Marco, but the pigeons of Paris are a particularly reviled breed. There are estimated to be some 80,000 of the birds in central Paris, or a pigeon for every 25 inhabitants.[17] By far the most common is the variety known as *pigeon biset*, a scraggy grey fowl that haunts the city all year round, and which has grown fat on the crumbs of *croque-messieurs* thrown by tourists from park benches. But there is also the pinkish-brown variety known as *pigeon ramier*, which migrates in the winter and returns to the city in the spring, gorging on green shoots to produce a particularly vicious, acidic green guano that eats away at the edifices

SHIT IN A SILK STOCKING

The word *merde* first appeared in the twelfth-century satirical collection of tales, *Le Roman de Renart*. The French often refer to it euphemistically as *le mot de Cambronne* ('the word of Cambronne'). This is a reference to General Pierre Cambronne (1770–1842) who, when called upon to surrender at the Battle of Waterloo by the British general Sir Charles Colville, is famously said to have responded with this single, forceful expletive. The incident was recounted by Victor Hugo in *Les Misérables* (1862).

Cambronne's supreme commander wasn't averse to using the term, either. Napoleon is reputed to have once told the diplomat Charles-Maurice de Talleyrand, whom he suspected of betrayal, '*Tenez, vous êtes de la merde dans un bas de soie!*' ('Why, you're just shit in a silk stocking!'). As soon as the Emperor had made his exit, Talleyrand supposedly plucked up the courage to observe: 'What a pity, sirs, that such a great man was so badly brought up!'

In contemporary French, *merde* is most frequently used as a mild swear word rather than designating the bodily excrement of man or canine (the latter would more likely be described as *crottes de chien*). It is still used, however, by actors to wish each other luck on stage – the equivalent of the British phrase, 'break a leg'. The origins of this usage seem to date from a time when the success of a play was gauged by the long line of carriage horses drawing up outside the theatre, depositing an impressive quantity of dung on the thoroughfare.

and monuments of the ancient city. Paris in the springtime, in fact, is not so much a time of romantic drizzle as of a precipitation of pigeon poo. The arches of the famous bridges of the Seine, the struts supporting the overground train stations, the pavements under the tree-lined boulevards… all have to be subjected regularly to the ritual ablutions of a high-pressure water jet to remove their peppery dressing.

In contrast to their ineffectiveness in the face of the *crottes de chiens*, however, the Parisian authorities seem to have cracked the *problème des pigeons*. Around the city, discreet pigeon houses are beginning to appear in major avian haunts. Graced with the rather crudely graphic name of *pigeonniers contraceptifs* ('contraceptive pigeon lofts'), these bird shelters provide a measured dose of feed to their occupants, while at the same time limiting their reproductive output (birds are allowed one brood a year, and any additional eggs are discreetly shaken to prevent them hatching). Meanwhile, the battle to save Paris' monuments from the ravages of acidic pigeon excreta grows ever more high-tech, the latest innovation being the installation of electromagnetic devices on statues which emit pulses insensible to the human visitor, but apparently highly repellent to pigeons.

Moving from flying rats to the scuttling variety, land rats are the city's bronze medallists among its excretory pests. At a rough estimate, Paris plays host to some 6–8 million of these rodents. Every second, more than 9 kilos of rat droppings are released in the capital's sewers, amounting to about 800 tonnes a day and 292,000 tonnes a year.[18] The problem is particularly acute in the winter – when the rodents sneak up to apartment buildings seeking warmth – and in the summer, the traditional time for building work, when the creatures flee from the drilling and seek new haunts. It is estimated that 25 per cent of fires of unknown origin in Paris are due to vermin gnawing their way through electrical circuits. Given that rats have a phenomenal breeding capacity – they become fecund from the tender age of two months and drop three to four litters of six to twelve rat babies annually, resulting in the potential creation of 5,000 new squealers by just a single couple in a year[19] – it is hardly surprising that the city conducts a yearly rat cull. The poor relation of the *Rattus rattus* – *Mus musculus*, the humble house mouse – is just as prevalent in the French capital, reaching even the top floors of Parisian apartment blocks, thanks to its greater climbing abilities. No spot is spared unwelcome visitations, however luxurious: a client propped at the bar of the celebrated Parisian hotel *Le Crillon*, host to many a world leader, is alleged recently to have spotted a mouse relaxing on the luxurious scarlet carpet, completely at ease. But the mouse, at least, has a slightly less nefarious image than its larger cousin: immortalized in countless French children's folk tales and nursery rhymes, it also fulfils the role of the French equivalent of the tooth fairy.*

Day and night, year in and year out, the machines of the Paris municipal authority whir and chug, disinfecting, disinfesting, sterilizing, scouring and scrubbing the arches, tunnels, sewers and squares of the city to expunge the unwanted waste products of the city's wild and domestic fauna. Certain French commentators have seen in this constant battle with nature the aseptic, clinical character of the city space, the disciplining and reduction of the natural world to the garish hanging baskets of the garden city.[20] Others – having just ruined another pair of stilettos by skidding in poo – might complain that the Parisian city space is not aseptic enough. Whatever the truth of the matter, it may be as well to observe some golden rules in Paris in the Springtime, that were unfortunately omitted from the famous Sinatra song. That is: always look at your feet, never loiter under a tree, and never leave the gruyère out on the table top.

Myth Evaluation: *True. Paris is not only the European capital of canine excreta, but also a good contender for European capital of pigeon and rat excreta as well.*

---

* French children leave milk teeth under their pillow in the expectation that they will magically be replaced by coins deposited not by a fairy, but a mouse. One of the most famous French children's nursery rhymes, *Une Souris verte*, involves dipping a mouse in hot oil. Believed to date from the early eighteenth century, the meaning of this rhyme – as with so many nursery rhymes – is uncertain. It may originally have carried a political significance that has been obscured by time.

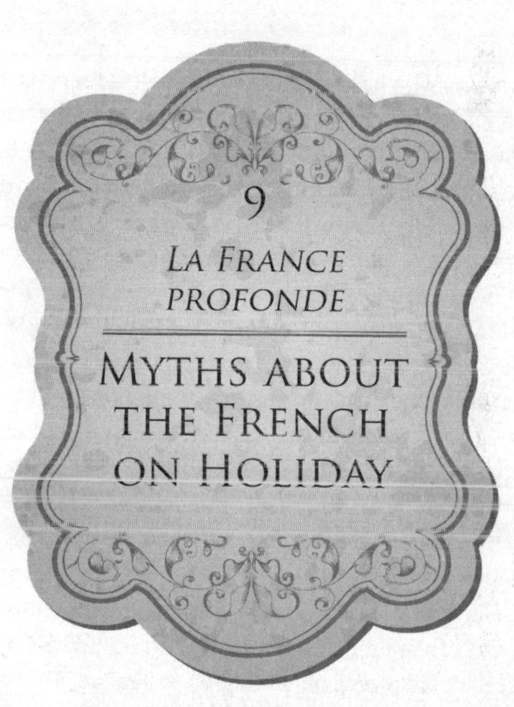

9

La France profonde

Myths about the French on Holiday

France shuts down for August

Vacations: the drug of the masses.
LOUIS CALAFERTE, FRENCH WRITER (1928–94),
CHOSES DITES, 1997

Anyone who has spent the summer in a French city, or in a town or village close to France's principal urban centres, will know the feeling. The miserable hunt for a baguette or a newspaper in deserted streets lined with shuttered storefronts, the interminable signs with the bleak statement, *fermeture pour congés annuels de 18 juillet de 18 août inclus,* or suchlike. The experience is fundamentally depressing. But – and this is less apparent to the foreign summer tourist – while such towns and villages will be moribund shadows of their customary selves, their counterparts on the coast and in the mountains will be buzzing with frenetic activity. In fact, France does not so much shut down for August as migrate on a massive scale: a great, seething mass of humanity, snaking from the cities down the *autoroutes* and *routes nationales* in an annual quest for sun, sea and sand. Was it always thus?

Hard as it may be to believe, given the enthusiastic attachment of the French to their time off, holidays for the masses are a relatively recent phenomenon in France. Tourism as we know it was essentially invented by the British, with the eighteenth-century gentleman's 'grand tour' – a stately progression through the cultural highlights of the Old Continent, accompanied by a pompous guidebook, and punctuated by seedy forays to assorted brothels along the way. Throughout the nineteenth and early twentieth centuries, little changed. Tourism remained the prerogative of the rich and leisured classes, labouring peasants, factory workers and servants having little time or energy available for sightseeing. It was not, in fact, until 1936 – with the coming to power of the Popular Front government, a coalition of left-wing parties led by the moderate Socialist Léon Blum that governed France just before the Second World War – that the first annual paid holidays were introduced for French workers by France's first minister for tourism, Léo Lagrange.* For the first time, French workers were entitled to fifteen days' paid holiday a year (this was extended over subsequent decades to end up with the present right to five weeks' annual paid holiday, introduced by the Socialist premier Pierre Mauroy in 1982). This leave had to be taken during the 'normal holiday period' – that is, the school holidays, which at that time ran from mid-July to the beginning of October.[1] But what were the working classes to do with all this newly available free time? Politicians, the Church, and other members of the French establishment all agreed that workers should spend their leisure time usefully rather than merely idling or loafing. Accordingly, they set about organizing a structured holiday experience that would ensure that the factory worker was as industrious at developing his mind and spirit in his time off, as he was at carrying out his duties in the workplace. Vacations were a time to be spent practising healthy outdoor sports, with plenty of sun and fresh air to counteract the enervating effects of sunless days at the assembly line; a time for city workers to reconnect with rural family members in the provinces; most of all, they were a time to explore and rediscover the glorious patrimony of France, through the splendour of its scenery and ancient monuments. Tourism, as one newspaper declared, should 'make a Frenchman love his native soil, which he either doesn't know, or knows too little'.[2]

Holidays are meant for working people, but the lazy are the first to take them.

ANNE BARRANTIN, *DE VOUS À MOI*, 1892

And thus began, in France, the golden age of tourism for the masses. In the summer of 1936 alone – the first year of *congés payés* – 600,000 of the newly issued *billets populaires de congés annuels*, or cut-price holiday train tickets for the working classes introduced by Léo Lagrange, were sold. The French philosopher Simone Weil, who witnessed the trainloads of those first-time holidaymakers, gave a touching description of their excitement in her notebooks:

* His official ministerial title was 'under-secretary for sport and the organization of leisure'.

'I had never noticed, until that point, to what extent habitual travellers on the great express trains affected a blasé and indifferent demeanour. Those we were accompanying, on the other hand, made one think of a village wedding: they wept with joy, sang, and made such innocent comments as, "Here's to life!"'[3]

Many more cut-price holiday train tickets were to be purchased in the decades to follow, ferrying their bearers to discount holiday villages and campsites run by organizations like the state-subsidized *Villages vacances familles*, or the newly-founded *Club Med*. Established in 1950 – fifteen years after Billy Butlin opened his first holiday camp at Skegness on the east coast of England – France's famous club with the trident logo started its days in a whirl of hedonistic idealism. Originally a non-profit-making association, the first *Club Med* holiday resorts pooled resources, banned the use of the formal *vous* form of address, and traded in seashells rather than money.[4] Previously élitist activities such as camping – originally invented as a British aristocratic pursuit allied with mountaineering – radically changed image to become the symbol of the French working-class holiday, with 20 per cent of people choosing family camping holidays by 1972. The mountains, too, were turned into new playgrounds, albeit for a more exclusive clientèle, with huge projects in the 1960s to create ski slopes and mountain resorts in the Northern Alps (Tignes, Val d'Isère, Les Trois Vallées and Les Arcs came into existence in this period). Film-makers such as Jacques Tati immortalized the uptight middle classes of those first holiday cohorts in his film *Les Vacances de M. Hulot* ('*M. Hulot's Holiday*'), unable to let go of their inhibitions in this strange, novel holiday mode. A very French institution – the *colonies de vacances* – also took off in the 1950s and 1960s, offering organized stays for children at full-boarding holiday camps in the regions. Initially designed for working-class children from cities to be exposed to fresh air and the countryside, these later spread to the middle classes, and exist to this day.* Many French people have fond recollections of

* The first *colonie de vacances*, or residential holiday camp for children, was organized in Switzerland by a pastor, Hermann Bion, in 1876. The pastor arranged for 68 working-class Swiss children between the ages of 9 and 12 to be exposed to fresh air and country life, staying in the homes of peas-

their childhood days in the *colo*, as epitomized by the jolly 1966 *chanson* of French crooner Pierre Perret, '*Les jolies colonies de vacances*':

Les jolies colonies de vacances
Merci maman, merci papa
Tous les ans, je voudrais que ça r'commence
You kaïdi aïdi aïda.

(The happy holiday colonies!
Thank you mummy and daddy
Every year I should like to go again,
Hip-hip-hooray!)[5]

Not everybody joined in the joyful chorus of *hi-di-hi*, however. As honking hordes in Citroën 2CVs flooded roads such as the classic holiday *Route nationale* 7 in the summer (the main road leading from Paris to the Riviera, immortalized by the French crooner Charles Trenet), the rich quietly packed their bags and fled to pastures new. Meanwhile, the conservative French press railed against the new invasion of the proles, or 'cloth-capped scoundrels', in the traditional playgrounds of the rich. To take the pressure off hotspots such as the Côte d'Azur, the French government in the 1960s attempted to divert the crowds of sun-seekers to the adjacent coast of Languedoc-Roussillon, leading to the development of the massive concrete piles lining the coast at resorts like La Grande-Motte (see page 270).

The question remains whether the French still up sticks every August and queue on the motorways leading to the same, over-crowded hotspots on the coast in traditional fashion, even in the days of low-cost airlines and cheap foreign package holidays.

---

ants. The holidays were funded by donations from charitable bodies, trade unions and employers. The idea took off in Europe, the United States (where the 'summer camp' remains an institution of childhood), South America and Japan. In 1913 more than 100,000 French children stayed in a *colonie de vacances*, more than 420,000 in 1936, and more than a million in 1955. Their number declined from the 1980s onwards. Summer camps have never formed part of the childhood experience in the UK to the extent that they have in France and the United States.

I am infuriated with certain employees who make sure that they never schedule their depressions at the same time as their vacations.
PHILIPPE BOUVARD, FRENCH JOURNALIST AND HUMORIST (b.1929)

The answer is, yes, they do. In fact, in many ways, things have not greatly changed since the 1950s. The French still consider a holiday to be a fundamental necessity of life: indeed, the right of everybody to at least one annual holiday is now enshrined by French law, as a 'cultural right'.* Two-thirds of the French population goes on at least one annual holiday a year; not to do so is considered the sign of the most humiliating social exclusion. France is still today the world champion of so-called 'social tourism', or state-assisted holidays, and one of the main objectives of the ministry of tourism is to ensure that as many people as possible realize their right to an annual vacation. Thus the French state indirectly subsidizes (through tax breaks) literally millions of euros of 'holiday vouchers' given by employers to their employees, and there are hundreds of bursaries and subsidies available to assist those unable to pay to get away. Low-cost, state-subsidized holiday camps and villages still exist, and dozens of charities make it their mission to help the children of poor families or broken homes get away for a break every summer. A standard advertisement for such a charity will typically feature a group of children returning to school in September and eagerly talking about their summer holiday, with one forlorn child standing outside the group, excluded from the conversation. Moreover, everybody does tend to desert the city for the coast at about the same time. Hence, every August, the inevitable *journées rouges* ('red days'), when the arteries of the French road network will be clogged with queues of vehicles sporting Paris number plates, bound for the Riviera or Brittany.†

---

* i.e. *La Loi sur l'exclusion de Juillet 1998.*

† These days the cars are more likely to be Toyotas than the now-defunct Citroën 2CV. And the celebrated holiday road, *Route nationale 7* – France's version of Route 66 – has now been broken up. This has not, however, stopped enthusiastic owners of vintage Citroën 2CVs, VW Beetles and Fiat 500s from nostalgically re-creating the holiday traffic jams of their youth in vintage car rallies on the old route.

In many ways, the original purposes of the French holiday at its inception – to cement family relations, to build a love of *la patrie* – still endure, albeit subconsciously, to this day. A surprising 57 per cent of French people take their holiday in France, the majority in non-commercial accommodation (i.e. with family, friends, or in a second home).[6] One of the consequences of France remaining a relatively rural country until well into the twentieth century is that many French people – both middle- and working-class – still have relatives and houses in the regions, with which they connect during holiday times. It is also a venerable French tradition across all classes to buy a 'family home' in the country, for use of all extended family members during vacations.* Being walled up for a month every summer with the mother-in-law, stepbrother-in-law, and several second cousins twice removed, in a flock-wallpapered suburb of an obscure French town, would probably be an average Anglo-Saxon person's nightmare, but it is par for the course in France. Conversely, the more traditional French person would probably be bewildered at the idea of voluntarily undergoing the experience of an easyJet flight, to spend a 'weekend break' in a foreign country. Yet the budget airline and the package foreign holiday, generally booked online, are gradually taking off in France, especially among the younger generation. This trend has been boosted by aggressive expansion of budget airlines in French territory, in particular Ryanair, which is starting to undercut the supremacy of the previously unassailable Air France.† The general Gallic preference for holidaying in France – boosted by the reluctance of the French to speak English and the system

* It is a pleasantly refreshing fact that in France, people of all classes take similar types of holidays, albeit on a varying scale of comfort and luxury. Thus, working-class as well as bourgeois French people are equally likely to go skiing, own a family holiday home, or stay in a holiday village. Middle-class folk are perhaps less likely to go camping and more likely to risk leaving the embrace of the beloved *patrie* by venturing abroad.

† When the French do venture forth abroad, their tastes are (predictably) fairly conservative. The top European holiday destinations for French people outside France are Spain and Italy; and the top worldwide destinations are the French-speaking Maghreb along with, more adventurously, the USA.

of 'holiday vouchers' (generally only redeemable in France) is also good for the national economy. After all, when the French go on holiday, money simply moves from one part of France to another. When the British go on holiday, money flows out of the country.

One of the consequences of all this is that holidays in France – in particular the long August vacation – are part of the deep metabolism of French life. Nowhere is this more apparent than in Paris during August, when – whilst the tourist Meccas are buzzing with activity – the real, indigenous life of the city lies slumbering like a somnolent beast, ready to lumber into action in the last few days of the month. The very words – *la rentrée* ('the return') – are enough to send shivers down the spine, and induce a febrile quickening of the pulse. The French *rentrée* is much, much more than the mere return of schoolchildren to their classes. It is the renewal of the whole of French society.* It is also a return to the obligations of the real world after August's fling with freedom: like the middle-aged hero of the 1966 film *Paris au mois d'août* ('Paris in August'), who indulges in a delicious summer fling with a nubile young model in a deserted Paris, whilst his wife and children are away on holiday on the coast – only to be given the wake-up call when the *rentrée* comes around.†

While the 'official' French calendar year may begin in January, the 'real' year starts in September. It is now that the *rentrée politique*, when the political machinery of the state swings into action again, takes place, and the news finally turns its attention from silly-season interviews with Basque lambs to the serious issues affecting the country; there is the *rentrée littéraire*, when hundreds of new books appear on the bookshelves (no fewer

* Much more so than New Year, which in France tends to be a fairly low-key affair of a quiet family dinner, rather than an excuse to down vast amounts of alcohol and vomit on the pavement outside a nightclub.

† *Paris au mois d'août* starred the celebrated French actor/singer Charles Aznavour and, somewhat bizarrely, the British actress Susan Hampshire. The film is noteworthy for one of the most sexually intense yet restrained sex scenes in cinema, in which for a full five minutes one sees nothing but the left hand of Susan Hampshire moving dextrously over a bed sheet.

than 646 in 2012); and there is even a *rentrée médiatique*, when the television channels present their new presenters and programmes to the public. No doubt because they are hoping that a good rest will have put everybody in a good mood, this is also often the time when the public transport authorities announce the latest hikes in ticket prices. This, naturally, produces a rash of protests and demonstrations, all of which are an assurance that the *rentrée sociale* is underway. Turning up at the office without a deep tan and a dozen holiday stories at this point is tantamount to social declassification. Of course, in many other countries of Europe – including the UK – it is customary to take all or some of August off. But only in France is this considered an absolutely necessary condition of human social existence, those who are unable to take flight becoming the object of heartfelt pity and commiseration. Likewise, while there is a muted 'buzz' of renewed activity in England in September, it is as nothing compared to the seismic upheaval of the *rentrée* in France.

Recent signs, however, are that the classic French model of *Homo touristicus* may be very slowly changing. As France yields to a creeping individualism, the traditional pattern of 'long' family vacations taken at prescribed times, such as August, is slowly giving way to a 'fractional' pattern of more frequent, shorter holidays, as seen in the UK and the rest of Europe.[7] France, it seems, is finally succumbing to the 'weekend break', booked online with a 'hip hotel'. As a result, many traditional French holiday villages have had to scale down their operations (as in the case of *Villages vacances familles*, which privatized almost half its sites in 2006), or find pastures new (as with *Club Med*, which has reacted to a dwindling market share by going fiercely upmarket, driving its prices up and a lot of its old customers away). The *colonies de vacances* have also experienced a reduction in numbers of children since the 1980s, many working French parents opting nowadays to send children to stay with grandparents during the holidays, or attend the flourishing state-run holiday day centres. Nevertheless, in 2011 1.3 million French children still spent some time during the holidays at a *colo*, or holiday boarding-house.[8] Campsites and mobile homes are still going strong as a budget holiday destination, although even here, one is more likely nowadays to find pilates and tennis as the listed activities, than dancing to the 'Birdie Song' or a contest for Miss Camping. As in Britain, the days of knobbly knees and glamorous granny contests are drawing to a close, replaced by karaoke evenings and all-night discos.

Wherever they go or whatever they do, however, August remains for the French a bright beacon in the year, a train for which everybody waits with childlike, impatient hope and expectation. None of which helps the frustrated visitor who ventures out of central Paris to the residential *arrondissements* or ordinary towns and villages during the hallowed holiday month, only to find the place as deserted as a ghost town in a Western. The only solution, if one wants to be assured of one's daily baguette in August, is to follow the French: switch off the mobile phone, take the car and a stash of musical entertainment for a long day's queuing, point the GPS in the direction of the nearest stretch of coast, and hit the road.

Myth Evaluation: *False. France does not shut down for August, the French simply migrate from the cities to the coast.*

French beaches are polluted

Gusts of wind blow on the Breton coast, where the huge petrol tankers are to be dreaded.
MICHEL COLUCCI ('COLUCHE'), FRENCH COMEDIAN (1944–86)

For years, the Anglo-Saxons have been casting aspersions on the standards of hygiene and environmental friendliness of southern European beaches. On the strands of Nice and Deauville, it is conceded, you may be guaranteed a hotspot in the sun and in a centre of stylishness, as opposed to the naff kitsch of a blustery weekend playing crazy golf on the pier at Brighton or Blackpool. But what about the dangers that the eye can't see? What lies beneath the allure of the Côte d'Azur? Can you be sure that, on the far side of that picturesque and rocky headland, there isn't an open drain or chemical factory pumping its contents into the sparkling sea? In short, Continental beaches may have the edge on their Anglo-Saxon counterparts in terms of chic; but the question of safety is a rather different matter…

There is no doubt that French beach resorts have traditionally headed the Continental ranking in terms of their reputation as swinging centres of fashion. In the late nineteenth century, when the first seaside holiday spots were beginning to emerge from the spas and therapeutic bathing centres of the early 1800s, resorts such as Deauville in Normandy, the 'queen of the Norman beaches' and the 'Parisian Riviera', drew in the rich and fashionable set like a magnet with its fast train link from Paris, casino, racetrack, and then – from the 1920s onwards – chic shopping outlets such as Coco Chanel's famous boutique retailing her iconic adaptation of the Breton/Norman striped fisherman's shirt.* This was the rich and fashionable set satirized by Proust in *À la recherche du temps perdu* ('Remembrance of Things Past', 1913–27), epitomized by the snobbish and bourgeois Madame Verdurin, for whom the whole of Normandy is an 'immense

* For more on the transformation of the striped fisherman's shirt into a fashion icon and subsequent symbol of Frenchness, see page 14.

English park', haunt of the despised fashionable Parisian holiday-maker flooding into the seaside towns of the *Côte fleurie*: Trouville, Deauville, Cabourg, and of course, the fictional Balbec, scene of part of the novel's action. And then there was of course the Riviera proper, which had long been the winter watering-hole of Europe's jetset, with the famous *Promenade des Anglais* at Nice standing testimony to the city's early and well-heeled visitors from across the Channel.

With the advent of the first paid holiday leave in 1936, however, the complexion of the French coastline was to be changed forever.* The thirst of newly liberated factory workers for a space to lay a towel in the sun – however minuscule – led to the massive development of the French littoral along all three coasts – the Channel, Atlantic and Mediterranean – in the postwar years, with much of the Riviera and adjoining coast of Languedoc-Roussillon turning into wall-to-wall concrete. Take, for example, the resort of La Grande-Motte in Hérault, in the south of France. Attracting over 2 million visitors a year, this monument to 1970s kitsch boasts a ring of massive, pyramid-shaped tower blocks encircling the beach, with names like La Grande Pyramide, Le Temple du Soleil and Fiji. La Grande-Motte boasts a tradition of all-night beach parties of 3,000 ravers or more, giving Ibiza a run for its money. A place, therefore, to be avoided (unless Las-Vegas-sur-Mer happens to be your thing). Similarly, at the resort of Fos-sur-Mer in Bouches-du-Rhône, the site of a major port development west of Marseilles, the visitor can enjoy the competing local tourist attractions of a steelworks to the east, an oil refinery to the west, and a fleet of supertankers belching their way across the waves beyond the town's substantial acres of sandy beach. And you will still have to fight for a place to put your parasol.

Unsightly development is not the only problem facing French beaches. Environmental issues have been looming large in recent years, notably the threat posed by huge banks of slimy seaweed, known to the French as *algues vertes*, which now form a bilious

* For more on the introduction of paid holiday leave and tourism for the masses, see pages 260–1.

green girdle around the shores of Brittany. Environmental campaigners had been harping on about the issue for ages, but the French press maintained its usual discretion on the subject until 2009, when a local vet riding on a Breton beach took a tumble as his horse mysteriously collapsed and died beneath him. Tests on the horse found that it had been asphyxiated by hydrogen sulphide (a poisonous gas that famously stinks of rotten eggs), produced as part of the decomposition process as the bright green seaweed rots on the beach.[9] When, during the summer of 2011, a total of thirty-six wild boar and dozens of seabirds were found asphyxiated on Brittany's seaweed-covered beaches, even the French authorities couldn't sweep the problem under the (bright green) carpet.

What could have caused the emerald invader to attack this most picturesque part of the northern French coastline? Environmentalists pointed the finger at Brittany's massive sheep, cattle and chicken farming industry. The problem, it was claimed, lay with the vast amount of nitrates from manure leaching into the sea on a daily basis, stimulating the uncontrolled growth of the green slime. France's powerful farming lobby vehemently denied this. Faced with a panicked exodus of holidaymakers from Brittany, the government announced an action plan including the daily removal of seaweed from affected beaches (those beaches where seaweed could not be removed on a daily basis were to be closed), and 'information' campaigns assuring alarmed visitors that the seaweed, if removed before decomposition, posed no threat to bathers or beachcombers. Indeed, according to the touchy-feely description on the Breton Tourist Board's website, the new 'sea lettuce' is not an invader but a 'natural part of the Breton ecosystem', so called because it resembles a 'giant salad and is edible'. Not that it has featured thus far on many Breton restaurant menus.

Nobody, not even the French, is describing the creature that has invaded the Mediterranean coastline since the early 2000s in touchy-feely terms, however. With their

If the Breton beaches are tarred with oil slick this summer, at least our clogs will not be filled with sand.

LAURENT RUQUIER, FRENCH JOURNALIST (b.1963), *JE NE VAIS PAS ME GÊNER* (2000)

bell-like, eerily glowing purple bodies and trailing tentacles studded with bright red stinging cells, the number of jellyfish of the species known scientifically as *Pelagia noctiluca* (and popularly as 'mauve stingers') visiting the Riviera has exploded in recent years. Overfishing of their natural predators (tuna, sardines, mackerel and turtles) and global warming of the oceans have seen them grow plump and plentiful. A single bank of *P. noctiluca*, drifting by the seashore, has been known to stretch for over seven miles. Many a Mediterranean holidaymaker has fallen victim to these toxic invaders: in certain areas of the Côte d'Azur, there have been up to 500 emergency cases reported in a single day, and 70,000 people were stung in Spain in 2007. The authorities have been quick to point out that their stings aren't as toxic as those of the notorious Portuguese man o'war; symptoms of those affected include light nausea, vomiting and diarrhoea, or at worst a touch of lymph-node swelling, abdominal pain, numbness, tingling, and/or muscle spasms. But it's still not what you came on holiday for.

Global warming, together with effluent from pig manure, have transformed part of the Breton coast into a reservoir for seaweed.
JEAN-MARIE GUSTAVE LE CLÉZIO, FRENCH-MAURITIAN WRITER (b.1940) *JOURNAL DE L'AN 1*

In recent years, however, the advent of a new European directive on bathing water quality – which all European countries are required to implement by 2015 – has caused a certain amount of panic. As a consequence, many coastal resorts in France have begun to clean up their act. According to the European Environment Agency's annual report on bathing water quality for 2011, French beaches scored below the European average in terms of water quality, with just 60.8 per cent of French resorts tested having excellent water (the European norm was 77.1 per cent). The European country with the cleanest bathing water was Cyprus, and the country with the dirtiest was the Netherlands. The United Kingdom came near the top of the league in 2011, with 82.8 per cent of bathing water deemed 'excellent'. (However, heavy rainfall in the non-summer of 2012, which washed a lot of pollution from towns and cities into the sea, together with

tougher reporting requirements, meant that British standards of bathing water cleanliness plummeted 20 per cent in 2012.)[10]

The question, therefore, remains. How can you tell, before you book a holiday on that idyllic stretch of coastline, that you really will be basking in the glow of the Provençal sun and not in that of an oil refinery? That you will be bathing in the azure of a crystal sea and not the nitrates discharged by an industrial silo into the *Merditerranean*? The answer is to do your homework. There are a number of classification systems that rank beaches according to cleanliness and access to decent sanitation facilities – such as the Blue Flag international scheme (although, given that Fos-sur-Mer and La Grande-Motte both have blue flags, one wonders about the criteria for awarding them). There is also a rather useful European Environment Agency website in collaboration with Google Earth, which will give a water quality rating for most resorts in Europe. Or – if you really want to avoid bathing in the waste products of the industrial world – you could always head for a far-flung resort such as Bora-Bora in French Polynesia, or the French island of Réunion in the Indian Ocean (although, in the latter case, you might well be attacked by sharks instead). If it's 'eye pollution' that you are most concerned about, you could stick with one of the beaches regularly featured in the top ten most beautiful in France by various polls – such as that of the travel agency TripAdvisor in 2012 (picturesque Porto-Vecchio in

Corsica came out top in this vote, followed by the rather more sprawling Biarritz).*

In any event, you can console yourself that, whatever the quality of the water, state of pollution, or sleaziness of a French beach, it will come nowhere near the squalor, say, of beaches in Thailand. Nor will you have to compete for the choicest sunspots with cows (as in Goa), or with teeming masses of humanity (as on the beaches of China, the most overcrowded in the world). Moreover, in an early evening off-season, it is still possible to drive along the French coast and find spots of breathtaking beauty – such as the rugged coast of Finistère, or the vast sand dunes of Arcachon in the Gironde – where the primitive power of the landscape defies even the most assiduous attempts at desecration. Or, as Proust's narrator Marcel describes the wild Norman coast of his imagination:

'You still feel there beneath your feet… (and even though hotels are now being superimposed upon it, without power, however, to modify that oldest ossature of the earth), you feel there that you are actually at the land's end of France, of Europe, of the Old World. And it is the ultimate encampment of the fishermen, the heirs of all the fishermen who have lived since the world's beginning, facing the everlasting kingdom of the sea-fogs and shadows of the night.'

Myth Evaluation: *Partially true.*

* TripAdvisor Travellers' Choice Awards, 2012. The complete list, in descending order, was: Porto-Vecchio, Biarritz, Calvi, Cassis, Juan-les-Pins, Antibes, Cannes, Nice, Saint-Malo, and Saintes-Maries-de-la-Mer.

French beaches are packed with topless women

All youth ends on the glorious beach, at the edge of the water, there where women appear to be finally free, there where they are so beautiful that they no longer need the lies of our dreams.
LOUIS-FERDINAND CÉLINE, FRENCH WRITER (1894–1961), *VOYAGE AU BOUT DE LA NUIT*, 1932

It's the ultimate fantasy of your average male backpacker in France: to wind up on miles of white sand somewhere on the Côte d'Azur, on a café terrace caressed by a cool breeze, a troop of bronzed and semi-naked girls appearing out of the waves…

Nor does this image have to remain confined to the realms of fantasy. Not if you pick the right beach. Don't, whatever you do, head for a windswept stretch of the Norman or Breton coastline (unless you want to spend the afternoon fossil-hunting). For those more interested in living specimens, the only way to go is the Riviera. St Tropez remains the top destination: a place where tops on beaches are largely optional, 'bikini' means sporting bikini bottoms and a sunhat, and the yachts moored along the coastline are draped with topless beauties who clearly spend a lot of money (mostly not their own) on the arts of pampering the flesh.

Men are born naked and live in clothes, just as they are born free and live under laws.
ANTOINE RIVAROLI, COMTE DE RIVAROL, FRENCH WRITER (1753–1801)

France was not always so laid-back about *le topless,* or indeed sunbathing on the beach in any attire. Tanning, or *le bronzage,* was frowned upon in polite society in the nineteenth century, being considered the hallmark of lowly farm labourers. That all changed in the early twentieth century, when most farm labourers decamped to factories and began to look pale and anaemic. Suddenly, a tan became *très cool,* the ultimate status symbol to signal that one spent one's time on yachts or at spa towns rather than slaving in the dim light of the assembly lines. Coco

Chanel created a rage for tans when she returned from the Côte d'Azur in 1920 with a bronze sheen, and the Afro-American dancer Josephine Baker (whose tan was genetic rather than sun-derived) inspired the Paris fashion élite to mimic her dusky look and minimal attire. But while Josephine Baker titillated Paris by dancing topless on stage in the 1920s, the bourgeoisie of the regions were shocked by the hedonistic rebels who were starting to take to the beaches in scanty attire (scanty, at least, by the standards of the day. Early swimsuits shrouded the body from head to toe, and were closer to the modern-day burkini than a bikini). From the 1920s on, family associations and societies for the propagation of morality confronted beachgoers in fisticuff battles, and lists of 'immoral beaches' were published for public consultation. In 1927, for example, in a small village in Brittany, a group of Breton housewives tore branches from the trees by the beach and whipped a posse of nubile female sun-worshippers in whom their husbands had become a little too interested.[11]

It was not, in fact, until the 1950s, with the advent of mass tourism and an annual summer exodus to the beaches, that sunbathing really caught on. Even so, the dress code on beaches was strictly a capacious one-piece. Unsurprisingly, the bikini was a French invention, the brainchild of fashion designer Louis Réard in the 1940s. What is more surprising is that he was also an automobile engineer. (Or perhaps not; after all, Jack Ryan, the man who gave us the Barbie doll, also invented the Sparrow and Hawk missiles.) Réard engaged in a battle with another French designer, Jacques Heim, to create the world's smallest swimsuit. Heim had already effectively created the predecessor of the bikini, called the 'Atom', marketed as the 'world's smallest swimsuit' (a rather heavy two-piece, it had modest panties closer to shorts). Réard trumped Heim with a far racier number: two triangles held together with string on top, and a g-string below. He called his creation the 'bikini' after Bikini Atoll, a group of islands in the South Pacific where the United States began testing nuclear weapons in the summer of 1946. Marketed as 'smaller than the smallest swimsuit' and taking up only 45 square centimetres of cloth, the first bikinis were sold in

RAGTIME AND RESISTANCE: THE REMARKABLE MS BAKER

It is a strange irony that the woman who made toplessness on the Paris stage fashionable and *avant-garde* (as opposed to mere pornography) was originally American: the great African-American performer and political activist Josephine Baker (1906–75). Born into desperate poverty in the back streets of St. Louis, Missouri, Baker was spotted at the age of 15 by a travelling vaudeville showman as a ragged child dancing on street corners. Huge success as a chorus girl on Broadway followed, and when she appeared at the newly opened *La Revue nègre* on the Champs-Elysées in 1925, Paris was smitten.

Baker's star turn – for which she is remembered to this day – was an erotic, topless dance in a banana-skin skirt. She was frequently accompanied on stage by her pet cheetah Chiquita, sporting a diamond collar, who added to the audience *frisson* by occasionally escaping into and terrorizing the orchestra pit.

But Baker was much more than just a topless dancer. Having taken French citizenship, married a Frenchman and settled permanently in France in 1937, she played a key role in the French Resistance during the war years. She also supported the Civil Rights movement in America in the 1950s and 1960s, refusing to perform before segregated audiences. Josephine Baker died peacefully in 1975, after a sell-out retrospective show. As the first American-born woman to receive the highest French award for gallantry, the *Croix de guerre*, she was buried with full military honours.

a matchbox to prove the point. They caused a scandal. A fleet of regular models turned down the assignment, so the only woman Réard could find who was willing to model his creation was a topless cabaret dancer, for whom the skimpy garment was presumably more of a cover-up than usual. The bikini was officially launched on 5 July 1946, five days after the explosion of an atomic bomb of 23,000 tonnes on Bikini Atoll. It was immediately banned in Italy, Spain, Belgium and France.[12]

It took until the 1960s for Réard's bombshell to explode with the devastating effect he intended, in the form of a nubile Brigitte Bardot at St Tropez. Clad in scanty string bikinis made of girlish fabrics such as pink gingham and *broderie anglaise*, Bardot ensured that henceforth there was only one dress code for the French beach: *le minimum*. Soon, she was being caught in snapshots without her top on, and the *monokini* was born.* The hip crowd flocked to the beaches of St Tropez, which, despite the efforts of the local *mairies*, became havens of bare-breasted sun-worship (there were in fact as many placards banning the *monokini* as there were women flaunting them). Jean-Luc Godard went so far as to put a shot of a topless bather in his 1964 film *Une Femme mariée* ('A Married Woman'). It was edited out by the censors. Finally, after the upheavals of May 1968 – a year when the whole of France rebelled and everybody from women to students took to the streets to protest – the battle for freedom of the boobs was won, and many French beaches either officially or unofficially condoned topless bathing.

Today, most beaches in St Tropez are 'bikini tops optional'. Foremost among them is the famous Tahiti Beach, a pioneer in the 1960s battles over topless bathing. Nor do you need to limit yourself to *le topless*: there are beaches where the dress code is strictly your birthday suit, including the risqué Cap d'Agde. Here, if you wear clothes on the beach you are asked to leave, and women in trousers are banned from the swingers' clubs. Although the Germans invented naturism and remain the nation most likely to bare all on the beach, France has one of the largest number of nudist beaches and resorts in the world. It

* That is, the French version of the *monokini,* which was simply to dispense with the bikini top. An American designer did invent a garment called the 'monokini', but it did not catch on.

might seem somewhat odd that the world's best-dressed country should be so obsessed with taking off its clothes, but the fact remains that the French are fascinated by nudism. A hugely successful 1960s French comedy series, *The Policeman from Saint-Tropez*, featured the French actor Louis de Funès (see page 154) as a local gendarme in charge of a Dad's Army of bumbling policemen, forever engaged in 'clothing fights' with nudists on the beaches. The nudists won. Even today, prime-time French TV dramas are set on naturist beaches, where naked bathers shock bourgeois families who stumble upon them by mistake.*

Yet despite France's post 1960s liberal attitude to nudity and the naked breast, it seems that the times are a-changing. The younger generation of French women is, it appears, much less inclined to let it all hang out on the beach than their mothers. Nobody can explain this reticence for bosom-baring among younger bourgeois women (noted and much lamented by French intellectuals and the press). One theory is that the beach today is no longer a space of liberation from social norms, but just another forum for a tooth and (manicured) nail competition. One of the most celebrated slogans of the May 1968 student rebellion was *sous les pavés, la plage…* ('under the paving stones, the beach' or, to paraphrase, 'under the oppressive rules of civilization lies freedom').† But is the beach so free and easy these days? The fanatical cult of the body beautiful in the 1990s meant that, for many women, the annual summer holiday, with its obligatory striptease, became as much a prospect of dread as anticipation. And nowadays on the beaches of the Côte d'Azur, there is so much competition from fake boobs and bottoms that the real thing looks *un peu triste* in comparison. As more and more foreign imports flood the Riviera and strut their (inflated)

---

* As in, for example, the television drama *À Dix minutes des naturistes*, broadcast on the French channel TF1 in June 2012.

† The reference is to the fact that when the protesting students prised up paving stones to hurl at the police in Paris, they found beneath them the sandy shelf on which the city was built. The slogan was widely used by the Situationists, a Marxist *avant-garde* group that reached its peak in the 1968 revolution.

Not only does the practice of nudism not lead to immorality, but it is a good way to combat it.
DR GASTON DURVILLE,
LEADING FRENCH NATURIST
(1887–1971)

stuff, the genuine French article beats a dignified retreat.

Whatever the cause of their new-found modesty, 50 per cent of French women in a recent poll stated that they were bothered by total nudity on the beach, and 37 per cent were discomfited by the sight of naked breasts or buttocks.[13] Today's bikinis are more likely to be scarily high-tech, silhouette-reforming contraptions with inbuilt breast-enhancers, stomach-flatteners and buttock-lifters, than the artless strings of the 1960s. And, for the first time in decades, the old-fashioned one-piece has become a market leader once again, as increasing numbers of French women refuse to enter the battle for the best body on the beach. Even on Paris Plage – the simulated beach created on the Seine every summer – topless sunbathing is now punishable by a fine. Interestingly, the reticence over topless bathing on ordinary French beaches contrasts with a boom in nudism itself, with increasing numbers of families taking to 'official' nudist beaches. Which suggests that it's not so much a question of whether, but rather where, to let it all hang out.

Does this mean an *au revoir* to the heady heyday of *le topless*, when Brigitte Bardot and her first husband Roger Vadim strolled carelessly on the then still-virgin beaches of the Pampelonne? Not quite. You'll still find plenty of naked breasts on certain beaches of the French Southeast. Just don't expect them to be Made in France.

Myth Evaluation: *Partly true. Many women do go topless on French beaches, but increasingly few of them are actually French.*

French villages are so quaint

This is French country life at its finest – with outdoor markets, charming village cafés and relaxed friendly people.

ADVERTISING BLURB FOR A FRENCH LANGUAGE SCHOOL IN THE SUBURBS OF PARIS

Ah, the 'typical' French village: a cluster of mellow stone cottages clinging to the top of a hill; a patchwork of mossy rooftops; picturesque window shutters adorned with a riot of brightly-coloured geraniums… Who hasn't at some point or another dreamt of this haven of peace and tranquillity? The French village is the quintessential fantasy of life in the slow lane, a place where time stands still, where the only noise is the Sunday morning toll of the church bell, the clink of glasses in the local village café, and the click of rolling boules as a few old men in berets play *pétanque* on the dusty village square… Just don't forget the Ford showroom, Buffalo Grill and Carrefour hypermarket round the corner.

There is no doubt that unadulterated French countryside can be absolutely magnificent. France's geographical position, straddling latitudes both temperate and Mediterranean, means that it rejoices in perhaps the most varied landscape in Western Europe. Villages so preternaturally pretty that they appear to have been plucked from the pages of Marcel Pagnol's *Jean de Florette* really do exist in France, in regions as diverse as Périgord and Provence, Brittany and Burgundy, the Ardennes and the Ardèche. In all likelihood, in such villages there will be a picturesque – although somehow disconcertingly quiet – centre with an old market square, church and the local town hall or *mairie*. Then – within a couple of miles of this idyll – you will usually find low-cost concrete housing, homogeneous holiday villas, grain silos and warehouses – in short, anything useful (and usually hideous) that the local authority decides needs to be there.

The French don't, as a rule, fetishize their countryside like the British (perhaps because there is so much more of it in France

– at least, for the moment). In Britain, anxiety that the countryside was about to be swallowed up wholesale in postwar urban sprawl saw the introduction of 'green belts' around British cities as early as 1947, and planning restrictions enshrining the principle that new developments should harmonize with local landscape and architecture. Powerful lobbyists such as the National Trust and vociferous activists like the Campaign to Protect Rural England are ever vigilant, waiting to pounce on any proposal that might blot the idyllic garden of England with a dark, satanic mill. In France, on the other hand, there is no heritage-preserving body with the sheer landowning might of the National Trust; the closest equivalent – the *Fondation du patrimoine* – mainly helps owners of historic houses maintain and repair their properties with grants. Grassroots environmental protest in France is more muted than in England, with the exception of certain high-profile projects that have created a furore. A salient example being the current brouhaha over the French government's plan to build an airport near the small farming community at Notre-Dame-des-Landes in Loire-Atlantique, the economic and environmental logic of which admittedly seems questionable, given that it involves spending 600 million euros to convert 1,600 hectares of rural land into an airport for a city (Nantes) that already has one.

The relative lack of vociferous local environmental campaign groups means that, although designated areas and buildings of historical significance are zealously protected in France, if a village falls outside these cultural exceptions, it will largely be at the mercy of the planning department of the local *mairie*. In most cases, this will have a PLU (*plan local d'urbanisme*) that predetermines permitted residential, commercial or public development. So if a factory or a hospital, a fire station or a block of flats, is required, it will simply be built according to the provisions of the PLU – even if that happens to be in a direct line of sight from your back garden, which previously enjoyed an uninterrupted view of the Provençal hills.

Of course, in this respect France is facing a challenge no different from the UK: namely, how to provide enough low-cost housing to accommodate an expanding and increasingly industrialized populace with a thirst for their own detached home, without wrecking the countryside in the process. And, as with so much in France, double standards apply. The 'official' rule is that all local authorities, or *mairies*, are required to have at least 20 per cent social housing, to preserve France's hallowed principles of equality, or *mixité sociale*. In practice, the most exclusive communes – like the *haute bourgeois* village of Le Vésinet in the western suburbs of Paris – have traditionally refused to do this, opting to pay an annual fine instead. Exclusive domains in the suburbs west of Paris such as Le Vésinet, Maisons-Laffitte, and the 'royal' communes of Versailles and St Germain-en Laye, were in fact some of the earliest suburban developments in France. Back in the nineteenth century, when railway lines were just beginning to criss-cross the country, suburbs such as these arose from the auctioning of building lots on the grounds of broken-up châteaux. A slow trickle of suburban developments followed, stimulated by reduced-rate loans for the construction of private suburban housing by French governments in the 1920s.[14] France, however, still remained a largely rural population, a people rooted in the hills and mountains of *le terroir*.

The poor who did migrate to the French towns in the 1960s were packed like sardines in the newly constructed housing estates of tower blocks or *cités*, which loom ominously to this day like brooding giants around the major cities of France. Piled on top of each other and relegated to the periphery of urban life, the *cité* dwellers

One fine morning, the people of France woke up and found that a baobab had sprung up in their garden… In less than half a century, in almost total silence, the map of France had changed. Rubbing their eyes, the citizens of France had to take in the evidence: the famous town–country opposition, which was how people had thought of the territory for centuries, was no longer applicable. In its place, another form of territorial occupation, at the same time more complex and vague, incontestably difficult to assess in voting terms… suburbia…

FRENCH NEWSPAPER *LE MONDE*, 'LE FRANÇAIS, CET HOMO PÉRIURBANUS', 31 MAY 2012

dreamed of their own little patch of paradise: a detached house with a garden. And in the 1970s and 1980s, that dream began to come true. Huge areas around small towns and villages, formerly occupied by agricultural land, farms and ancient châteaux, began to be snapped up by developers and turned into private housing estates. It was easy: all potential purchasers needed to do was choose from a range of ready-made homes from a catalogue. With names like Romance, Evolution or Azure, these homes were really identikit boxes, cubes of concrete with uniform roofs and differently coloured shutters. Dubbed in estate agents' jargon with the ludicrously pompous name of *pavillon* (the word for the private hunting lodges of the old kings of France), they are France's version of the Barratt home. You can buy one for as little as €50,000, picking up the keys on completion of the necessary paperwork at one of the 'model home' villages outside Paris and other major cities, such as Domexpo and Homexpo. Today, 85 per cent of all new French houses constructed are *maisons de catalogue*.

Naturally, the forest of new private housing estates mushrooming all over France needed a network of new roads to connect their suburban home-owners with the cities in which they no longer wished to live, but to which they still needed access in order to work. With the *loi Pasqua* of 1998, the French government grandly promised that every citizen should find themselves within forty-five minutes of a motorway. That dream (or nightmare) is swiftly being realized. Soon, every large city – then medium-sized city – then village – had its unholy trinity of motorway, shopping complex and new concrete private housing estate on its outskirts. Today, France has more than 1,400 hypermarkets bigger than 2,500 square metres, over 8,000 supermarkets, and more than 30,000 roundabouts.[15] (In fact, over half of the world's roundabouts are to be found in France, which has more roundabouts than any other country in the world.) Twenty-six square metres of agricultural land are gobbled up by development in France every second.

By 1998, the number of village and small-town grocery stores in France had declined to one-sixth of the number in 1966, the number of local butchers by two-thirds. One village in two no longer has any local shops.[16] Meanwhile, as the village centre turns into a museum, the outskirts are turning into a vast shopping mall. At the entry to the average French village, you are as likely to encounter a forest of placards advertising the local Intermarché, McDonald's or Décathlon, as you are a rustic stone bridge over a babbling brook.* Move on from the picturesque centre and you will be sure to be directed to the massive out-of-town shopping complex, or *hangar*. Take the example of the village in which I live, formerly a hamlet nestling on the outskirts of Paris. The past three years have seen the construction there of an estate of catalogue *pavillons* in the medieval village centre; an underpass on the main road at the village entrance; and a new, 30,000-square-metre shopping complex (to join the one that was already there), ironically called the Orchards (in memory of the fruit orchards it replaced).

For most foreigners, the classic French home is a smart Parisian apartment or a rustic cottage: urban chic or rural picturesque. The reality is that it is neither. In France, 56 per cent of people live in a house. Many are *maisons de catalogue*, or *pavillons* in the suburbs. And indeed, this is not only the real, but also the dream, French home. According to a 2004 survey, only 10 per cent of French people questioned wanted to live in the centre of a large city, and a mere 16 per cent wanted to live in a village. The majority – 49 per cent – dreamed of living in the suburbs.[17] In other words, the average French fantasy home is not a cottage surrounded by lavender fields in Provence, or a Haussmann-esque apartment on a chic Parisian boulevard, but rather… a two-up, two-down in a cul-de-sac. And the French countryside is beginning to reflect that dream: less and less like *A Year in Provence* and more and more like *Neighbours*.

The increasingly suburban character of the French landscape

---

* In this respect France perhaps resembles the United States more than the UK, which has largely evaded the horror of the edge-of-town roadside hoarding. Much of French suburbia, in fact, more closely resembles America than Britain, with features characteristic of the US suburban landscape – long strings of vast shopping malls housed in concrete bunkers, for example.

is something that has not gone unnoticed by French commentators. It has been swooped on by environmentalists, who point out that the new, matchbox-like houses springing up all over the countryside have a carbon footprint bigger than King Kong, gobbling up acres of French farmland and guzzling vast amounts of energy, not to mention the exhaust fumes generated by two sets of family cars shuttling back and forth to Paris twice a day. But by and large, the French intelligentsia has tended to treat the suburban landscape as invisible (which, given that most of them live in central Paris, it effectively is). There is no poet of the French Metroland – no Buddha of Suburbia to chart an escape from the prison of the *pavillon* to the city, no John Betjeman to mourn the misty elm trees that once clustered around shopping complexes like the mammoth commercial park in the western suburbs of Paris (which someone with a black sense of humour called Plaisir). Nor is there a French version of films and TV dramas such as *American Beauty*, *Desperate Housewives* or *Weeds* to reveal the true goings-on behind the twitching net curtains of the suburbs.*

But all is not lost for the French village. A clutch of pioneering mayors have instigated imaginative schemes like *Opération coeur de village* ('Operation Village Heart'), a system of subsidies designed to breathe new life into moribund village centres by renovating former schools, factories or shops, and converting old buildings into houses or flats, rather than just going for the easy (and lucrative) option of plonking a new development of *maisons de catalogue* on the outskirts. But such projects require flair, imagination, and – hardest of all – hard cash. And so the question remains. How do you ensure that the *gîte* in

* This chapter is about 'village suburbia', that is suburbia as it is commonly understood in the UK and USA, as the sprawl of mainly private housing around the outskirts of a city, town or village. This, in French, is called *périurbanisme*. The other type of 'suburbia' in France is the *banlieue* or *cité*, consisting of vast housing estates built on the edges of the cities, to house the poor and immigrants. These would be known as 'inner-city' areas in the UK, and much has been written about them in all areas of French media and the arts (in contrast to the suburbia of the private housing estate). The *cités* are not the subject of this chapter, or indeed of this book, as they demand special consideration worthy of a book on its own.

the 'picturesque French village', as touted on your travel agent's website, really is located in the village of your holiday dreams? How can you know for sure that it nestles in the shadow of a a castle-crowned hilltop, and not downwind of a hypermarket *hangar*? Research is the answer. There are a number of organizations which certify that a village really does come off the set of films like *Chocolat*: for example, unofficial guides like *Les Plus Beaux Villages de France*, or official listings like *Village de caractère*. (*Chocolat*, incidentally, was shot in the village of Flavigny-sur-Ozerain, in Burgundy. Don't expect to see the river there, though, as those scenes were shot in Wiltshire.) Or you could try out France's favourite village, as chosen from a shortlist of twenty-two in 2012 by an audience of millions on national television: Saint-Cirq-Lapopie in the Lot, a tear-jerkingly beautiful cluster of amber stone houses huddled against a cliff in a stupendous valley (see page 287). To get an idea of numbers: *Les Plus Beaux Villages de France* certified 157 villages as making the 'Beautiful' grade in 2012. There are a total of 31,927 villages of under 2,000 inhabitants in France. Of course, classifications aren't everything, and there are plenty of picturesque little places off the beaten track in France, just waiting to be discovered. Just remember that round the corner, also just waiting to be discovered, there will probably be an Auchan hypermarket or an El Rancho grill.

Myth Evaluation: *Partly true (with a lot of exceptions).*

French country style is so chic

For two hundred thousand dollars, one can buy an 'authentic' French country home on Philadelphia's Main Line.

DEAN MACCANNELL, *THE TOURIST: A NEW THEORY OF THE LEISURE CLASS*, 1999

For the middle-class Anglo-Saxon who dreams of owning a few acres of Lot-et-Garonne, the French farm or country house calls to mind an immediately recognizable style of interior decoration. Simple yet elegant, it speaks with the muted tones of bare walls (perhaps washed with lime or a thick layer of russet *crépi*,* weathered through years of buffeting by the *Mistral*); the quietly sophisticated greys or *vert-de-gris* of furniture handed down through generations, upholstered in faded *toile de jouy*;† the crisp simplicity of a red-checked tablecloth, mismatching yet harmonious cream tableware, or starched linen napkins. Above all, there will be an understated elegance: fine wine will be served in a plain carafe, a salad bursting with regional produce in a solid glass bowl, local charcuterie on a heavy, white oval platter. It is a look of rustic yet refined simplicity, bearing witness to an innate sense of exquisite taste and quality that, undaunted, shines timelessly through the worldly weathering of the objects that give it expression.

But where does this image of 'French country style', as we think we know it, come from? Certainly, you would be hard-pressed to see it in real French farms or country houses, except for a handful of top-class *gîtes* and *chambres d'hôtes* (many owned by foreigners). The typical French *gîte* – though it may offer a fetching vista of tumbledown stone and French grey

* *Crépi:* a roughcast traditional form of plaster rendering for French walls, often a fetching russet colour when mellowed by age.

† *Toile de jouy*: a linen cloth in an off-white colour imprinted with complex and usually pastoral designs, originally developed in eighteenth-century France and now indelibly associated with French country interiors.

shutters on the exterior – will, inside, likely be a hideous riot of brightly tiled, 1970s-coloured walls and floors, IKEA furniture, frilly curtains, chicken wire, and/or linen tablecloths embroidered with hearts. Have the French never heard of Farrow & Ball? Is it possible that they are unaware of the potential of sisal matting? Are all those interiors magazines with mouthwatering pictures of tastefully renovated French country homes (usually owned by British people) lying? The answer is that they are – or at least in part.

'French country style', as we understand it, has very little to do with rural France.[18] It is, essentially, an interior decorators' invention. As early as the late eighteenth century, Louis XVI's queen, Marie-Antoinette, amused herself in her fake rustic village near the Petit Trianon at Versailles, milking cows with monogrammed silver buckets, collecting eggs in ribboned baskets, and pretending not to notice the court functionaries dressed as peasants who swept the horseshit out the way as she approached. Real French peasant homes were rude and functional, using local materials as best they could. What we know as 'French country style' today draws its inspiration not from peasant homes, but rather from what became known in France as 'French provincial style' – the style developed by the affluent middle classes in the French provinces, in imitation of the grand interiors of the châteaux of the aristocracy. In essence, it was the style of Versailles – of Louis XIV, XV or XVI – scaled down, made more domestic and familiar.[19] It was a look that spoke of a comfortable gentility, of links to the past. And for American visitors to Europe in the late nineteenth and early twentieth centuries, it was exactly what they were looking for.

In the late nineteenth century, the American writer Edith Wharton – better known as a novelist than for her ideas about interior decoration – was one of the first to see in the country houses of England and France models of inspiration for the American middle-class home, already equipped with all the creature comforts but lacking a sense of history.[21] Later, in the early twentieth century, the Manhattan socialite Elsie de Wolfe also spotted the potential of French décor and furnishings to

lend American homes a touch of the past. A former actress, Elsie was probably the first woman to dye her hair blue, perform handstands at society gatherings, and cover eighteenth-century footstools in leopard-skin prints (on first seeing the Panthéon, she is alleged to have said, 'It's beige – my colour!'). She was also almost certainly the world's first interior designer. In her iconic 1913 book *The House in Good Taste*, Elsie described her various projects of house renovation – from a crumbling New York brownstone to her beloved house in Versailles.[21] Inspired in particular by eighteenth-century French design as embodied by the château at Versailles, Elsie opened up the early twentieth century American house from the gloomy, claustrophobic prison of Victoriana to the light, open, reflective and trellised spaces that inspired her in the Hall of Mirrors and the Orangerie. Heavy, dark furniture was replaced by light, painted pieces adorned with *découpage* and chinoiserie motifs, some inspired by Monet's blue and yellow dining room at Giverny; silk, damask and velvet made way for light, airy chintzes, including of course the fabled *toile de jouy*. *The House in Good Taste* is brimming with photographs illustrating the homes of wealthy Manhattanites redecorated by Elsie, where Louis XIV, XV and XVI furniture sits happily next to ample, squishy contemporary sofas, abundant lighting, and all the best of modern conveniences: in short, a version of Versailles with scatter cushions.

In this process of modernization and synthesis, 'French country style' was being manufactured in a similar way to 'British country style', the creation of another American, Nancy Lancaster.[22] Like Elsie, Lancaster's hugely popular renovations of British country mansions in the 1940s also created an essentially American marriage of artful clutter, tasteful memorabilia and allusions to a glorious heritage, with creature comforts that would have been unknown to the aristocratic incumbents of the icily draughty originals.* Fabric designers in the 1950s and 1960s were quick to spot the potential of the country house dream factory: in France, Pierre Frey's luxurious prints featuring sprays of flowers and assorted hounds were guaranteed to give any window the noble feel of a country château, as were the 'country house' fabrics produced in England by Liberty and Laura Ashley.

The most satisfactory of all chintzes is Toile de Jouy. The designs are interesting and well drawn, and very much more decorative than the designs one finds in ordinary silks and other materials.

ELSIE DE WOLFE, AMERICAN ACTRESS AND INTERIOR DESIGNER (1865–1950), *THE HOUSE IN GOOD TASTE*, 1913

The displacement of furniture, fittings and design motifs from their original homes – the châteaux and country houses of England and France – to locations as far flung as New York's Upper East Side, created what were to become global 'styles' in the interior decorator's portfolio. It is now completely possible to have 'French country style' in a villa in Palm Springs, or 'British country house style' in a tower block in Tokyo. When the (now half-empty) luxury archipelago, the Palm Island in Dubai, was created, the property developer's catalogue included houses in a range of different 'styles', including 'French style'. Nor are French or British 'country house' styles any longer the preserve of the wealthy. The interior designer Terence Conran, reminiscing about the sensational colours, scents and sounds of his first road trip to France in 1952, has said that this French experience was fundamental to his inspiration for the first Habitat collection.[23] With Cath Kidston's reinvention of British 'vintage' and Rachel Ashwell's French-inspired 'shabby chic' (available to the mass market through the American retail giant Target), French and English 'country style' can be recreated as easily in a Man-

* The English country house as a national myth acquired totemic significance just as the country house itself as an institution was on the decline, around the time of the publication in 1945 of Evelyn Waugh's classic portrayal of decaying aristocratic splendour, *Brideshead Revisited*. Over time the myth has been fed by a host of National Trust properties and such television series as the BBC adaptation of *Brideshead*, which inspired a generation of languid, floppy-haired men clutching teddy bears at Oxford. Nor has its appeal diminished, as witnessed by the worldwide success of the ITV drama *Downton Abbey* since 2010.

hattan loft as a semi-detached in Surbiton. French brands such as Comptoir de Famille and Jardin d'Ulysse make a fortune flogging painted furniture, frilly lampshades, chicken-wire larders, wrought-iron wall sconces, porcelain roosters, checked tablecloths, monogrammed tableware, *toile de jouy* cushions, and enamel coffee pots, to consumers the world over.

Which brings us back to the tricky question of the possibly not-so-dreamy interior décor of that dreamy-looking *gîte*. It looks so very pretty from the outside. But what will the inside be like? Will it cut the *moutarde* for the English visitor? The answer is, it depends… on the preferred 'world decorating style' of the owners. They might be into 'French country style' (especially if they are not actually French). If so, and you strike lucky, you might get the tasteful version of this style – a few weathered and well-chosen items, carefully orchestrated to accord with a backdrop of the inevitable Farrow & Ball. If you're unlucky, you will get the tat that comes with the cheap version of the style – clashing floor and wall tiles in 1970s colours, an extravaganza of overwrought crystal chandeliers, chicken wire over every cupboard door, *froufrou* frilly lampshades, the obligatory porcelain rooster, clocks made of seashells and embroidered hearts and bows on everything in sight (this is most likely if the owner is French, in particular an elderly French couple letting out their holiday cottage). On the other hand, the owners will just as likely be into neither of these styles; they may be into boho eclectic, Japanese zen garden, African tribal sculpture, or just dirt-cheap IKEA and whatever junk wouldn't fit into their own home. There's just no way of telling. There is, however, a glimmer of hope on the horizon. After all, if you really want 'French country style', you don't need to go to France any more. You are just as likely to find it in Paris (Texas) or Versailles (Florida).

Myth Evaluation: *Partly true.*

10
The Best of Enemies
Myths about the *Entente Cordiale*

The French think British food is revolting

There is only one word to say when faced with English cuisine: pass!
PAUL CLAUDEL, FRENCH POET (1868–1955)

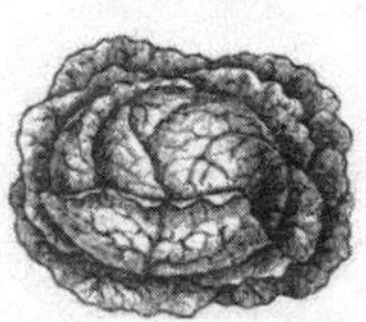

Has anybody a good word to say for British cooking? Historically, the answer has to be no. British cuisine has traditionally been one of the longest-running world jokes (to Britons as much as everybody else). The sharp-toothed Italian scholar Alberto Denti di Pirajno (1886–1968) remarked that the British, incapable of giving flavour to their cooking, relied on ketchups to give to their food what 'the food does not have', which explained the prevalence of bottled sauces and chutneys that 'populate the tables of this unfortunate people'. In the twentieth century, Virginia Woolf lamented the 'abomination' that is British food, the boiling of cabbage, leathery meat, and viscous granular sauce that passes for 'gravy'; and the American journalist Martha Harrison speculated that 'what motivated the British to colonize so much of the world is that they were just looking for a decent meal'.

The English have only one sauce, melted butter.
COMMENT MADE BY VOLTAIRE TO THE SCOTTISH PHILOSOPHER AND ECONOMIST ADAM SMITH (RECORDED IN JOHN RAE, *THE LIFE OF ADAM SMITH*, 1895)

The French are no exceptions to this general world tide of derision. An old saying in France says of *la cuisine anglaise* that 'if it is cold, it's the soup; if it is warm, it's the beer'. The great French politician and diplomat Talleyrand (1754–1838) observed: 'In France, we have three hundred sauces and three religions. In England, they have three sauces and three hundred religions.' The novelist Émile Zola, forced into unhappy exile in England in 1898 for publishing his controversial open letter accusing the French army of obstructing justice in the Dreyfus affair, considered that whatever matters the English and French might agree upon in the future, cuisine would never be one of them (see page 299). Nor did French opinion seem to soften greatly over the next hundred years. 'You can't trust people who cook as badly as that,' President Jacques Chirac was overhead saying of the British to President Vladimir Putin on the sidelines of a meeting in Kaliningrad, Russia, in 2005. 'After Finland, it's the country with the worst food.' He went on to comment that the only thing the British had contributed to European agriculture was 'mad cow disease', and that his problems with NATO originated when he was made to try haggis by the then NATO Secretary General, George Robertson, a Scot.*

Talk to any French exchange student on their return from a stay with an English family, and they will invariably claim to have been traumatized by the experience. Not only did it rain every day, but the host family (inhabiting some terrible pebble-dashed semi near a petrol station) spent every night in front of the television watching soap operas and consuming endless cups of revoltingly milky tea. The poor student will have been made to eat fish and chips, or overcooked lamb served with a bizarre mint vinaigrette, or beans in an orange sauce made of vinegar and cornflour, or a revolting tartrazine-yellow substance called *la jelly* (or very possibly, all four at once). A guide for French waiters published in 2004 by the French Tourist Board describes British cuisine as 'simple, founded on popular food culture, based on leftovers'. Signature dishes are apparently 'les pies', 'les puddings' and 'les dumplings'. Waiters are advised to 'de-animalize' meat as much as possible with British tourists, i.e. on no account even to hint at the identity of the animal from which the meat came; to serve meat without a trace of blood (that is, overcooked in French terms); to steer them away from offal, frogs' legs or snails; and to avoid making snide comments about British food.†[1]

From where did British food get its abysmal world reputation? English food in the Middle Ages, as food historians have noted,

---

† The traditional British horror of red meat is odd, given that it was the celebrated London restaurant Simpson's that is said to have first served bloody meat at the end of the nineteenth century. But the French Tourist Board's 2004 guidance suggests that the British are not alone in their aversion to a bleeding steak: the Americans, Germans, Spanish, Italians, Japanese, Dutch and Polish apparently share this repugnance.

had a Europe-wide reputation for its delicious cuts of meat and adventurous use of spices.[2] Whilst the precise reasons for the decline in British food are the subject of simmering academic debate, one of the more convincing theories is that the rot first set in with the Reformation, and was later exacerbated by the Puritan influence on British society from the seventeenth century onwards. Gastronomy – with its hedonistic and sensuous delights – became allied with Gluttony, for Protestants one of the worst of the Seven Deadly Sins that were the subject of weekly tirades from the pulpit. The G words were the mark of the traitor and the Papist – those noble, recusant families who persisted in eating the rich dishes of the pre-Reformation era, redolent of Romish luxury. The plain food of the Protestant became the food of the righteous and God-fearing Englishman: unadorned, wholesome fare without frills or fancy. Gastronomy (an art) gave way to cookery (a branch of domestic science). The Industrial Revolution simply made matters worse, cutting off thousands of workers in the fast-growing urban sprawl from their former food sources. Then, with the Second World War, came the final death-blow to an already ailing cuisine: rationing. For fourteen years, the British were severely restricted in their access to milk, butter, eggs, sugar, and dozens of other foodstuffs. A whole generation grew up without having tasted a lemon or seen a banana – let alone learning traditional British skills such as pot-roasting a partridge or pressing an ox-tongue. Whatever remnants of culinary credibility Britain had left were killed off by the war. Into the vacuum stepped the pioneers of early processed food: Fray Bentos, Nescafé and the producers of the first sliced loaf, Wonderbread.

George Orwell, however, predicted that British food would rise again after the punishment of rationing, and sure enough British food today ain't what it used to be.[3] 'Modern British' has whisked away the stodgy past, with gastropubs now serving dishes such as buttered Manx kippers and bacon with Burford brown eggs in place of traditional pub fare like pies, chips and beans and chicken in a basket. There are farmers' markets, shelves of organic produce, and a battalion of television chefs

THE UNHAPPY EXILE

On the evening of 18 July 1898, the French novelist Émile Zola (1840–1902) was bundled onto a train and packed off to England in the deepest secrecy. The reason for his flight was his conviction for slander over the newspaper publication of '*J'accuse*', an open letter in which he attacked the highest levels of the French army for the antisemitism and corruption it displayed in the Dreyfus affair. Zola was to spend just under a year in exile in England, first in Weybridge and then in Upper Norwood. During this time, he kept a diary (later published as *Pages d'exil,* 'Notes from Exile'), which revealed how miserable he was in his adopted home. He missed his dog, mistress, children and wife (possibly in that order), and spoke barely a word of English. Most of all, he loathed British food:

'I confess that I am finding the cooking here harder to get used to. It's true that my cook is a hearty lady, who has only cooked for modest folk. But that at least tells me much about how modest folk eat here. Never any salt in anything. All the vegetables boiled in water and served without butter or oil. The large cuts of roasted meat are good, but the braised cutlets and steaks are inedible. I'm so suspicious of the sauces that I've totally banned them. And the bread – oh my God! – the half-cooked English bread, soft as a sponge!... I live pretty well on roast meat, ham, eggs, and salad. And it's not in order to complain that I talk about the cooking, but rather to express my astonishment – philosophically speaking – at the gulf that exists between the French pot-au-feu and the English oxtail soup. We may at some point bring these people together, but we will never get them to agree on cooking. Even when we are brothers, we'll still be quarrelling on the question whether potatoes should be served with or without butter.'

From *Pages d'exil*, 1898–9.

THE FRENCHMAN WHO CHAMPIONED BRITISH FOOD

Marcel Boulestin (1878–1943) is barely remembered today, but it was he who first brought French country cooking to England. Born in Poitiers and growing up in the regional kitchens of the Southwest, Boulestin was an Anglophile who attempted to make his father's household in Poitiers appreciate the sublime flavours of mint sauce with mutton and Anglo-Indian curry. In Paris he is said to have searched out mince pies and marmalade, persuaded the writer Colette to partake of the pleasures of a festive plum pudding, and drunk whisky instead of wine at a dinner in the Parisian restaurant Fouquet's.

Boulestin arrived in England in 1906 and, having failed in a decorating business, turned to writing cookery books after the First World War. His first book – *Simple French Cooking for English Homes* – was a huge success on publication in 1923. He was also the first television chef. Boulestin did not have a professional qualification as a chef, but as he said himself, 'I had eaten well all my life, and like the majority of my compatriots of the south-west, I had an instinct for cooking.' Abhorring the *faux* French cooking of London hotels and restaurants, where 'nondescript dishes boast of pretentious names, and where there is always a white sauce for fish and a brown one for meat', he placed an emphasis on the fresh ingredients and simplicity of the French country kitchen. His unfussy dishes suited the pared-down lifestyle after the war, and inspired cookery writers such as Elizabeth David. The restaurant he founded in Covent Garden survived, under various ownerships, until the 1990s.

busily working at defining a 'New British' cuisine. No longer is it an act of humiliation for the red-blooded British male to don a pinny and sweat heirloom organic onions in Suffolk goose fat. But have the French registered any of this *outre-Manche* culinary activity? Are they eating humble pie and changing their minds about the horrors of *la cuisine anglaise*? To some degree, yes. The new enthusiasm of Her Majesty's subjects for the finer things in life has been noted approvingly by the French Bible of gastronomy, the Michelin Guide (a formidably tough nut to crack). The 2012 Guide awarded the coveted three stars to four British restaurants: Heston Blumenthal's Fat Duck and Alain Roux's Waterside Inn (both at Bray in Berkshire), Restaurant Gordon Ramsay in Chelsea, and Alain Ducasse at The Dorchester, Mayfair. In a humiliating defeat for French cuisine, in the 'Top 100' review for 2012 by *Restaurant Magazine*, Blumenthal's Knightsbridge restaurant Dinner was placed ninth, three places above the highest-ranking French restaurant, Joël Robuchon's restaurant L'Atelier. And, to add insult to injury, the menu at Dinner spurns French *haute cuisine* in favour of dishes painstakingly researched from Britain's culinary archives. Some English classics have even made it into Gallic restaurants: crumble, for example, can now be found nestling on French bistro menus alongside the more traditional *crème brûlée* and *tarte aux pommes*.

All in all, the signs are that the French gastronomic élite *is* aware of an aroma of change wafting from the culinary shores of Albion. But what of the French person in the street? Are they eating their words too? Sadly, it seems not. Surveys and the recorded views of French visitors to Britain are depressingly negative. 'Water is the basic ingredient of English cooking,' the French pop singer Daniel Darc observed, after a visit to the UK. The typical French visitor's view seems to be that – however avid consumers of food literature the Brits may be these days, and however cutting-edge the fanciest London restaurants – glossy recipe books and posh eateries with pretentious single-word names do not a nation of gourmets make. French online guides to London advise that, in all but a handful of top-end restaurants, one should ask for one's steak to be 'underdone' or, even better, 'imported'. English supermarkets are accused of being stocked with hermetically sealed, out-of-season, flavourless fruit and veg; they lack even basic dairy produce (no plain *petites suisses* or *fromage blanc*); they

One cannot help wondering if an English salad is the result of ignorance or the aim of a curiously perverted taste.
MARCEL BOULESTIN, FRENCH CHEF (1878–1943)

fail to provide a good selection of meat or seafood (no veal, rabbit, sea urchins or live lobsters). Ultimately, of course, in the opinion of French visitors and expats, the best English cuisine is always French. 'The English may have taught the world table manners,' conceded the contemporary French-Greek writer Pierre Daninos, 'but the French taught the world how to eat.'

Among the French at home, the impact of British food on the national palate appears to be nil. In a 2011 survey of French people's preferred foreign cuisine, the top-rated foreign food was Italian, followed by Chinese and then Japanese (a particular favourite for the younger and hipper French). British food did not even figure.[4] But to cheer the British up, there is one British meal that is the cream of the crop for every nation in the world: breakfast. A survey of 2,400 hotel guests in 2011 found that the full English breakfast was voted the best breakfast in the world, with even French people agreeing that it was their favourite hotel wake-up meal.[5] So if there is one meal at least that saves the bacon for British cooking, it is the great British fry-up. In the words of Somerset Maugham: 'To eat well in England, all you have to do is take breakfast three times a day.'[6]

Myth Evaluation: *Partly true. The French cognoscenti are changing their minds on the awfulness of British cuisine, but the view that 'Modern British' is now quite pukka has yet to filter down to the man in the rue.*

The English have taken over the French countryside… and the French have taken over English cities

The French are a logical people, which is one reason the English dislike them so intensely. The other is that they own France, a country which we have always judged to be much too good for them.

ROBERT MORLEY, ENGLISH ACTOR (1908–92)

Invasions of France by the English are nothing new. In fact, at various times in the turbulent history of the two countries, parts of France have come under English rule. The English have longed to own a piece of French soil ever since Henry of Anjou – the future Henry II – inherited vast swathes of territory in the western half of the country through his marriage in 1152 to that most eligible of French brides, Eleanor of Aquitaine. Most of these Plantagenet lands (except Gascony in the Southwest) were lost to the French crown in the early years of the thirteenth century – partly owing to the incompetence of bad King John – and it was to recapture them that the bellicose King Edward III embarked on a hundred years of war with France in 1337. Indeed, English monarchs from that time forward styled themselves Kings of England and France, and the English royal coat of arms historically included the insignia of pretenders to the French throne, the *fleur-de-lys*. The *fleur-de-lys* was only removed from the royal coat of arms after George III, in a brief moment of sanity, finally relinquished the centuries-old claim of English kings to the French throne after 1802. In all likelihood, George III's largesse was motivated by self-preservation; after all, by then France had undergone a Revolution and dispatched its own royal family to the scaffold.*

* The relinquishing of the British monarchy's age-old claim to the French throne by George III was part of an attempt to reach a peaceful accommodation with Napoleonic France, which had just successfully defeated a coalition of European monarchies (including Habsburg Austria and Russia), and

Of the love or hatred God has for the English, I know nothing, but I do know that they will all be thrown out of France, except those who die there.

ATTRIBUTED TO JOAN OF ARC, FRENCH NATIONAL HEROINE (c.1412–31)

The nineteenth and early twentieth centuries marked a break with the previous five hundred years, in that England finally lost interest in ruling France, and concentrated on ruling much of the rest of the world instead. But that did not mean that the English lost their dream of colonizing their neighbours by stealth, if not by the sword. As early as the second half of the eighteenth century, the upper classes of England had flocked to the natural beauty and sunny Mediterranean clime of the French Riviera, which became the traditional winter resort of the wealthy and fashionable English set. Nice's celebrated *Promenade des Anglais* is testimony to the presence of these early, well-heeled and aristocratic British good-lifers.* In the later nineteenth and early twentieth centuries the Anglo-Saxon adventurers began pushing further inland, invading the lavender fields and rustic villages of Provence: a new type of resident was beginning to arrive, in the form of the arty and bohemian English-speaking middle-classes. In the 1920s and 1930s, Provence and the Côte d'Azur became the home of American writers such Edith Wharton (a lifelong fan of all things Gallic, Wharton bought Castel Sainte-Claire on the hills of Hyères in 1927, and spent winters and springs there until her death in 1937); or F. Scott Fitzgerald, who visited Hyères, Cannes and Monte Carlo in the 1920s, finally stopping at St Raphaël, where he wrote *The Great Gatsby* and began *Tender is the Night*. The British writer W. Somerset Maugham also bought a house – the Villa Mauresque – at Saint-Jean-Cap-Ferrat in 1928, living much of his life there save for a brief period of exile during the Second

---

was generally frightening the life out of conservative, monarchical Europe. For more on British contemporary reaction to the French Revolution, see the chapter on the French as a nation of Revolutionaries, pages 180–8.

* Even today, the 'season' for the fashionable jet-set to frequent the French Riviera is in the autumn/winter, leaving August to the tourist scrum. The discreet arrival of elegant yachts at St Tropez in time for October's *weekend des voiles* ('weekend of sails', or yacht racing week) is testimony to the fact.

World War. The publication of Elizabeth David's phenomenally successful cookery books brought the flavours and aromas of provincial France to an entire generation of postwar British middle-class, who also began to purchase homes in Provence. As that region became prohibitively expensive, due to the vast influx of foreigners, they spread out to the equally picturesque, albeit cheaper, neighbouring department of Gard, and then out to the Southwest of the country (especially the Dordogne and the Lot).

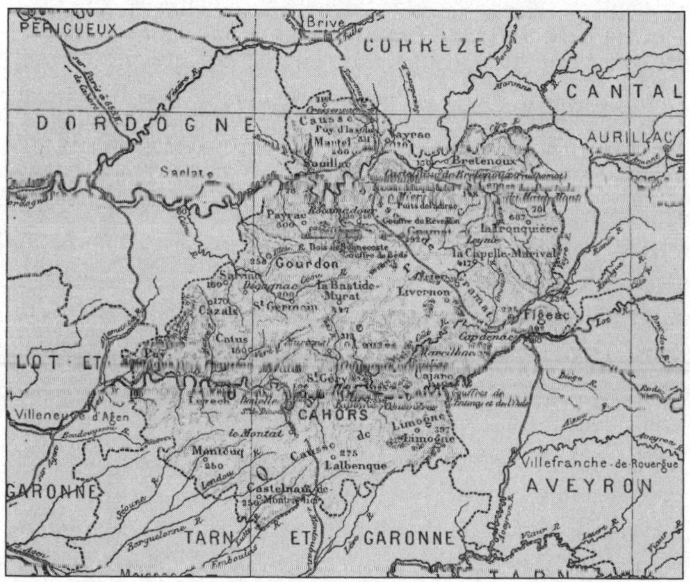

The English emigrants to France in the early twentieth century were for the most part Francophile, middle-class, affluent and at least reasonably conversant with French language and culture. In the 1980s, however, a new type of visitor began to arrive from the shores of Albion. Spurred on by former advertising executive and sex-manual writer Peter Mayle's hugely successful 1989 book, *A Year in Provence*, subsequent television series such as *A Place in the Sun*, and the new accessibility via discount airlines of what had previously been *la France profonde*, the new invaders came not on horses armed with swords, but rather on easyJet armed with cricket bats, Farrow & Ball paint, and jars of Marmite. Many knew not a word of French beyond *bonjour* and *au revoir*, nor did they feel they needed it: they were of course coming to France for the *lifestyle*, not the language, politics or culture. The peak of the influx was in the decade after easyJet's foundation in 1995: the initial trickle of retired folk quickly became, in the early 2000s, a deluge of families seeking dirt-cheap dilapidated farmhouses or châteaux to convert, from which to run *gîtes*, keep goats, or even run an English chippy. It got to the point that in certain regions – such as the fabled Dordogne(shire) – the English population was beginning to compete with, or even exceed, the French.* In the Dordogne village of Eymet, for example, there is a local *épicerie anglaise* selling such nostalgic treats as Wagon Wheels, Angel Delight and Frank Cooper's Oxford Marmalade (Thick Cut); the local pub offers curry and chilli con carne alongside the local *salade de chèvre*; and the summer afternoons are punctuated not by the clack of *boules*, but rather the gentle thud of cricket balls hitting turf and willow and the clink of glasses of Pimm's.

In all, there are estimated to be some 200,000 British expats living in France.[7] But what about the other side of the coin – the French people living in Britain? Estimates on this count vary wildly, but figures from the French embassy in London suggest that there are as many as 300,000 Gauls living in Albion.[8] Of these, two-thirds live in London (now said to be the sixth-largest French city), but there are Gallic enclaves in Scotland (the Scottish French Institute describes itself as 'a little corner of France in the heart of Edinburgh'), East Anglia (there is now a regular French market in Norwich flogging everything from *brioches* to Corsican sausages), and Wales (the *Madame Fromage* cheese shop in Cardiff sells the best and stinkiest of French curds). In London, the exclusive area around the French Institute and Lycée Charles de Gaulle in South Kensington – including the

* According to tax records, the highest proportion of British expats who arrived in France in the past five years live in Paris/Île de France; next comes the mild, western region of Poitou-Charentes; and then the Midi-Pyrénées and Aquitaine.

street officially known as Bute Street, SW7 and unofficially as Frog Alley – is a place where the cafés sell more early-morning *tartines* than bacon and eggs, and earnest young men in turtlenecks discuss Sartre in the French bookshop. The number of French people living in Britain, in fact, has increased every year from 1991, jumping by over 10,000 in 2006 – the largest leap in two decades. England is now the preferred destination for French people in Europe, just as France is for the English.

What lies behind this latest French mania for *la vie anglaise*? A study by the French newspaper *Le Figaro* in 2011 found that for the majority of French expats in England, the biggest attractions are the job opportunities, levels of pay, and individual freedom (on all of which counts England was rated far more highly than France).[9] French expats in London can't get over the fact that, in England, you can get a job as a bartender without a PhD in oenology; that you can set up a new company in a day for a few quid, as opposed to several weeks of complicated form-filling and hundreds of euros in accountants' and lawyers' fees; and that when you make a profit, two-thirds of it doesn't end up being paid out in tax and employee charges. In France, businessmen who start their own thriving enterprises are regarded as vulgar upstarts, the object of envy and resentment; the brightest French students kill themselves to win a place as a civil servant or PDG* of a top French company, not a *nouveau riche*, self-employed wheeler-dealer.† The French are fond of sneering at the British tendency – of which the former Conservative premier Margaret Thatcher was an especially ardent proponent – of elevating the lower middle class and its aspirations to a national totem: the 'nation of shopkeepers', as Napoleon once famously dismissed it. But it gets ever harder for the French to curl the lip when the country's brightest and best are voting with their feet, and opting for the nation of shopkeepers over the oligarchy of pen-pushers.

---

* i.e. 'President Director General', the French equivalent of a CEO.

† If George W. Bush really did once say that the French don't have a word for *entrepreneur*, he was right in spirit, if not in the letter.

Nor is Britain the only adoptive home for French expats. Whilst England is the top destination for French expats in Europe, the top world destination for France's children in travelling shoes is Canada, in particular the French-speaking province of Québec. Over the last decade Québec has seen as explosion in French immigrants, now totalling over 110,000, and in the past thirty years French immigrants have come before those from Algeria, China and Morocco. The number of French people registered with the French embassy in Québec has doubled in the last ten years.[10] The reasons for this influx are similar to those underlying the exodus to London – job opportunities, freedom to be oneself – without the linguistic challenge of life in London. But unlike the majority of French immigrants in England – who usually thrive in their host country once the language barrier has been overcome – a lot of French would-be settlers in Québec come back to the Motherland disgruntled. Why? Because of mistaken assumptions as to what Québec is, it appears. The average French emigrant dreams of a land of log cabins and sled-pulling huskies peopled by jolly provincial Frenchmen: in short, an acre of France in America. The reality – to their shock and chagrin – is to be faced with America in French. With a strongly individualistic ethic, a free-market economy, and cuisine that has developed far beyond its French roots and embraced much of its American heritage, the *Québecquois* turn out to be – frighteningly – Anglo-Saxon. Perhaps it is little wonder that, of the 3,000–4,000 French emigrants to Québec every year,[11] 18–20 per cent return home within five years.[12]

Nor is it just the bright young things rich in ideas and poor in cash who are leaving France for pastures new. Just as in 1981 – after the election of the Socialist president François Mitterrand – there was a stealthy flow out of the richest *arrondissements* of central Paris, so in 2012–13, following the election of a new Socialist president with an aggressive tax agenda, there is once again a discreet packing of Louis Vuitton bags and a row of limousines snaking along dark roads to private aerodromes. French businessmen, celebrities (including the actor Gérard Depardieu) and industry bosses are quietly finding domiciles elsewhere, shifting assets, taking Swiss or Belgian nationality (or, in Depardieu's case, Russian). The biggest storm was caused when the boss of the multinational luxury goods conglomerate LVMH,* Bernard Arnaud – the richest man in France – took Belgian nationality in 2012, allegedly to avoid paying the new wealth tax of 75 per cent for incomes over €1 million (a claim that he denied). 'Get lost, you rich jerk!' (*Casse-toi, riche con!*), screamed the headline in the French left-wing daily *Libération* on Monday 10 September 2012, in an explosion of vulgar invective worthy of the Murdoch press in Britain.

Now that there are as many pavement cafés and French bookshops in Paris-on-Thames as there are tea-shops and pubs in Dordogneshire, it seems that the Gauls have at long last taken sweet revenge on the invading Britons. Except that it seems they are booting out their brightest and best across the Channel, while becoming a retirement home for elderly Brits. Hardly the fairest swap. But then, who do the French have to blame?

Myth Evaluation: *True, although more French people are fleeing Gaul these days than Britons leaving Blighty.*

---

* i.e. the group Louis Vuitton Moët Hennessy, proprietor of some of France's most famous luxury brands, including Moët et Chandon, Louis Vuitton, Hennessy, Christian Dior and Veuve Clicquot.

The British are the champions of gardening

One channels Nature, one does not change it.
VOLTAIRE (FRANÇOIS-MARIE AROUËT; 1694–1778), FRENCH WRITER

They may have lost an empire and not won football's World Cup for nearly fifty years, but there is one (hugely popular) area of human endeavour in which the British still pride themselves on being world champions – and that is gardening. In fact, gardening in Britain is a national obsession, whether one has a garden or not (perhaps especially if not), and an Englishman or Englishwoman is never so happy as when on his or her knees in a herbaceous border, doing unmentionable things in wellies with a pair of secateurs. The French, on the other hand (or so the Anglo-Saxon wisdom goes) consider it all a bit of a bore – gardens are for the peasantry, and with such jaw-dropping countryside, what need is there to bother getting grubby with a spade or fork? The average Parisian apartment dweller is perfectly content with a window box of geraniums, knowing those fields of lavender and olive groves are just a TGV trip away. To prove their supremacy on the horticultural front, the British generally point to the great tradition of English landscape gardening that began in the 1730s and subsequently became the model for aristocratic estate gardens and municipal parks throughout the world: from the majestic vistas of rolling hills, winding rivers and humpback bridges of the great early landscaped parks such as those at Stowe and Stourhead, to the later, more intimate, cottage-garden-inspired drifts of humbler blooms in the gardens designed by Gertrude Jekyll in the early twentieth century.

The pre-eminence of English landscape garden design in Europe from the mid-eighteenth century tends to obscure the fact that, in terms of gardening history, it is the French who were once the uncontested champions of gardening. At the turn

of the seventeenth century in Europe, the only kind of garden to be seen dead in was the *jardin à la française*. The classical French garden had its roots in the Italian Renaissance gardens of the early sixteenth century, which, with their geometrical *parterres*,* fountains, mazes and statuary, were designed to evoke the harmony and balance that were key to this most optimistic and enlightened of eras. French Renaissance gardens like those at Fontainebleau and the châteaux of the Loire Valley (such as Chenonceau and Villandry) featured intricate knots of cropped box hedges, coordinated floral displays, and rows of pollarded trees interspersed with fountains; the regimented order of the planting merely exemplified the triumph of the civilizing force of man over the natural world.

The order and discipline of the classical French garden became, over the ensuing centuries, the pattern copied by noble estates throughout Europe. Greatest of all, naturally, was the garden of the Sun King himself: the vast network of tree-lined paths and fountains that made up the gardens of Versailles, constructed from the latter part of the seventeenth century onwards. Not that the Versailles gardens were, strictly speaking, Louis XIV's own idea. In fact, he nicked the concept from a courtier. The unfortunate man in question was Nicolas Fouquet, Louis' minister of finance. For many years, Fouquet had been busy embezzling state money to build the most spectacular estate the world had ever seen: Vaux-le-Vicomte, southeast of Paris. This was a massive baroque extravaganza of a palace and sumptuous gardens, designed by the celebrated master of French garden design, the landscape gardener and architect André Le Nôtre (incidentally requiring the purchase and demolition of three villages for its construction). Revealing hubris equal to Icarus himself, in 1661 Fouquet had the temerity to invite the Sun King to his spectacu-

* An ornamental garden with paths, hedges and flowerbeds arranged in a geometrical pattern.

Everything is good when it leaves the hands of the creator... everything degenerates in Man's hands.

JEAN-JACQUES ROUSSEAU, FRANCO-SWISS PHILOSOPHER AND WRITER (1712–78), *ÉMILE OR, ON EDUCATION*, 1762

lar new abode. The result was inevitable – a wing-clipping that landed him in jail for the rest of his life, his palace and gardens requisitioned by the king, and his head gardener poached to work on Louis' new work-in-progress at Versailles.

With Fouquet languishing on permanent gardening leave, Le Nôtre was free to devote his green-fingered magic to the gardens of his horticultural competitor at Versailles. The result was the glorious, showy masterpiece that even to this day continues to delight and amaze millions of visitors every year. Le Nôtre brought the principles of classical French garden design – order, symmetry, the triumph of man over nature – to a dizzy apogee with a spectacular display of fountains, parterres, lakes and statuary, synthesized to form an anthem to the sun god Apollo (alias the Sun King) himself. Intimacy in this vast space came from the enclosed walls and secret chambers of the celebrated *bosquets* that harboured secluded benches and grottos, perfect places for romance, intrigue and secret assignations.*

The gardens of Versailles remained the playground of the French aristocracy for over a century, until the royal family was forced to return to Paris in the wake of the French Revolution of 1789. Then, just as the sun was setting on the Sun King's legacy, so it set on his garden also. After the Revolution the gardens of Versailles fell into disrepair, the hedges unclipped and the grand pools requisitioned by local villagers to wash their linen. But in any event a new, rival gardening style had already begun to usurp the position of the French classical garden fifty years before the fall of the gardens of Versailles, from the 1730s onwards. This revolutionary style was quite different from the formal geometry of the classical French garden. It was based on

* Literally a 'group of trees', *bosquet* became the term used to define the rows and clusters of tall, clipped hedges and later trees that formed external alleyways and chambers in the gardens of Versailles and other classical French gardens of this period.

rolling hills, clumps of trees, and winding rivers – a 'landscape' garden that strove both to imitate and perfect nature. The originator of this rival style was the architect William Kent, who had introduced tumbling ruins and picturesque Italianate landscapes to parks such as that at Stowe House (1730–8), to complement the Palladian architecture of the new mansions he was building. Kent's legacy was developed and expanded by one Launcelot Brown, immortalized in history as 'Capability Brown' because of his habit of telling his wealthy clients that their gardens were 'capable' of improvement. Under the stern axe of Brown and his successors from the 1740s onwards, hundreds of acres of formal French-style gardens in England in the eighteenth century had already been guillotined in a green revolution every bit as shattering in its own way as the real one that took place fifty years later across the Channel. The sacrilegious wit and poet Richard Owen Cambridge even dared to whisper the hope that he would die before Brown, so as to get to heaven before it was 'improved'.

The landscaped, 'gardenless garden' soon caught on in Europe as the latest fashion, not least because acres of rolling, sheep-cropped grass were a lot easier to maintain, in a war-torn and post-revolutionary continent where obedient peasants were in short supply, than the clipped box hedges of the classical French style. Not that the French ever admitted that it was the English who invented the new style. Even to this day, they tend to prefer to call the English landscape garden the *jardin anglo-chinois* (Anglo-Chinese garden). And strangely, recent research shows that they may have a point. Among the myriad influences that came together to culminate in the eighteenth-century landscape garden, there were the tales brought back by Jesuit priests from the court of the Chinese emperor, of magnificent gardens with stately pleasure domes inspired not by art but nature, where

Every culture has an attitude towards nature. I think the French feel that you have to fit into nature and control it, but live along with it. You cannot violate it without paying for it. It is not necessarily hostile, but you have to be careful to keep nature civilized.

LAURENCE WYLIE IN *CONTEMPORARY FRENCH CULTURE AND SOCIETY*, 1981 covered corridors linked sequences of pavilions with 'viewing platforms' cunningly set up so that the observer could witness the sound of the wind in the bamboo, rain on banana leaves, or a shaft of moonlight streaking the fins of a leaping goldfish. The philosophy of Chinese gardening essentially drew its inspiration from the natural world, of 'art imitating nature' rather than the other way round, as in classical French garden design. The explosion of interest in *chinoiserie* in the early eighteenth century could well have led the English to the appreciation, then subsequent imitation, of Chinese garden design; but they were never to admit it. The Whig politician Horace Walpole, along with his friend the poet Thomas Gray, were virulent about scurrilous French attempts to characterize the English gardening style as a copy of the Chinese. According to Walpole, the naturalistic English gardening style could only have come from the 'opulence of a free country'. Richard Owen Cambridge also weighed in: 'Whatever may have been reported, whether truly or falsely, of the Chinese gardens,' he wrote sniffily, 'it is certain that we are the first Europeans to have founded their taste.'[13]

Whatever the truth of its origins, the English (sorry, Anglo-Chinese) garden was to replace Versailles as the new European norm, laying the parameters of landscape gardening and subsequently public parks in the centuries to come. It was to be the basis of many mid- and late-eighteenth-century French parks and gardens, such as Rousseau's garden at Ermenonville, the Désert de Retz at Chambourcy in the Île de France, and the romantic Parc Monceau in the 8th *arrondissement* of Paris. The French, however, somehow never made 'natural' really look natural: even in the case of Parc Monceau and the fabulously fantastical ravines of the garden at the Désert de Retz, the panoramas of French landscape gardening are highly stylized, and there are a few too many of the ubiquitous follies or *fabriques* dotted about. (Parc Monceau alone boasts scaled-down versions of an Egyptian pyramid, Chinese fort, Dutch windmill and Corinthian columns.) Nevertheless, it is all too easy to forget that, while the naturalistic landscape park may have been originally an English (and/or Chinese) invention, the French did influence its later development. This is particularly true of the English landscape gardener Gertrude Jekyll, whose work with the architect Edwin Lutyens in the early twentieth century reduced the vast proportions of the old, Capability Brown-style parks to the more intimate, manageable proportions of a garden suited to the Edwardian home. It was Jekyll who replaced Brown's giant vistas with intimate spaces ('rooms') clustered with cottage-garden roses, drifts of bulbs and herbaceous borders; it was she who introduced the now classic formulation of 'hot' and 'cool' colours for plantings; and she was in no little measure inspired by the works of Impressionist painter Claude Monet in the painterly strokes of her colour schemes. (Monet's garden at Giverny, created in the 1890s, contains the water-lily pond made famous by his sequence of paintings that take it as their subject. The vivid colour-blocks of the plantings in Monet's garden are reminiscent of the gardens of Gertrude Jekyll.)

Turning to the present day, in terms of public spaces, French gardening style has not grown out of the rather strict, disciplinarian regime under which it (like French children) grew up. Trees in French public parks (except those specifically denoted as rebellious Anglo-Chinese gardens) are usually marshalled in elegant rows, subject to annual pollarding; flowers are whipped into shape in geometric parterres; hedges clean-shaven. There's none of the hippie abandon of Hampstead Heath or Wimbledon Common. (Unsurprisingly, most of the words for disciplining and training trees – *espalier, pleach, cordon* – are originally French.) The French obsession with disciplining and formalizing nature is evident in the annual autumn ritual of pollarding every single tree in sight, creating miserable rows of amputees along the great roads carved by Napoleon. The former French president Charles de Gaulle – a perhaps unlikely commentator on horticultural matters – once wrote in praise of French gardening style. His eulogy is telling:

'In a French garden, no tree seeks to stifle the other trees by overshadowing them, the flower beds flourish although they are geometrically trained, the pool of water does not long to be a waterfall, the statues do not seek to show off to the detriment

THE GREEN-FINGERED GAULS

Contrary to popular belief about the alleged French disdain for the spade, perhaps not surprisingly for a country newly in love with suburbia, the French actually love gardening. If recent surveys are anything to go by, they are at least as (if not more) fond of gardening as the British. According to figures from the Office of European Statistics, French and British women both spend about 3 per cent of their domestic time gardening; however, French men spend 13 per cent of their time getting down and dirty, whereas British men apparently spend only 9 per cent. It seems, then, that if anybody is the champion of gardening these days, it is French men.

As to the dream garden of the French, the answer is somewhat surprising. It is neither the classical French, nor the Anglo-Chinese version. In fact, according to the most recent studies, the ideal garden that most French people fantasize about having is no other than the humble *jardin de curé* – the traditional walled village curate's garden, with its grass paths bordering diamond-shaped potagers planted with vegetables for the kitchen, simple hardy flowers to decorate the altar, a vine or two to supply church wine and some medicinal herbs. Nothing grand, formal, pseudo-natural or triumphalist, but a simple return to something quite basic and utilitarian – not so very far removed, in fact, from the English cottage garden, or the recent allotment revivals in Britain.

Sources: EUROSTAT Free Time survey, 2004; French Union of Businesses for the Protection of Gardens and Green Spaces survey, 2004.

of the other elements of the garden. There is a feeling of noble melancholy about the garden. Perhaps it comes from the feeling that each element, if it were seen alone, could be shown off to better advantage. But it would have been to the detriment of the whole unit, and the person who strolls through the garden congratulates himself on the order that imparts to the garden its magnificent harmony.'[14]

Order, discipline, hierarchy, the subordination of individual desire to the collective good, versus the luxuriant chaos of rampant individualism… the polarities in French and English gardening styles seem to mirror the difference between the two countries and cultures. On the one hand there is the formal, planned rigidity of the French garden; on the other, the pretty, disorganized yet somehow harmonious chaos of the English cottage garden. Just as Paris is still the splendidly planned, rational city of Baron Haussmann's boulevards, and London a messy, glorious Dickensian hotchpotch of 'villages'. Both sets of rival aesthetics, like both sets of politics, have helped shape the lens through which we see and live the world today; but neither, in the end, has been the ultimate victor in the turf wars.

Myth Evaluation: *False. The French and English have been champions of gardening at different periods of history.*

Digestif

The Almighty in his infinite wisdom did not see fit to create Frenchmen in the image of Englishmen.
WINSTON CHURCHILL (1874–1965), BRITISH STATESMAN

When my final French 'myth' had been mercilessly set on the operating table, examined, dissected and either saved or relegated to the trash bin, I sat down to ponder. What had I learned from this forensic exercise? My examination of the myriad myths, legends and stories surrounding the people of Gaul had taught me an awful lot about France and the French. But it had also taught me even more about myself – or rather, I should say, about us, the Anglo-Saxons. Because, underlying almost all of these myths we construct about France, there lies a romantic and indefinable yearning… a sense of emulation, jealousy and desire. It is as though we cannot simply accept the French as a different race and culture, analysing them objectively – as, for example, we have no problem doing, say, with the Japanese. No, when it comes to the French, we must romanticize, idolize, emulate, envy or – when they defy our attempts at definition – condemn. They are either the object of wild and senseless worship, or equally vitriolic censure. We somehow have to possess and define them, as a projection of our own dreams. And they defy our attempts at possession.

But, you might ask, why spoil our romantic notions about the French by an investigation? What harm does it do, dreaming about a Gallic Neverland conjured up by a book with a pink dustjacket, cheering up a cold and wintry English afternoon? The first answer to that argument must be that truth – however difficult, shocking or unpalatable – has got to be ultimately more satisfying than fiction. Nor are all myths about the French bad. History is full of fables and tall tales, and the construction of narratives is integral to life itself. Stories about the fabulous discovery of *tarte tatin*, the legendary chefs of French history, or the discovery of Roquefort, enrich our cultural experience of

French food, and indirectly of France itself. Who cares if they are probably not true?

Myths that become distorted into stereotypes defining a whole nation, on the other hand, merit a closer inquiry. We ought to ask ourselves whether myths that are frankly offensive or derogatory – such as that of the French not washing – really are true. Other stereotypes are more subtle. Myths such as that of French women not getting fat, French children not throwing food, or the idyllic French village, would seem to be pretty harmless – and even complimentary to the French, on the surface. But what if they are masking an incipient obesity issue, or concealing the wholesale destruction of the French countryside? What of the disappointment that we feel when we arrive at that dream rustic holiday *gîte*, only to discover a Carrefour hypermarket at the entrance to the village, and a cottage interior stocked with IKEA furniture? France is a land of beauty and delight, but in a country that is a major industrial power, those unspoiled, picturesque corners and sublime experiences are becoming rarer and more hidden, requiring a determined expedition off the beaten track to find them. To be forewarned is to be forearmed. The most important thing is not to be disappointed.

In any event, we should perhaps be asking ourselves a different question. That is, not whether France lives up to our expectations, but rather whether we have the right to impose such expectations on it. After all, doesn't France have the right to be an industrial power like any other – blotted and scarred with the battles of immigration, industrialization, fast food, overcrowding and mass-market culture? Why should she be a mausoleum imprisoned forever in a cheese-eating, garlic-munching, glamourously thin-woman Neverland, just to satisfy the Anglo-American desire for a dream? An interesting point to note is that whilst a great deal of material from different authorities was amassed in researching this book, most of the material comes from published sources readily available to those actually living in France, with a sound grasp of the French language and a good general knowledge of issues of live interest to the French today. I did not need to bribe French government officials to find out

the figures for female obesity in France, or secretly interview unnamed sources in the education sector to find out that French children *do* throw food. And yet, the 'Froglit' authors – those messengers to their compatriots in the UK and USA, whose winged missives so many Anglo-Saxons await with breathless expectation – do not report these truths which, in many cases, are completely apparent to anybody living in France for any length of time, and with a modicum of familiarity with French culture. Instead, they insist on recycling the same tired yet (admittedly) eminently marketable clichés. Just like those countless romantic movies about Paris – Woody Allen's *Midnight in Paris* included – which, in their portrayal of the City of Light, totally ignore the Corbusian ugliness of tower blocks like those at La Défense, apparent to everybody when they actually arrive in town. Our vision of France is always distorted, skewed, tailored to what we want to see.

Our image of the French, more than of any other nationality, tends to be based on a series of 'paradoxes'. For example, French women drink wine, eat *foie gras*, and yet don't get fat; the French work less than most other countries, yet they have one of the highest productivity rates. These contradictions fuel our perception of the French as a mysterious people, endowed with miraculous qualities beyond Anglo-Saxon comprehension. But in reality, once the so called 'paradoxes' are unpackaged, they are always explicable. In fact, their existence is testimony not to any mystical abilities on the part of the French, but rather to our incomprehension of them. In particular, Anglo-Saxons – fuelled by the Froglit sub-genre – have a tendency to focus on aspects of French lifestyle subject to massive idealization (long holidays, short work hours, a culture of intimate local shopping experiences, lengthy lunches), while ignoring the French politics and policies that make this lifestyle possible. Take one example. France is a haven of small, independent bookshops: there are 3,000 in the country, of which 400 are in Paris, compared to only 1,000 in England (a mere 130 in London). Why? Because the French state imposes the same price on all books, regardless of whether they are sold via the Internet, chain bookstores or the corner bookshop. The same is true for all those markets and local *boulangeries* buzzing at the weekend: laws preventing the big supermarkets trading on Sunday to date have helped them survive. The role of the French state also explains the apparent 'miracle' by which French women have loads of children and yet manage to hold down their jobs: a network of low-cost crèches, holiday and after-school care, along with massive child benefits and tax breaks for children, helps women manage a work–life balance with relative ease. At the same time, France is an intensely macho society which is only just getting round to abolishing the title of 'Miss', defining a law of sexual harassment, and a country in which one of the major functions and duties of the female sex always has been to embellish and ornament the public space. These attitudes and assumptions are fundamental to, and therefore cannot be dissociated from, French female style. But would we want to adopt them as our own?

Next time you read a book that promises the secrets of French women's style or eulogizes the French way of life, ask yourself a few searching questions. Are you willing to pay €16 for a book for the privilege of buying it in a small bookshop? Are you prepared to pay twice as much tax, so that women can put their kids in a crèche? Are you willing to sacrifice the freedom of being able to sneak to the supermarket on a Sunday morning in tracksuit bottoms and trainers? If the answer is no, it doesn't matter how much cabbage soup you drink, how many clothes you buy from *Agnès B,* or whether you try to follow the precepts of *la pause* to make your baby sleep. You will never master the basics of the French way of life. Because, in many ways, the 'French way of life' – formal, hierarchical, state-controlled and prescriptive – is diametrically opposed to the individualism and freedom that lies at the heart of Anglo-Saxon society.

I have now lived for almost a decade in France. My three children have lived their childhood here, cheer for France in rugby matches, and will be sitting the *baccalauréat,* the great examination originally invented by Napoleon. They themselves do experience occasional problems negotiating the vast psychological differences between the cultures that they straddle, but somehow they seem to be muddling through. As for myself, over the years I have acquired a great affection for my host country, considerable respect, and some reservations.

But one thing is certain, and that is that we Anglo-Saxons will never be French; nor should we wish to be. As Queen Elizabeth II once said in a public address (in very good French, incidentally): *vive l'entente cordiale, et vive la différence!*

Acknowledgements

A book like this could not have been written without a great deal of assistance and advice from different experts in the many fields it covers, including of course those most expert in its principal subject: the French! My first acknowledgement should be to the many historians, sociologists and other experts, both French and English, who have examined the subjects treated in this book in depth, and whose learned dissertations and treatises have shed light on the many 'myths' explored in this book (full details of works relied upon can be found in the Notes and Bibliography). Then there are the many people who have either lent me a helping hand with their expertise, or cogitated, ruminated, argued and procrastinated with me on the many issues explored: to all of you, a heartfelt thank you! Special thanks are due to (in no particular order):

Jean-François and Hélène Bourdet of JFB Architectes; Martine Bourelly, Dr Christine Moisan at Obépi/Roche; Delphine Siino Courtin; Paul Bichot; Nina Wasilewska-Bichot; Mégane Quere; Alain Huisier; the team at SizeUK; Catherine Dawson at Clifford Chance Europe LLP; Charles Dalglish; Lord Eatwell at Queens' College, Cambridge; Katharine Axten; Pascal Petit, Director of Research at CNRS, Université Paris 13; Azouz Guizani; Shelley Thevathasan; Veerle Miranda and Julie Harris at the OECD; Dominique Le Martret; the staff at Cambridge Tutors College, London; Nicholas Baker and James Cathcart at the Lycée International de Saint-Germain-en-Laye; Arlette Garih at Maternité Port Royal de Paris; Professor Stoffel Munck; Didier Pleux, Director of the French Institute of Cognitive Therapy; Julie Marabelle of Famille Summerbelle; Sarah Ardizzone; Julie Muret of *Osez le féminisme*; Ella Gaffuri; and the representatives of *Allegro Fortissimo*.

It goes without saying, of course, that all views, opinions and conclusions in this book are entirely my own.

To my indefatigable agent, Andrew Lownie, I am eternally

grateful. And a heartfelt thank you to my editor Richard Milbank, who has made this book so much better than it otherwise would have been.

Finally, I should thank my mother, Sarah Das Gupta, for keeping the faith at all times, and my long-suffering husband, Nikolaï Eatwell.

NOTES

APERITIF

1 ***the last traditional French beret manufacturer.*** i.e. Béatex, taken over in July 2012 by the army uniform manufacturing group Cargo-Promodis.

2 ***wet sock on my head.*** See *L'Armée US abandonne le béret, Le Figaro* 14 juin 2011.

CHAPTER 1

1 ***Vatel incident.*** See *Lettres de Madame de Sévigné de sa famille*, Vol. I, Paris: Hachette 1863, pp. 286–8.

2 ***'lighter food, less of it, costing more.'*** Elizabeth David, *French Provincial Cooking*, Penguin 1970, p. 476.

3 ***French cuisine was ranked number two.*** Survey by Kantar market research, May 2010.

4 ***hippophagy in France was socially engineered and a relatively recent phenomenon.*** For a detailed discussion about the campaign to make *hippophages* of the French in the nineteenth century, see Pierre, Eric: *L'hippophagie au secours des classes laborieuses*. Communications, 74, 2003, pp. 177–200.

5 ***the menu was as follows.*** See *Larousse Gastronomique* (English edition), Hamlyn/Octopus Publishing Group Ltd 2009, p. 549.

6 ***feasts in Britain, in Ramsgate.*** See Frederick J. Simoons, *Eat Not this Flesh: Food Avoidances from Prehistory to the Present*, University of Wisconsin Press 1994, p. 190.

7 ***Yesterday, I had a slice of Pollux for dinner.*** From *Diary of the Besieged Resident in Paris* by Henry Du Pré Labouchère, Hurst & Blackett, 1871.

8 ***consumption of horsemeat increasing 77 per cent.*** See *La Viande Chevaline: un patrimoine, juridiquement encadré, indispensable à la filière cheval*, Fédération Nationale du Cheval, May 2008, p. 5.

9 ***nine thousand horses, mules and donkeys.*** See Simoons, *Eat Not this Flesh*, op. cit., p. 190.

10 ***low status and poverty.*** See Simoons, op. cit., p. 190.

11 ***110,290 TEC of horsemeat were consumed in 1964.*** See *La Viande Chevaline: un patrimoine, juridiquement encadré, indispensable à la filière cheval*, op. cit., p.17.

12 ***In 2004, France consumed 25,380 tons of horsemeat.*** Figures from *Production Viande Chevaline, chiffres clés*, Fédération Nationale du Cheval, Supplément à Tendances No. 164, December 2006.

13 ***Just 0.4 kg per French person per year in 2005, compared to 22.5 kg of beef.*** See *Production Viande Chevaline, chiffres clés*, op. cit.

14 ***two-thirds of French light horses and ponies are now protected in this way.*** See *Production Viande Chevaline, chiffres clés*, op. cit.

15 ***Jean-Claude Ribaut.*** In *Le Monde à table*, 10 February 2013.

16 ***Expert on the history and culture of food.*** See *Pourquoi la viande de cheval est un tabou en Grande-Bretagne, Le Monde*, 12 February 2013.

17 ***the association between the French and jumping amphibians.*** For further elaboration of the historical association between the French and frogs or toads see E. Cobham Brewer (1894), *Brewer's Dictionary of Phrase and Fable – Revised and Updated Edition*, 19th revised edition, Hodder Education, 31 August 2012.

18 ***'Nic Frog' was once a nickname for a Dutchman.*** See Jonathon Green's *Dictionary of Slang*, Chambers Harrap 2012, entries for *Frog* and *Froglander*.

19 ***redcoats.*** The term *habit rouge* became a slang term for Englishman after Waterloo: see *Le Grand Robert de la langue française*.

20 ***homards or lobsters.*** Recorded use in this sense in 1847; see *Le Grand Robert de la langue française*.

21 ***The biggest European importer of frogs' legs is not France.*** See Altherr, S. et al. (2011): *Canapés to extinction – the international trade in frogs' legs and its ecological impact*. A report by Pro Wildlife, Defenders of Wildlife and Animal Welfare

Institute (eds), Munich (Germany), Washington DC (USA).

22 ***close to a billion snails eaten every year.*** See *Escargot: une industrie ralentie par la sécheresse*, Les Marchés (l'agroalimentaire au quotidien), 9 juin 2011.

23 ***the average Frenchman eats around 26kg of cheese a year.*** Per capita cheese consumption figures for France, UK and the USA for 2010 (total per capita consumption) from Canadian Dairy Information Centre.

24 ***protected by the AOP label.*** The French *AOC* label began with wine then caught on with food, to be replaced by the European *AOP* label for dairy products in 2012. In practice, *AOC* and *AOP* mean the same thing.

25 ***the genius of Roquefort.*** See Curnonsky, *Lettres de Noblesse*, Les Éditions Nationales 1935, p. 29.

26 ***Raw milk cheese made up only 15 per cent.*** See *Enquête annuelle laitière 2009*, Agreste Primeur No. 264, June 2011; *Les petits entreprises du commerce depuis 30 ans*, INSEE No. 831, February 2002.

27 ***The Lyonnaise cheese known as la galette des Monts-d'Or.*** See *La bataille pour la survie des fromages français*, Laprovence.com, 30 mars 2008.

28 ***the feta-loving Greeks.*** Total per capita cheese consumption figures for 2010 from the Canadian dairy Information Centre, as above.

29 ***Russian penicillin.*** See Alix Lefief-Delcourt, *L'Ail Malin*, LEDUC.S Éditions 2011, p. 17.

30 ***Henri IV.*** See Alix Lefief-Delcourt, op. cit.

31 ***Temple of Cybele.*** Alexandre Dumas, *Grand Dictionnaire de cuisine.*

32 ***French word chandail.*** See *Dictionnaire Étymologique*, Larousse 2001, p. 16.

33 ***US military pamphlet issued in 1945.*** See *112 Gripes about the French*, US military occupation forces pamphlet, 1945, Kessinger Legacy Reprints.

34 ***10 kilos per capita annually.*** Figures from LMJ International Limited; see also Andy Mukherjee, *South Korea's Mr Garlic strives for openness*, Bloomberg June 7, 2004.

35 ***China.... followed by India and South Korea.*** See *Economie et marché de l'ail*, Matthieu Serrurier, Centre Technique Interprofessionel des Fruits et Légumes, 16 mars 2011.

36 ***Recent figures show that the biggest consumers of garlic in France today are the elderly and middle-aged.*** See *Economie et marché de l'ail*, 2011, op. cit.

37 ***Americans eat three times as much garlic as they did in the 1980s.*** *Garlic – tracing its country of origin*. US Customs today, Vol 38, no. 8.

38 ***mercantile empires of standardization and conformism.*** Cited by Richard F. Kuisel, *The French Way: How France Embraced and Rejected American Values and Power*, Princeton University Press 2010, p.183.

39 ***France is the second-biggest market in the world for McDonald's.*** See Caroline Castets, *A la Une egalement – French paradox*, Le Nouvel Economiste.fr, 27 avril 2011.

40 ***Every day, 1.7 million French people eat at McDonalds.*** Key figures for meals sold and turnover for the year 2011 from McDonald's.

41 ***one of the principal purchasers of French beef.*** See Caroline Castets, op. cit.

42 ***fast food represented 7 out of 10 meals.*** See *Le boom de la restauration rapide*, Le Figaro, 10 février 2010.

43 ***The French are now the second-largest consumers of hamburgers in Europe.*** According to a study conducted by market researchers NPD Group, the French consume on average 14 hamburgers per year in restaurants per person, behind the British (17) but ahead of the Germans (12), Spanish (9) and Italians (5) (*Les Français, deuxième plus gros consommateurs de hamburgers en Europe*, L'Express, 16 juillet 2012).

44 ***over a third of French people were overweight.*** That is, 32 per cent in the Paris-Île de France region and 36 per cent elsewhere. See INSEE report *Un tiers des Franciliens présente un excès de poids*, 2007.
45 ***the poet Charles Baudelaire.*** From *Du vin et du haschich* (1851).
46 ***France is still the world's biggest wine producer.*** Figures for world wine production and consumption for 2010 from The Wine Institute, California.
47 ***plummeting from 50 billion litres in 1980 to 32 billion litres in 2008.*** Studies by VINIFLHOR/INRA (Scientific Institute for Agricultural Research) (2008) on wine consumption in France.
48 ***And whereas in 1970 the French drank over twice as much alcohol as mineral water or fruit juice.*** See *Boissons alcoolisées: 40 ans de baisse de consommation*, INSEE no. 966, mai 2004, p. 3.
49 ***A 2011 study by researchers at the University of Toulouse.*** See Lorey, T. and Poutet, P. (2011), *The representation of wine in France from generation to generation: a dual generation gap, Int. J. Entrepreneurship and Small Businesses*, Vol. 13, No. 2, pp. 162–80.
50 ***UK wine imports.*** See WSTA (Wine and Spirit Trade Association), 2012 UK wine and spirit market overview, p. 5.
51 ***the most spectacular increases are in Australia and Chile.*** See *L'Avenir de la viticulture française: entre tradition et défi du Nouveau Monde.* Sénat, 4 octobre, 2012. In the period 1998–2001, land devoted to vines increased by 21 per cent in Chile and 63 per cent in Australia.
52 ***He (in)famously once said.*** Interview with William Langewiesche, correspondent for *The Atlantic*, in *The Atlantic Monthly*, December 2000: *The Million-Dollar Nose* – 00.12; Volume 286, No. 6; page 42–70.
53 ***China is now the number one buyer of Bordeaux wines.*** See FranceAgriMer, VINS/COMMERCE EXTERIOR, Bilan 2011/du 1er janvier au 31 décembre, p.13.
54 ***the French poet Paul Verlaine.*** Letter to Edmond Lepelletier, cited in Lepelletier, *Paul Verlaine: sa vie, son œuvre*, Réimpression de l'édition de Paris, 1923, p. 299.
55 ***Roland Barthes.*** From *Mythologies* (New York, The Noonday Press, 1957), p. 59.
56 ***The French rules of savoir-vivre.*** See Dominique Picard, *Politesse, savoir-vivre et relations sociales*, Presses Universitaires de France, 1998, p. 31.
57 ***On the other hand, the rules of savoir vivre are closely linked to place.*** See Dominique Picard, op. cit., p. 42.
58 ***As the author of the leading French book on etiquette.*** See Baronne Staffe, *Usages du monde: règles du savoir-vivre dans la société moderne* (1891), Éditions Tallandier, 2007, p. 257.
59 ***the principal cause of death among French youth.*** According to the French health insurers SMENO.
60 ***In a 2011 survey of European youth by the pan-European agency ESPAD.*** See ESPAD (European School Survey Project on Alcohol and Other Drugs) 2011, results for France, United Kingdom and Europe as a whole.

CHAPTER 2

1 ***Key rules include:*** For a comprehensive exposition of the rules of *savoir-vivre* relating to personal appearance, see Dominique Picard, *Politesse, savoir-vivre et relations sociales*, P.U.F. 1998, pp. 30–4.
2 ***it's important not to be noticed too much.*** Poll conducted by Kairos Future for the *Fondation pour l'innovation politique*, 2008.
3 ***the ObÉpi survey.*** *Enquête épidémiologique nationale sur le surpoids et l'obésité* (ObÉpi 2012), Inserm/Kantar Health/Roche.
4 ***Vital Statistics Table.*** Figures from *SizeUK* (UK National Sizing Survey) 2004, and from *Résultats de la campagne nationale de mensuration*, 2 février 2006. All figures have been converted from metric to imperial and rounded.

5 ***global averages conceal large discrepancies.*** See *L'Obésité en France: les écarts entre catégories sociales s'accroissent*, INSEE report Feburary 2007. The strong links between education/class, geographical region and weight are also recorded in the ObÉpi/Roche report, op. cit.
6 ***Women without the baccalauréat.*** See INSEE report, op. cit., p.3.
7 ***An OECD report.*** See *Obesity and the Economics of Prevention: Fit not Fat – France Key Facts.* OECD, 2011.
8 ***Manual of etiquette.*** Baronne Staffe, *Usages du monde: règles du savoir-vivre dans la société moderne* (1891). Éditions Tallandier, 2007, p. 257.
9 ***Madame Robertot.*** From Elizabeth David, *French Provincial Cooking* (1960), Grub Street 2007, pp. 22–4.
10 ***It is a law of most societies.*** See Stephen Mennell, *All Manners of Food: Eating and Tasting in England and France from the Middle Ages to the Present.* Univ. of Illinois Press 1996, p.201.
11 ***At a meeting in Paris in 1893.*** See Martine Bourelly, *Le Pouvoir dans la cuisine*, Fondation Gabriel Péri, 26 octobre 2009, p. 3.
12 ***As late as 2006, only 6 per cent of French chefs were women.*** See Martine Bourelly, *Le Pouvoir dans la Cuisine*, op. cit.
13 ***According to a 2011 survey by the polling agency Ipsos***. See *Les Français et la cuisine*, Ipsos/Logica Business Consulting, 21 septembre 2011.
14 ***an OECD survey of 29 member countries in 2011.*** See Miranda, V. (2011). *Cooking, Caring, and Volunteering: Unpaid Work Around the World.* OECD Social, Employment and Migration Working Papers, No. 116, OECD publishing, p. 25 Figure 12.
15 ***with the highest birth rate in Europe and one of the highest percentages of women at work.*** According to French Foreign Ministry figures, over 80 per cent of French women are working. (See *La France, championne d'Europe des naissances*, French Foreign Ministry circular, March 2011.)
16 ***no rankness of the wild goat.*** Ovid, *Ars Amatoria* Book III Part IV lines 1-2, translated by A.S. Kline, 2001.
17 ***her pudendum did not match.*** See Mary Lutyens' biography, *Millais and the Ruskins*, John Murray 1967, p. 156, footnote.
18 ***The postcard of this painting.*** See *Courbet : l'enquête à l'œuvre* by Claude Habib, *L'Express*, 3 August 2006.
19 ***it has the distinction.*** See *'L'Origine du monde' de Courbet interdit de Facebook pour cause de nudité*, A.F.P. 16 février 2011.
20 ***In Yugoslavia, for example.*** See Marc-Alain Descamps, *L'invention du corps*, P.U.F. Paris 1986, p. 124.
21 ***a landmark advertisement appeared.*** For an informative although polemical feminist account of the 'underarm campaign' of the early twentieth century in American women's magazines, see Christine Hope, *Caucasian Female Body Hair and American Culture, Journal of American Culture*, Vol. 5, Issue 1, Spring 1982, pp. 93–9.
22 ***A survey of American women from 20 to 81 years old in 1991.*** See S.A. Basow, *The hairless ideal: women and their body hair.* Psychology of Women Quarterly, 1991, 15, pp. 83–96.
23 ***postwar arrival of the nylon stocking.*** Descamps, op. cit., p. 124.
24 ***An inquiry conducted in 1972.*** Descamps, op. cit., pp. 124–5.
25 ***Ipsos for the depilatory brand Nair in 2006.*** *Enquête sur les Français et l'épilation: opinions, attitudes, et comportements, Ipsos, mai 2006.*

CHAPTER 3

1 ***His biographer notes***. L. Daudet, *Clemenceau*, 1942, p. 116.
2 ***the Dominican Republic***. See Bruce M. Rothschild, *History of Syphilis*, Clinical Infectious Diseases 2005:40 (15 May).

3 ***The first major epidemic of the great pox broke out in Naples in 1495.*** For the following and a more detailed account of the spread of syphilis in Europe to Asia, see Aine Collier, *The humble little condom: a history*, Prometheus Books 2007, pp. 47–54.

4 ***slang phrases containing the word 'French'.*** See Jonathon Green's *Dictionary of Slang*, Hodder Education 2010.

5 ***A 2010 survey by the French polling group Ifop.*** *Les Français et la sexualité dans le couple*, Ifop, septembre 2010.

6 ***the Durex 2005 Global Sex Survey.*** See *Give and Receive Global Sex Survey*, Durex, 2005.

7 ***the favoured sexual position.*** *LifeStyle*, 2011; Channel 4 *Great British Sex Survey*, 2011.

8 ***Continental people have sex-life.*** See George Mikes, *How to be an Alien*, Penguin Books 1966, p. 29.

9 ***grandes horizontales.*** For an illuminating discussion of the development of extra-marital relations in France in the nineteenth century, see Alain Corbin, *La Fascination de l'adultère, Marianne l'Histoire hors-série*, juillet–août 2012, pp. 68–73.

10 ***middle-class salon.*** See Corbin, op. cit.

11 ***A 2009 survey by the French magazine Madame Figaro.*** See *Infidélité: les Français passent aux aveux, Madame Figaro*/CSA poll, 23 juillet 2009.

12 ***The United States, on the other hand.*** See Stephen T. Fife and Gerald R. Weeks, *Extramarital Sex/Infidelity*. In J. T. Sears (Ed.) *The Greenwood Encyclopedia of Love, Courtship, and Sexuality Through History, Vol. 6, The Modern World* (pp. 126–9). Westport, CT: Greenwood Pub. Group.

13 ***Giscard/milk float incident.*** See Dimitri Casali & Sandrine Gallotta, *Sexe & Pouvoir: secrets d'alcôves de César à DSK*, Éditions de la Martinière, Paris, 2012.

14 ***'drive-and-tell' book.*** Jean-Claude Laumond, *Vingt-cinq ans avec lui*, Ramsay, 11 septembre 2001.

15 ***number one reason for divorce in France.*** See L'Union des Familles en Europe, *les enfants du divorce*, février 2011.

16 ***heinous consequences.*** For example *Madame Bovary* (Flaubert) and *Thérèse Raquin* (Zola).

17 ***The French birth rate, at 2.01 children per woman on average.*** Figures from the French Office of Foreign and Diplomatic Affairs, *La France, championne d'Europe des naissances*, March 2011.

18 ***And while most French families average two children.*** Figures from the report *Does Fertility Respond to Work and Family-life Reconciliation Policies in France?* by Olivier Thévenon, CESifo Conference on Fertility and Public Policy, 1st February 2008, pp. 9–10.

19 ***The French philosopher Montesquieu.*** From *De l'esprit des lois*, 1758.

20 ***Louis introduced in 1666 an edict.*** See Louis Boucoiran, *La famille nombreuse dans l'histoire de nos jours*, 1921, p. 39.

21 ***Revolutionary tax breaks.*** See Boucoiran, op. cit., p. 45.

22 ***Posters sprung up featuring Madonna-like materfamilias.*** See for example the 1920 poster, *Journée Nationale des Mères de Familles Nombreuses*, preserved in the *Musée d'histoire contemporaine/BDIC* (Paris).

23 ***since 1967 it has been legal to take the Pill.*** The 1920 law banning contraception was finally reversed in 1967 (in the lead-up to the May 1968 revolution), after a great deal of feminist campaigning, by the law commonly known as *la Loi Neuwirth* in 1967. Abortion was finally sanctioned, under certain conditions, by a law promulgated by the celebrated French writer and feminist Simone Weil (*la Loi Weil*) in 1975.

24 ***Spending upwards of 27.5 per cent of GDP per capita on family allowances.*** See Olivier Thévenon, *Family Policies in OECD Countries : A Comparative Analysis*. Population and Development Review 37(1): 57–87 (March 2011), p. 78 (Appendix Table A1).

25 ***Child benefit starts.*** Figures as at January 2012 (Centre of European and International Liaisons for Social Security database).
26 ***All in all, while France may not be at quite the level of the Nordic countries.*** See Thévenon, 2nd op. cit.
27 ***Chinese parenting.*** As in the somewhat scary *Battle Hymn of the Tiger Mother* by Amy Chua (Bloomsbury, February 2012).
28 ***21–38 per cent of French children aged 1–2 years woke up at night.*** M.J Challamel and Marie Thirion, *Mon enfant dort mal*, Éditions Retz-Pocket, 1993.
29 ***72 per cent of French children aged between 16 and 24 months had sleep issues.*** H. Stork, *Le sommeil du jeune enfant et ses troubles. Une étude clinique comparative entre trois cultures*, in *Neuropsychiatrie de l'enfance et de l'adolescence*, février 2000, 48(1): 70–9, cited by Nathalie Roques, *Dormir avec son bébé*, L'Harmattan 2002, p. 52.
30 ***an unsuitable diet.*** See study by SFAE/BVA 2009 : *Les parents insuffisamment conscients de ce qui se joue au moment du repas.*
31 ***an estimated 25–45 per cent of French babies and toddlers have food issues at some point or other.*** See M.F. Le Heuzey, *Troubles du comportement alimentaire du jeune enfant: 0–6 ans* in *Troubles du comportement alimentaire de l'enfant du nourrisson au préadolescent*, Elsevier Masson 2011, p.31.
32 ***La fessée… which 64 per cent of French parents in a recent survey were not ashamed to admit to using.*** According to a poll conducted by the television channel France 5 after a screening of a television debate on *la fessée* in the daytime series *Les Maternelles*, 3 May 2012 (*Eduquer sans fessée*). Out of 1080 parents who voted, 57.5 per cent smacked their children 'from time to time', and 6.94 per cent 'often'.
33 ***Severe corporal punishment.*** See Prof. Dr. Kai-D. Bussmann, Claudia Erthal, and Andreas Schroth, *The Effect of Banning Corporal Punishment in Europe: a Five Nation Comparison*, University of Wittenberg, October 2009.
34 ***the ritual humiliation of those unable to keep up.*** For an eloquent and passionate critique of the French education system, see Peter Gumbel, *On achève bien les écoliers*, Grasset 2010 (available in English as a Kindle edition, *They shoot school kids, don't they?*).
35 ***Like 'rats in a cage.'*** Lucy Wadham, *The Secret Life of France*, Faber and Faber 2009, p. 123.
36 ***ranked France fifth from the bottom of 66 countries.*** See OECD Pisa in Focus, *Has discipline in school deteriorated?* 2011/4 (May), p. 2.
37 ***A UNICEF study of French primary schoolchildren.*** *Une enquête de victimation et climat scolaire auprès d'élèves du cycle 3 des écoles élémentaires*, Unicef France, March 2011.
38 ***Almost a third of French children aged between 10 and 15 years smoke.*** See Fédération Française de Cardiologie, *Les jeunes et leur coeur*, 13 mars 2012.

CHAPTER 4

1 ***the only known global tourist toilet survey.*** See *The Titanic Awards*, Doug Lansky, Perigee, 2010.
2 ***Our fathers crapped there…*** Pierre-Jean Grosley, *Ephémérides troyennes*, 1758–1769, cited in Roger-Henri Guerrand, *Les Lieux : Histoire des Commodités*, Éditions La Découverte, 2009, p. 17.
3 ***Today, there are some 400 Sanisettes in Paris.*** Mairie de Paris website.
4 ***descent into hell.*** Martin Monestier, *Histoire et bizarreries des excréments… des origines à nos jours*, Le Cherche midi, 1997, 2012, p. 158.
5 ***French and US surveys conducted in the 1990s.*** Studies conducted in California in 1993 and in France in 1994–1996, cited by Martin Monestier, op. cit., pp. 24–5, p. 61. The studies also found that (somewhat

intriguingly) the majority of Americans remained seated when wiping their bottoms (58 per cent) versus the majority of French, who stood up (61 per cent).

6 ***2008 survey for the SCA group.*** *Hygiene Matters: the SCA Hygiene Report* 2008.

7 ***In the words of one Japanese analyst.*** Seiichi Kitayama, study comparing French and Japanese toilets, cited by Monestier, op.cit., p. 159.

8 ***Tobias Smollett.*** See Tobias Smollett, *Travels through France and Italy*, 1766.

9 ***Henri IV to his mistress.*** Cited in Michel Musolino, 150 *Idées Reçues sur la France*, First Éditions 2012, p. 133.

10 ***But our pride… succumbed to the unwashed barbarians.*** *New Scientist*, 6 November 1975, p. 348.

11 ***British per capita soap consumption.*** See Jan de Vries, *The Industrious Revolution: Consumer Behaviour and the Household Economy, 1650 to the Present*, Cambridge University Press 2008, p. 197.

12 ***Frances Trollope.*** Vigarello, Georges, *Concepts of Cleanliness: Changing Attitudes in France since the Middle Ages*. Translated Jean Birell, CUP 1988, p. 180.

13 ***girls in convents.*** Vigarello, *Concepts of Cleanliness*, op. cit., pp. 174–5.

14 ***As early as 1940… Bradford.*** See John Hassan, *History of Water in England and Wales*, Manchester University Press 1998, pp. 54 & 55.

15 ***Only 10 per cent of homes in the 1950s.*** See Jean Watin-Augouard, *Dop: le plaisir de passer un savon, Historia* 31 mars 2004, Mensuel No. 688, p. 84.

16 ***English wife of the Vicomte de Baritault.*** Cited in Katherine Ashenburg, *Clean: An Unsanitised History of Washing*, Profile Books 2008, p. 192.

17 ***The French don't bathe… not as clean as the Germans.*** See *112 Gripes about the French*, US Military leaflet, 1945, Gripe Nos. 45 and 70.

18 ***complaints about French plumbing.*** *112 Gripes about the French,* op. cit., Gripe Nos. 42 and 44.

19 ***The Sun campaign.*** See Stephen Clarke, *1,000 Years of Annoying the French*, Random House eBooks p. 483.

20 ***liquid soaps and shower gels.*** Yves Stavridès, *Les Français se lavent, L'Express*, 9 février 1995.

21 ***BVA/Tork survey, 2012.*** *Les habitudes d'hygiène des Français*, BVA/Tork September 2012, reported in *The Daily Mail* on 17 October 2012.

22 ***United Minds/Tena/SCA survey,*** **2010.** Reported by *France* 24 on 28 June 2011.

23 ***SCA 2008 survey.*** *Hygiene Matters: the SCA Hygiene Report* 2008, p. 29.

24 ***dictations… I wash my hands.*** See Ashenburg, op. cit., p. 196.

25 ***Alain Corbin.*** Corbin, *The Foul and the Fragrant : Odour and the French Social Imagination*, trans. Miriam L. Kochan, Roy Porter and Christopher Prendergast (Cambridge, Harvard University Press 1986), p. 173.

26 ***Bidets were probably invented in Italy.*** See Katherine Ashenburg, *Clean: an unsanitised history of washing*, Profile Books 2009, p. 151.

27 ***the earliest reference to one.*** See Julia Csergo and Roger-Henri Guerrand, *Le Confident de dames. Le bidet du XVIIIe au XXe siècle: histoire d'une intimité*. Éditions La Découverte, 1997, 2009, p. 36.

28 ***One of Madame de Pompadour's many bidets.*** See Ashenburg, op. cit., p. 151.

29 ***The word bidet.*** See *Le Grand Robert de la langue française*.

30 ***George Brassaï.*** See Brassaï, George. *Le Paris secret des années 30*, Paris, Gallimard, 1976. (Translated as *The Secret Paris of the 30s* by Richard Miller, Thames & Hudson, 2001), chapter entitled 'Ladies of the Evening'.

31 ***discreetly skirt around the word bidet.*** See Csergo and Guerrand, op. cit., pp. 22–3.

32 ***eau de bidet or bidet water.*** See *Le Grand Robert de la langue française*.

33 ***Bidet data.*** Csergo and Guerrand, op. cit., pp. 187–8. Also *God save le bidet*, *Libération*, 16 août 1995.

CHAPTER 5

1 ***As one of the hundreds of guides to French etiquette.*** See A. Goujon, *Manuel de l'homme de bon ton* (1825), cited by Frédéric Rouvillois in *Histoire de la politesse: de 1789 à nos jours*, Éditions Flammarion, septembre 2008.

2 ***those who wear yellow gloves, and those who do not.*** Alphonse Karr, *Revue Anecdotique*, 1858, Vol. VII, p. 551, cited in Rouvillois, op. cit.

3 ***Sylvia Plath.*** Plath, *Unabridged Journals*, August 26, 1956, p. 260.

4 ***Temple Fielding.*** *Fielding's Travel Guide to Europe: 1953–54*, p. 321.

5 ***John Steinbeck.*** Steinbeck, *One American in Paris*, in *Holiday in France*, by Ludwig Bemelmans (Cambridge : Houghton Mifflin, 1957), p. 148.

6 ***IPSOS poll 2012.*** See 'Rude surprise: French fed up with own incivility', *The Guardian*, 27 July 2012.

7 ***The German philosopher Martin von Kempe.*** *Opus Polyhistoricum de Osculis* (Frankfurt, 1680). Cited by Keith Thomas in Karen Harvey, ed., *The Kiss in History*, Manchester University Press 2005, p.187.

8 ***Anglo-Saxon men have never gone in for this kissing performance.*** D.M.C. Rose, Lieutenant-Colonel, letter in *The Spectator*, 10 May 2003.

9 ***In general, Parisians will limit themselves to two kisses.*** See Frédéric Rouvillois, *Histoire de la politesse de 1789 à nos jours*, Edition Flammarion 2008, p.428.

10 ***average Gaul cringing with disgust.*** See for example Hélène Crié-Wiesner, *La bise, un ritual 'so chic' qui déroute les Américains*, Rue89, 24 juillet 2012.

11 ***sucking each other's saliva and dirt.*** Henri A. Junod, *The Life of a South African Tribe*, cited in Karen Harvey, op. cit., p. 187.

12 ***the French do not smoke as much as the world's biggest puffers, the Greeks.*** See OECD key tables on health, *Tobacco consumption: Percentage of population who are daily smokers*, 21 December 2011 (figures are from 2008 as this is the last year when comparable country statistics were available).

13 ***24 per cent of 15–19 year-old-French teenagers smoke.*** See Inpes (Institut national de prévention et d'éducation pour la santé), *Premiers résultats du baromètre santé 2010 : Evolutions récentes du tabagisme en France*, 28 janvier 2010, p. 3.

14 ***Today, 38 per cent of French women aged between 20 and 25 smoke.*** See Inpes, op. cit., p. 4.

15 ***a slightly worrying 24 per cent of pregnant women.*** Inpes press release, *Première hausse du tabagisme chez les femmes depuis la Loi Evin selon le Baromètre santé 2010.*

16 ***€47 billion or 3 per cent of GDP.*** See CNCT (Comité National Contre le Tabagisme), *Le tabac coûte cher à la société.*

17 ***state-owned cigarette monopoly SEITA.*** See Eric Godeau, *Comment le tabac est-il devenu une drogue?* Vingtième Siècle no. 102, avril–juin 2009.

18 ***a study by the market-research group Ipsos.*** See Ipsos, *Tabac et cinéma*, 1 juin 2012.

19 ***a 'Paris Exception' on the dining front.*** See P. Singer and J. Mason, *The ethics of what we eat*, New York, Rodale, 2006.

20 ***Out of the eight favourites dishes of France.*** See *Les plats préférés des Français*, Study by TNS Sofres for *Vie Pratique Gourmand*, 21 october 2011, p. 5.

21 ***Less than 2 per cent of French people are vegetarian.*** Figures from the European Vegetarian Union.

22 ***The second-biggest leisure pursuit in France.*** According to the French Hunters' Federation (*Fédération Nationale des Chasseurs*).

23 ***the majority of hunters in France.*** Information from the French Hunters' Federation. According to the Federation, 40 per cent of hunters are manual labourers (*ouvriers*).

24 ***a cushy deal for French farmers.*** See *Des chasseurs accusés de ne pas tuer assez de lapins, Le Figaro* 14 septembre 2012.

25 ***the French are the biggest pet owners in Europe.*** Figures from study by the animal insurers Santé Vet, May 2011.

CHAPTER 6

1 ***William Wordsworth.*** See Wordsworth's poem, 'French Revolution as it Appears to Enthusiasts', 1804.

2 ***Hobsbawm quotation.*** See Hobsbawm, E. J., *Echoes of the Marseillaise: Two Centuries Look Back on the French Revolution*, London: Verso 1990.

3 ***Zola was accused.*** *Le Gaulois*, July 1886. Cited in Alain Rustenholz, *Les grandes luttes de la France Ouvrière*, Éditions Les Beaux Jours 2008, p. 102.

4 ***Léon Trotsky.*** See Léon Trotsky, *Their Morals and Ours* (1938).

5 ***Georges Sorel.*** Georges Sorel, *Réflexions sur la violence* (1908).

6 ***Alain.*** Alain, *Propos*, 1934, *Droit des fonctionnaires.*

7 ***Etymology of the word grève.*** See *Le Grand Robert de la langue française.*

8 ***women textile workers at Cerizay.*** See Alain Rustenholz, op. cit., pp. 70–1.

9 ***Percentage of French workers who belong to a union.*** See Ministère des Affaires, étrangères, site franco-allemand, *Les syndicats en France.*

10 ***public sector strikes.*** See Stéphane Sirot, *La grève en France: une histoire sociale (XIXe–XXe siècle)*, Éditions Odile Jacob, septembre 2002, p. 34.

11 ***French retirement age.*** See OECD *Pensions at a Glance* 2011, France.

12 ***taxis in Paris… in London.*** See Richard Darbéra, *Rapport Attali: les craintes des taxis étaient-elles fondées ?* Transport, No. 448, mars–avril 2008, pp. 86–91.

13 ***Birth remains in France one of the principal conditions of access to power.*** See François Denord et al., *Le Champ du Pouvoir en France, Actes de la recherche en sciences sociales*, 2011/5 – No. 190 pp. 24–57, p. 50.

14 ***bosses of the CAC 40 companies.*** See Hervé Joly, *Grand patrons, grandes écoles : la fin de l'endogamie?* Laboratoire de recherches historiques Rhône-Alpes, 13 mars 2008. Bosses who had inherited their position were not counted.

15 ***40 per cent of the French government… Le Siècle.*** See François Denord, op. cit., p. 52.

16 ***Balzac/particule.*** See *Honoré de Balzac* edited by Harold Bloom, Chelsea House Publishers 2003, p. 46.

17 ***Fabrice Luchini.*** As recorded by Christophe Barbier, 8 May 2010, for the French newspaper *l'Express.*

18 ***league table of holiday-happy states in the EU.*** See Clotilde de Gastines, *Congés payés: le classement européen*, Metis 16 juillet 2009; also Rebecca Ray and John Schmitt, *No-Vacation U.S.A. – a comparison of leave and holiday in OECD countries*, Centre for Economic and Policy Research, 2007.

19 ***average number of hours worked by the French.*** See OECD Better Life Index, Work-Life Balance – France.

20 ***leisure and personal care.*** See OECD Better Life Index, op. cit.

21 ***French productivity miracle.*** For a clear and succinct demystification of the so called 'French productivity phenomenon', see Olivier Passet, *Productivité: le faux record de la France*, Canal Xerfi, November 2012.

22 ***Taylor letter.*** See *Goodyear: Arnaud Montebourg répond au lettre du PDG de Titan, Le Monde*, 19 February 2013.

23 ***Métro, boulot, dodo.*** See Philip Gooden and Peter Lewis, *Idiomantics: the Weird World of Popular Phrases*, Bloomsbury 2012, pp. 104–5.

24 ***Ney quotation.*** Quoted in Raymond Horricks, *Marshal Ney: the Romance and the Real*, Midas Books 1982, p. 271.

25 ***World War I military deaths.*** The French figure of 1,397,800 is from a study published by the Carnegie Endowment for International Peace in 1931. The British figure of 886,939 is from the Commonwealth War Graves Commission Annual Report, 2009–10.

26 ***mass-produced feelings.*** Cited in Harvey Levenstein, *We'll Always have Paris: American tourists in France since* 1930, University of Chicago Press 2004, p. 133.
27 ***a craven act of desertion.*** See for example Pierre-Olivier Lombarteix, *Pourquoi les Français n'aiment pas les Anglais... et réciproquement*, éditions du temps 2008, p. 95.
28 ***70–80 per cent of European (including British) public opinion.*** See Robert Gibson, *Best of Enemies: Anglo-Saxon Relations since the Norman Conquest*, second edition, Impress Books 2004, Chapter 8.

CHAPTER 7

1 ***On the need and ways to annihilate dialects and universalize the use of French.*** *Sur la necessité et les moyens d'anéantir les patois et d'universaliser l'usage de la langue française*, Abbé Grégoire, 1794. Cited by Dennis Ager, *Identity, Insecurity, and Image: France and Language*, Multilingual Matters Ltd 1999, p. 24.
2 ***Federalism and superstition speak Breton, etc.*** Cited by Ager, op. cit., p. 25.
3 ***Revolutionary legislation.*** See Ager, op. cit., p. 28.
4 ***Hamburgers, cheeseburgers, and eggburgers.*** René Etiemble, *Parlez-vous franglais?* Paris: Gallimard 1964, p. 238.
5 ***90 per cent of French people in a 2012 survey.*** Survey of 1,015 people by OpinionWay for the French festival XYZ, October 2012. Cited in *Le Parisien*, 30 October 2012, p. 13.
6 ***Agadoo/The Birdie Song.*** Voted fourth and first most annoying songs of all time respectively in a poll conducted by the internet site Dotmusic in 2000.
7 ***The Birdie Song.*** The French version of 'The Birdie Song', '*La Danse des canards*', is ranked as the number 2 best-selling French pop single of all time (Infodisc).
8 ***a nightmarish... world... Johnny Hallyday doesn't exist.*** The film was *Jean-Philippe*, directed by Laurent Tuel.
9 ***drank too many cigarettes.*** Cited in Sylvie Simmons, *Serge Gainsbourg: a fistful of Gitanes*, Da Capo Press 2002, p. xii.
10 ***the French chanson is still a big hitter.*** Survey Opinion Way/Sacem 2011/2012.
11 ***a Monty Python sketch.*** *French Subtitled Film* from the BBC series *Monty Python's Flying Circus*, Season 2, Episode 10, 1 December 1970.
12 ***Jean-Luc Godard's 1967 movie Weekend.*** See *Weekend*, Jean-Luc Godard/Athos Films, 29 December 1967.
13 ***Three Colours Blue.*** *Trois Couleurs: Bleu*, Krzysztof Kieślowski/Eurimages/France 3 Cinéma/Canal +, 1993.
14 ***top-grossing films in France.*** Figures from J.P.'s Box Office.
15 ***the French hit film Camping.*** See *Camping*, Fabien Ontoniente/France 2 Cinéma/France 3 Cinéma/Pathé, 2006.
16 ***Intouchables.*** See *Intouchables*, Olivier Nakache/Eric Toledano/Gaumont (France), 23 September 2011.

CHAPTER 8

1 ***police prefect to spy on them.*** See W. Scott Haine, *The World of the Paris Café: Sociability among the French Working Class, 1789–1914*, Baltimore: Johns Hopkins University Press 1996, p. 7.
2 ***the visiting American journalist Edward King observed.*** See Robert L. Herbert, *Impressionism: Art, Leisure and Parisian Society*, New Haven: Yale University Press 1988, p. 65.
3 ***the wing of madness pass over me.*** See *Charles Baudelaire: Intimate Journals*, translated by Christopher Isherwood with an Introduction by W. H. Auden, London: Panther Books 1969, p.10.
4 ***everyone came there to keep warm.*** Cited in Colin Jones, *Cambridge Illustrated History: France*, CUP 1994, p. 277.
5 ***He was my worst client.*** Colin Jones, op. cit., p. 277.
6 ***The Café de Flore serves as a drugstore.*** Janet Flanner (Genêt), *Paris Journal 1944–55*, Harcourt Publishers 1988, p. 92.
7 ***the chanson Rive Gauche.*** From the album *Au Ras des pâquerettes*, Virgin 1999.

8 ***at €9,790 per square metre.*** *Marché immobilier à Paris: les prix par arrondissements.* Droits-finances, October 2012.

9 ***a favourite haunt of the actress Catherine Deneuve.*** See the documentary film *Catherine Deneuve Rive Gauche*, Loïc Prigent/Paris Première, September 2012.

10 ***British journalist John Lichfield.*** In *The Independent*, 19 December 1998.

11 ***should smell of itself.*** See Olivier Thiery, *La fabrication de l'atmosphère de la ville et du Métro*, ethnographiques.org, No. 6 – novembre 2004.

12 ***Zazie note.*** See *Romans II, Œuvres complètes de Raymond Queneau*, La Pléiade / Gallimard 2006.

13 ***New York versus Paris.*** See Layla Demay & Laure Watrin, *Une vie de Pintade à Paris*, 2009.

14 ***three Olympic swimming pools.*** Data from French environmental marketing agency Planetoscope/consoGlobe.

15 ***Parisians hospitalized.*** Planetoscope data, op. cit.

16 ***A French dog-owner.*** See Nathalie Blanc, *Les animaux et la ville*, Éditions Odile Jacob octobre 2000, p. 60.

17 ***a pigeon for every 25 inhabitants.*** Data from the Mairie of Paris.

18 ***more than 9 kilos of rat droppings***. Planetoscope data, op. cit.

19 ***5,000 new squealers.*** See *Les rats se plaisent à Paris, Le Nouvel Observateur*, 12 janvier 2011.

20 ***aseptic, clinical character of the city space.*** See Nathalie Blanc, op. cit.

CHAPTER 9

1 ***fifteen days' paid holiday a year.*** See Jean-Claude Richez and Léon Strauss, *Un temps nouveau pour les ouvriers: les conges payés (1930–1960)*, in Alain Corbin ed., *L'Avènement des Loisirs* 1850–1960, Aubier (Paris) 1995, pp. 376–412.

2 ***make a Frenchman love his native soil.*** See Richez and Strauss, op. cit., p. 393.

3 ***The French philosopher Simone Weil.*** See Richez and Strauss, op. cit.

4 ***a whirl of hedonistic idealism.*** See Stéphane Lecler, *Tourisme pour tous!*, *Alternatives Economiques* No. 271, juillet 2008.

5 ***Les jolies colonies de vacances.*** Pierre Perret, Vogue 1966.

6 ***Figures for type and location of French holidays.*** See French government strategic document, *Les vacances des français: favoriser le départ du plus grand nombre*, juillet 2011 no. 234.

7 ***fractional pattern.*** As reported in French government strategic document, op. cit.

8 ***1.3 million French children spent some time in a 'colo' in 2011.*** See report *Le gouvernement promet un bon déroulement des colonies de vacances cet été*, WEKA 29 mars 2012.

9 ***Asphyxiation of horse on Breton beach.*** See for example *Le Figaro, La mort d'un cheval relance le débat sur les algues vertes*, 5 August 2009.

10 ***European Environment Agency's annual report on bathing water quality for 2011.*** See European Environment Agency, *European bathing water quality in 2011*, EEA Report No. 3/2012.

11 ***whipped a posse of nubile female sun worshippers.*** *Le Petit Journal Illustré*, 11 September 1927. Cited by Christophe Granger in *Batailles de plage. Nudité et pudeur dans l'entre-deux-guerres.* Rives méditerranéennes 30/2008.

12 ***He called his creation the 'bikini'***. See Bernard Andrieu, *Bronzage: Une petite histoire du soleil et de la peau*. CNRS Éditions, Paris, 2008, p. 8.

13 ***50 per cent of French women in a recent poll.*** See *Les femmes et la nudité*, poll conducted by Ifop/Tena, 5 mai 2009.

14 ***reduced rate loans.*** i.e. the *Loi Loucher* of July 1928, providing financial incentives to build private housing in the suburbs.

15 ***hypermarkets... supermarkets... roundabouts.*** See *Comment la France est devenue moche*, Enquête Télérama 13/02/2010, Xavier de Jarcy and Vincent Remy.

16 ***One village in two no longer has any local shops.*** See INSEE, *Les Petits Com-*

merces depuis 30 *ans*, No. 831, February 2002.

17 ***The majority – 49 per cent – dreamed of living in the suburbs.*** Consommation et Modes de Vie, CREDOC, *Être propriétaire de sa maison*, September 2004.

18 ***very little to do with rural France.*** See Roland Beufre & Dominique Dupuich, *Dictionnaire Pratique et Illustré des Styles Décoratifs Actuels*, Éditions du Chêne 1997, p. 47.

19 ***French provincial style.*** See John Pile, *A History of Interior Design*, Laurence King Publishing Limited 2005 (2nd Edition), pp. 182–4.

20 ***Edith Wharton.*** See Edith Wharton and Ogden Codman Jnr., *The Decoration of Houses*, B.T. Batsford 1898, Chapter I: *The historical tradition.*

21 ***various projects of house renovation.*** Elsie de Wolfe, *The House in Good Taste*, The Century Co., 1913.

22 ***'British country style' … Nancy Lancaster.*** For a detailed discussion of the 'creation' of English country house style by Nancy Lancaster, see Louise Ward, *Chintz, swags and bows: the myth of English country house style* 1930–1990, in Susie McKellar and Penny Sparke, eds., *Interior Design and Identity*, Manchester University Press, 2004.

23 ***inspiration for the first Habitat collection.*** Terence Conran, *Terence Conran's France*, Conran Octopus Limited 1991.

CHAPTER 10

1 ***A guide for French waiters published by the French Tourist Board.*** *Désirs et pratiques alimentaires des visiteurs étrangers en France,* French Ministry of Tourism, June 2004.

2 ***English food in the Middle Ages, as food historians have noted.*** See for example the excellent analysis of British cooking throughout history by Colin Spencer, *British Food: an extraordinary thousand years of history*, Grub Street 2011.

3 ***George Orwell predicted.*** See George Orwell, *In Defence of English Cooking, Evening Standard*, 15 December 1945.

4 ***survey of French people's preferred foreign cuisine.*** *La cuisine italienne: cuisine étrangère préférée des français*. Mingle Trend, mars 2011.

5 ***the best breakfast in the world.*** See *The 'Full English' Crowned World's Favourite Breakfast*, Hotels.com press release, 14 July 2011.

6 ***in the words of Somerset Maugham.*** W. Somerset Maugham, quoted in Ted Morgan, *Somerset Maugham: A Biography*, 1980.

7 ***200,000 British expats living in France.*** Figures from the British embassy in Paris.

8 ***300,000 Gauls living in Albion***. Figures from the French Embassy in London.

9 ***A study by the French newspaper Le Figaro in 2011.*** See Cyrille Vanlerberghe, *Heureux comme un Français à Londres, Le Figaro* 22/04/2011.

10 ***French immigration to Québec.*** Figures from the French Embassy in Québec.

11 ***The 3,000–4,000 French emigrants to Québec every year.*** Figures from the French Embassy in Québec.

12 ***18–20 per cent will be back home in five years.*** See Fannie Olivier, *The Failures of French Immigration in Québec, The Wall Street Journal*, August 13, 2007.

13 ***Walpole… Gray… Richard Owen Cambridge.*** For a detailed examination of the Chinese influence on English garden design and indeed eighteenth-century aesthetics, see Yu Liu, *Seeds of a Different Eden: Chinese Gardening Ideas and a New English Aesthetic Ideal*, University of South Carolina Press, 2008.

14 ***Charles de Gaulle on gardens.*** Charles de Gaulle, *La Discorde chez l'ennemi*, Paris: Berger-Levrault, 1944.

BIBLIOGRAPHY

Ager, Dennis. *Identity, Insecurity, and Image: France and Language*. Multilingual Matters Ltd 1999.

Alac, Patrik. *La grande histoire du Bikini*. Parkstone Press 2002.

Andrieu, Bernard. *Bronzage: Une petite histoire du soleil et de la peau*. CNRS Éditions, Paris, 2008.

Ashenburg, Katherine. *Clean: An Unsanitised History of Washing*. Profile Books 2009.

Augé, Marc. *Un ethnologue dans le métro*. Hachette 1986. (Translated with an Afterward by Tom Conley under the title of *In the Metro*, University of Minnesota Press, 2002).

Basow, S.A. *The hairless ideal: women and their body hair*. Psychology of Women Quarterly 1991, 15, pp. 83–96.

Baudelaire, Charles. *Intimate Journals*. Translated by Christopher Isherwood with an Introduction by W.H. Auden. London: Panther Books 1969.

Beufre, Roland, & Dupuich, Dominique. *Dictionnaire pratique et illustré des styles décoratifs actuels*. Éditions du Chêne 1997.

Blanc, Nathalie. *Les animaux et la ville*. Éditions Odile Jacob, octobre 2000.

Boucoiran, Louis. *La famille nombreuse dans l'histoire de nos jours*, 1921, p. 3. Bibliothèque Nationale de France/Gallica Bibliothèque Numérique.

Bourelly, Martine. *Le Pouvoir dans la Cuisine*, Fondation Gabriel Péri, 26 octobre 2009.

Brassaï, George. *Le Paris secret des années 30*, Paris, Gallimard, 1976. Translated as *The Secret Paris of the 30s by Richard Miller*, Thames & Hudson, 2001.

Bussmann, Prof. Dr. Kai-D., Claudia Erthal, and Andreas Schroth, *The Effect of Banning Corporal Punishment in Europe: a Five-Nation Comparison*. University of Wittenberg, October 2009.

Campagne Nationale de Mensuration, Résultats. Dossier de presse, 2 février 2006.

Clarke, Stephen. 1,000 *Years of Annoying the French*. Random House eBooks.

Collier, Aine. *The humble little condom: a history*. Prometheus Books 2007.

Conran, Terence. *Terence Conran's France*. Conran Octopus Ltd 1991.

Convention on International Trade in Species. *Report on International Trade in Frogs' Legs*. March 2012.

Corbin, Alain, ed. *L'Avènement des loisirs 1850–1960*. Aubier (Paris) 1995

CREDOC. Consommation et Modes de Vie. *Être propriétaire de sa maison*. Septembre 2004.

CSA/Marianne 2. *L'Image des Parisiens auprès des Français. Marianne* 2, 26 février 2010.

Csergo, Julia, and Guerrand, Roger-Henri. *Le Confident de dames. Le bidet du XVIIIe au XXe siècle : histoire d'une intimité* Éditions La Découverte, 1997, 2009.

Curnonsky. *Lettres de Noblesse*. Les Éditions Nationales, 1 janvier 1935.

Delétang, Henri. *La Tarte Tatin – Histoire et Légendes*. Éditions Alan Sutton, 30 novembre 2011.

Denord, François, et al. *Le Champ du Pouvoir en France. Actes de la recherche en sciences sociales*, 2011/5 – no. 190, pp. 24–57.

Descamps, Marc-Alain. *L'invention du corps*. P.U.F. Paris, 1986.

de Vries, Jan. *The Industrious Revolution: Consumer Behaviour and the Household Economy, 1650 to the Present*. Cambridge University Press 2008.

de Wolfe, Elsie. *The House in Good Taste*. The Century Co. 1914.

Drouard, Alain. *Histoire des cuisiniers en France XIXe–XXe siècle*. Paris, CNRS Éditions 2004.

Druckerman, Pamela. *French Children Don't Throw Food*. Doubleday 2012.

Dumas, Alexandre. *Grand Dictionnaire de Cuisine* (1873). Reprinted General Books, 6 January 2012.

Durex. *Give and Receive Global Sex Survey*. Durex, 2005.

European Environment Agency. *European bathing water quality in* 2011. EEA Report 3/2012.

ESPAD (European School Survey Project on Alcohol and Other Drugs) 2011. Results for France, United Kingdom and Europe.

Eurobarometer. *Attitude of EU citizens towards animal welfare*. March 2007.

Fédération Nationale du Cheval. *La Viande Chevaline : un patrimoine, juridiquement encadré, indispensable à la filière cheval.* Mai 2008.

Flanner, Janet (Genêt). *Paris Journal* 1944–55. Harcourt Publishers 1988.

FranceAgriMer, VINS/COMMERCE EXTERIOR, Bilan 2011/du 1er janvier au 31 décembre.

Gibson, Robert. *Best of Enemies: Anglo-Saxon Relations Since the Norman Conquest*. Impress Books, second edition 2004.

Godeau, Eric. *Comment le tabac est-il devenu une drogue?* Vingtième Siècle no. 102, avril-juin 2009.

Gooden, Philip and Lewis, Peter. *Idiomantics: the Weird World of Popular Phrases*. Bloomsbury 2012.

Granger, Christophe. *Les corps d'été: Naissance d'une variation saisonnière XXe siècle*. Éditions Autrement 2009.

_______. *Batailles de plage. Nudité et pudeur dans l'entre-deux-guerres*. Rives méditerranéennes 30/2008.

Guerrand, Roger-Henri. *Les lieux : Histoire des commodités*. Éditions la Découverte 2009.

Guiliano, Mireille. *French Women Don't Get Fat: the Secret of Eating for Pleasure*. Vintage, 2 February 2006.

Gumbel, Peter. *On achève bien les écoliers*, Grasset, 2010 (available in English as a Kindle edition, *They shoot school kids, don't they?*).

Haine, Scott W. *The World of the Paris Café: Sociability among the French Working Class*, 1789–1914, Baltimore: Johns Hopkins University Press 1996.

Hallyday, Johnny, and Sthers, Amanda. *Dans mes yeux*. Éditions Plon, 2013.

Harvey, Karen, ed., *The Kiss in History*. Manchester University Press 2005.

Hassan, John. *History of Water in England and Wales*. Manchester University Press 1998.

Herbert, Robert L. *Impressionism: Art, Leisure and Parisian Society*. New Haven: Yale University Press 1988.

Hobsbawm, E. J. *Echoes of the Marseillaise: Two Centuries Look Back on the French Revolution*. London: Verso 1990.

Hope, Christine. *Caucasian Female Body Hair and American Culture. Journal of American Culture*, Vol. 5, Issue 1, Spring 1982, pp. 93–9.

Ifop. *Les Français et la sexualité dans le couple*. Septembre 2010.

Inpes (Institut national de prévention et d'éducation pour la santé). *Premiers résultats du baromètre santé 2010 : Évolutions récentes du tabagisme en France*. 28 janvier 2010.

INRA. *Qu'est-ce que le lait cru? Agriculture, alimentation, environnement*, janvier 2008.

INSEE. *Un tiers des Franciliens présente un excès de poids*. INSEE Île de France, 2007.

_______. *Les Petits Commerces depuis 30 ans*. INSEE no. 831, février 2002.

_______. *Boissons alcoolisées : 40 ans de baisse de consommation*. INSEE no. 966, mai 2004.

_______. *L'Obésité en France : les écarts entre catégories sociales s'accroissent*. INSEE no. 1123, février 2007.

Ipsos. *Enquête sur les Français et l'épilation : opinions, attitudes, et comportements*. Ipsos/Nair, mai 2006.

_______. *Les Français et la cuisine*. Ipsos/Logica Business Consulting, 21 septembre 2011.

_______. *Tabac et cinéma*. Ipsos/Ligue contre le cancer, 1 juin 2012.

Joly, Hervé. *Grand patrons, grandes écoles : la fin de l'endogamie?* Laboratoire de recherches historiques Rhône-Alpes, 13 mars 2008.

Jones, Colin. *Cambridge Illustrated History: France*. CUP 1994.

Kruck, William E. *Looking for Dr. Condom*. University of Alabama Press 1981

Kuisel, Richard F. *The French Way: How France Embraced and Rejected American Values and Power*. Princeton University Press 2010.

Labouchère, Henry Du Pré. *Diary of the Besieged Resident in Paris*. Hurst & Blackett 1871.

Larousse, *Le Grand Larousse Gastronomique*, French Edition. Larousse 2007.

__________. *Larousse Gastronomique*, English Edition. Octopus Publishing Group 2009.

__________. *Dictionnaire Étymologique*. Dubois/Mitterand/Dauzat. Larousse/VUEF 2001.

Lecler, Stéphane. *Tourisme pour tous! Alternatives Économiques*. No. 271, juillet 2000.

Lefief-Delcourt, Alix. *L'Ail malin*. Leduc S. 17 mai 2011.

Levenstein, Harvey. *We'll always have Paris: American tourists in France since 1930*, University of Chicago Press 2004.

Liu, Yu. *Seeds of a Different Eden: Chinese Gardening Ideas and a New English Aesthetic Ideal*. University of South Carolina Press 2008.

Lombarteix, Pierre-Olivier. *Pourquoi les Français n'aiment pas les Anglais… et réciproquement*. Éditions du temps 2008.

Lorey, T. and Poutet, P. 'The representation of wine in France from generation to generation: a dual generation gap', *International Journal of Entrepreneurship and Small Businesses*, Vol. 13, No. 2, 2011, pp. 162–80.

Madame Figaro/CSA. *Infidélité : les Français passent aux aveux*. 23 juillet 2009.

Marianne, L'Histoire. *Le Couple*. Hors-Série, juillet–août 2012.

McKellar, Susie, and Sparke, Penny, eds. *Interior Design and Identity*. Manchester University Press 2004.

Mennell, Stephen. *All Manners of Food: Eating and Tasting in England and France from the Middle Ages to the Present*, Univ. of Illinois Press 1996.

Mikes, George. *How to be an Alien*. Penguin Books 1966.

Miranda, V. *Cooking, Caring, and Volunteering: Unpaid Work Around the World*. OECD Social, Employment and Migration Working Papers, No. 116, OECD publishing 2011.

Monestier, Martin. *Histoire et bizarreries des excréments… des origines à nos jours*, Le Cherche midi, 1997, 2012.

Musolino, Michel. *150 Idées reçues sur la France*. Éditions First-Gründ, Paris 2012.

Nadeau, Jean-Benoît and Barlow, Julie. *Sixty million Frenchmen can't be wrong: what makes the French so French*. Portico 2008.

NHS Information Centre, Lifestyle Statistics. *Statistics on obesity, physical activity and diet* 2012.

ObÉpi/Roche. *Enquête nationale sur l'obésité et le surpoids*. Octobre 2012, 6ème édition.

OECD (Organisation for Economic Co-operation and Development). *Obesity and the Economics of Prevention: Fit not Fat – France Key Facts* 2011.

________. OECD Pisa in Focus, *Has discipline in school deteriorated?* 2011/4 (May).

________. OECD *Pensions at a Glance* 2011.

________. OECD key tables on health. *Tobacco consumption: Percentage of population who are daily smokers*. 21 December 2011.

________. OECD Better Life Index. Reports for France.

Orwell, George. *In Defence of English Cooking. Evening Standard*, 15 December 1945.

Ota, H. et al. 'Les Japonais en voyage pathologique à Paris: un modèle original de prise en charge transculturelle'. *Nervure : Journal de Psychiatrie*, 5:31–34.

Picard, Dominique. *Politesse, savoir-vivre et relations sociales*. Presses Universitaires de France 1998.

Pierre, Eric. *L'hippophagie au secours des classes laborieuses*. Communications, 74, 2003, pp. 177–200.

Pile, John. *A History of Interior Design*.

Laurence King Publishing Ltd 2005 (2nd Edition).

Poulain, Jean-Pierre and Neirinck, Edmond. *Histoire de la cuisine et des cuisiniers*. Éditions JT Jacques Lanore 2004.

Rambourg, Patrick. *Histoire de la cuisine et de la gastronomie françaises*. Éditions Perrin 2010.

Rogov, Daniel. *Rogues, Writers & Whores: Dining with the Rich and Infamous*. AmazonEncore 2007.

Roques, Nathalie. *Dormir avec son bébé*. L'Harmattan 2002.

Rothschild, Bruce M. 'History of Syphilis', in *Clinical Infectious Diseases*, 2005:40 (15 May).

Rouvillois, Frédéric. *Histoire de la politesse : de 1789 à nos jours*. Éditions Flammarion 2008.

Rustenholz, Alain. *Les grandes luttes de la France Ouvrière*. Éditions Les Beaux Jours 2008.

SCA. *Hygiene Matters: the SCA Hygiene Report* 2008.

Serrurier, Matthieu. *Economie et marché de l'ail*, Centre Technique Interprofessionel des Fruits et Légumes, 16 mars 2011.

Simon, François. *Pique-Assiette : la fin d'une gastronomie française*. Grasset & Fasquelle, 5 novembre 2008.

Simoons, Frederick J. *Eat Not this Flesh: Food Avoidances from Prehistory to the Present*. University of Wisconsin Press 1994.

Singer, P. and Mason, J. *The Ethics of What We Eat*. New York: Rodale 2006.

Sirot, Stéphane. *La grève en France: une histoire sociale (XIXe–XXe siècle)*. Éditions Odile Jacob, septembre 2002.

SizeUK (UK National Sizing Survey), 2004.

Staffe, Baronne. *Usages du monde : règles du savoir-vivre dans la société moderne* (1891). Éditions Tallandier 2007.

Steinberger, Michael. *Au Revoir to All That: The Rise and Fall of French Cuisine*. Bloomsbury 2010.

Thévenon, Olivier. *Does Fertility Respond to Work and Family-life Reconciliation Policies in France?* CESifo Conference on Fertility and Public Policy, 1 February 2008.

___. *Family Policies in OECD Countries: A Comparative Analysis*. Population and Development Review 37(1): 57–87 (March 2011).

Thiery, Olivier. *La fabrication de l'atmosphère de la ville et du métro*. ethnographiques.org, No. 6 – novembre 2004.

TNS Sofres/*Vie Pratique Gourmand*. *Les plats préférés des Français*, 21 octobre 2011.

Toklas, Alice B. *The Alice B. Toklas Cookbook* (1954). Abridged as *Murder in the Kitchen*, Penguin 2011.

Unicef France. *Une enquête de victimation et climat scolaire auprès d'élèves du cycle 3 des écoles élémentaires*, March 2011.

US military leaflet, *112 Gripes about the French*, 1945.

Wadham, Lucy. *The Secret Life of France*. Faber and Faber 2009.

Watin-Augouard, Jean. *Dop : le plaisir de passer un savon. Historia* 31 mars 2004, Mensuel No. 688.

Wharton, Edith, and Codman Jnr., Ogden. *The Decoration of Houses*. B.T. Batsford 1898.

Zola, Émile. *Germinal* (1885), translated with an Introduction by Havelock Ellis. Everyman's Library 1894.

PICTURE CAPTIONS AND ACKNOWLEDGEMENTS

PAGE 13 Breton onion sellers in South Wales, 1938; Getty Images.

PAGE 16 The singer Pierre Perret in his kitchen, 1979; Getty Images.

PAGE 22 Title page of *La Physiologie du goût* ('The Physiology of Taste') by Jean Anthelme Brillat-Savarin, 1848; Wikimedia Commons.

PAGE 30 Customers queue for horsemeat during the Siege of Paris, 1870–71; Art Archive.

PAGE 42 How does one govern a country with 246 different cheeses? President Charles de Gaulle receives a cheeseboard while visiting Mamers (Sarthe), 22 May 1965; Getty Images.

PAGE 61 Wine tasting in the Hospices de Beaune, c.1930–50; Getty Images.

PAGE 69 Two Frenchmen sleep off the effects of excessive wine-tasting, c.1950; Getty Images.

PAGE 73 Catherine Deneuve on the set of the film *La Chamade*, 1968; Getty Images.

PAGE 77 A model in a dress designed by Jacques Fath, c.1950; © TopFoto.co.uk.

PAGE 81 Caricature of Louis Philippe, King of the French, as Marianne, by Gustave Doré, 1871; Getty Images.

PAGE 89 Front cover of *Le Pot au Feu*, 15 July 1896; © TopFoto.co.uk.

PAGE 98 *La Liberté guidant le people* ('Liberty Leading the People'), 1830, by Eugène Delacroix (1798–1863); Shutterstock.

PAGE 100 'To live happily, live in bed', anonymous photograph for a postcard, c.1905; The Art Archive/Kharbine-Tapabor/Collection IM.

PAGE 102 Poster for the film *Emmanuelle* 2, 1975; Trinacra/Orphee/The Kobal Collection.

PAGE 106 *Rolla*, by Henri Gervex (1852–1929). Jacques Rolla, a young bourgeois, who has fallen into a life of idleness and debauchery, prepares to commit suicide by poison; The Art Archive/Musée des Beaux Arts Bordeaux/JFB.

PAGE 113 An irate husband, accompanied by the police, catches his wife and her lover in the act… Female adultery was always considered more seriously than male, as this 1905 French postcard entitled *Le Flagrant Délit* shows; The Art Archive/Kharbine-Tapabor.

PAGE 120 A French family at breakfast, 1939; Roger-Viollet/Topfoto.

PAGE 129 'The worst pupils in the class': cover photograph for the magazine *Guérir* ('Healing'), 15 March 1934. The French equivalent of the Dunce's Cap as a school punishment was the *bonnet d'âne*, or donkey's ears, and was widely used in French schools even into the twentieth century. It was often used as a punishment for talking in regional languages at school; The Art Archive/Kharbine-Tapabor/Coll. Jonas.

PAGE 132 A new model of urinal photographed by Charles Marville (1816–78) in the chaussée de la Muette, Paris (16th arrondissement); © Charles Marville/Musée Carnavalet/Roger-Viollet/TopFoto.

PAGE 136 A public urinal kiosk, illustration by Hondt for the catalogue of Tassart, Balas, Barbas et Cie, 1898; The Art Archive/Kharbine-Tapabor/Coll. Jonas.

PAGE 144 French engraving a toilet, bathroom and bathtub, c.1870, The Art Archive/Private Collection/CCI.

PAGE 146 A baby in the bath; postcard from the author's collection.

PAGE 149 'Femme à sa toilette', by Armand Jagaud, 1920s; Roger-Viollet/Topfoto.

PAGE 154 Louis de Funès in *Le gendarme de Saint-Tropez*, 1965; Keystone-France/Gamma-Keystone via Getty Images.

PAGE 163 The French custom of *maraîchinage*, or prolonged kissing, traditionally under an umbrella, blurred the distinction between the social and the passionate kiss; postcard from the author's collection.

PAGE 170 The French actress and dancer

Leslie Caron, London, 1966; Getty Images.

PAGE 178 Republican guards lining up at the rear entrance to the Palais de Chaillot, 1948; Time & Life Pictures/Getty Images.

PAGE 182 *La beauté est dans la rue* ('Beauty is in the Street'), poster from the student revolt in Paris, May 1968; Archives Charmet/Bridgeman Art Library.

PAGE 194 Title page of the 1929 edition of *Le Bottin Mondain*, Éditions Didot-Bottin; public domain.

PAGE 195 Photo by Nadar of the novelist Honoré de Balzac (1799–1850); Wikimedia Commons.

PAGE 197 Vintage French metal sign: *Désolé nous sommes fermés* ('Sorry, We're Closed'); Shutterstock.

PAGE 203 Illustration of a Frankish knight, created by Montfaucon, published in *Magasin Pittoresque*, Paris, 1842; Shutterstock.

PAGE 206 A French helmet of Second World War vintage; Shutterstock.

PAGE 210 The French actor Jean-Paul Belmondo, c.1960; Getty Images

PAGE 212 First page of the Sixth Edition of the *Dictionnaire de l'Académie française*, 1835; Wikimedia Commons.

PAGE 215 Guardians of the purity of the French tongue: learned members of the *Académie française* in earnest discussion of such crucial matters as the use of the circumflex accent; Roger-Viollet/Topfoto.

PAGE 224 Serge Gainsbourg and Jane Birkin, late 1960s/early 1970s; Keystone Archives/HIP/TopFoto.

PAGE 231 The original release poster for *À bout de souffle*, 1960; SNC/The Kobal Collection.

PAGE 244 Jean-Paul Sartre scribbling in a Left Bank café, 1940s; Gamma-Rapho via Getty Images.

PAGE 254 A dog owner carries her three Pekinese to a dog show in Paris, c.1935; IMAGNO/Austrian Archives (S)/TopFoto.

PAGE 258 Parisian schoolchildren leave the city for holidays in the mountains or by the sea, 1933; IMAGNO/Austrian Archives (S)/TopFoto

PAGE 273 Holidaymakers in Deauville (Calvados), 1983; Jean-Pierre Couderc/Roger-Viollet/TopFoto.

PAGE 278 So tiny, it fitted into a matchbox… Louis Réard had to use a topless nightclub dancer to model the first bikini, considered too risqué by regular models, 1946; Getty Images.

PAGE 283 New French housing estate; Wikimedia Commons.

PAGE 287 Saint-Cirq Lapopie in the Lot; Shutterstock.

PAGE 291 Elsie de Wolfe, from *The House in Good Taste*. The Century Company 1914.

PAGE 294 Winston Churchill and Charles de Gaulle, 1944; Roger-Viollet/Getty Images

PAGE 299 The novelist Émile Zola (1840–1902); Wikimedia Commons.

PAGE 305 Map of the department of Lot, Midi-Pyrénées, from *Dictionary of Words and Things*, Larive and Fleury, 1895; Shutterstock.

PAGE 311 The garden at the château of Villandry in the Loire, widely regarded as one of the greatest of the French Renaissance gardens; Shutterstock.

PAGE 320 The futuristic cityscape of La Défense; Wikimedia Commons.

All other images included in the book are from Shutterstock.